IATEFL 2010

Harrogate Conference Selections

44th International Conference
Harrogate
7–11 April 2010

Edited by Tania Pattison

Editorial Committee: Siân Morgan, Sandie Mourão, Amos Paran

Published by IATEFL
Darwin College
University of Kent
Canterbury
Kent CT2 7NY

First published 2011

British Library Cataloguing in Publication Data
Education
Tania Pattison (Ed.)
    IATEFL 2011 Harrogate Conference Selections

ISBN 978-1901095-33-3

For a complete list of IATEFL publications, please
write to the above address, or visit the IATEFL
website at www.iatefl.org

Copy-edited by Simon Murison-Bowie, Oxford.
Designed and typeset by Keith Rigley, Charlbury.
Printed in Britain by Information Press, Eynsham.

Contents

Editor's introduction

In his review of the 44th Annual IATEFL Conference and Exhibition, Ken Lackman says, 'I come all the way from Canada and pay my own ticket to IATEFL because I believe it's the best way to keep up with what is happening in my field'. This sentiment is undoubtedly shared by the 2,030 ELT practitioners who made the journey to Harrogate in April 2010 for the 44th Annual International IATEFL Conference and Exhibition. As many of us recognise, IATEFL conferences present wonderful opportunities for learning, sharing and networking, and the 2010 Conference was no exception.

Held at the Harrogate International Centre and adjoining Holiday Inn, the conference offered five days of presentations, symposiums, SIG programmes, posters, debates, publishers' demonstrations, and opportunities to catch up with colleagues from all over the globe. Evening events included David Crystal's 'Language Playtime', co-presented with his family; evenings of music, poetry and stories; and the third annual IATEFL *Pecha Kucha*. For those looking to experience Yorkshire beyond the conference room, IATEFL arranged several daytime excursions, notably a visit to Haworth, made famous by the Brontës. It was truly an exhilarating, if exhausting, five days!

While perennial favourites such as the Hornby Scholars' panel presentation and the *ELT Journal*/IATEFL debate remain, there were also some innovations this year. Most significantly, IATEFL 2010 saw the introduction of the Interactive Language Fair, an innovative forum through which the 21 presenters were able to explore their topics with participants through a variety of media, both computer- and paper-based. Also new this year was the Jobs Market, which enabled delegates to meet with potential employers from around the world. Both were enthusiastically received, and both will be continued at the 2011 Conference in Brighton.

As has become customary, IATEFL once again teamed up with the British Council to present Harrogate Online. Sessions and interviews were available for viewing through the IATEFL website, and materials from presentations were posted here, thus making the conference available to many IATEFL members all over the world who were not able to attend in person.

With over 500 talks on offer, every aspect of ELT was represented in Harrogate; as editor of *Conference Selections*, I was astonished by the diversity of the reports I received. Many parts of the globe are represented here, and in these pages you will meet a variety of learners and teachers of English. Many familiar names appear, yet there are also plenty of newcomers. Most writers have included their email address; while space limitations allow for only three references to be included with individual reports (plenary papers contain full references), readers are invited to contact individual writers to discuss a topic in more detail. In addition, in the short term, handouts and PowerPoint slides for some of the reports included here will remain available through Harrogate Online.

This year, *Conference Selections* received an enormous number of submissions, and space was tight. I am grateful to IATEFL for allowing us an increase in the number of pages. Even so, in order to make room for as many papers as possible, we have had to eliminate individual chapter introductions; instead a brief overview of each chapter is given here.

Chapter 1 comprises three reviews of the conference, from delegates based in Italy, Canada and the UK. Chapter 2 focuses on the psychological aspects of learning—motivation, identity, autonomy—and poses the intriguing question: what makes a 'good' language learner? In Chapter 3, the attention shifts away from the learner and onto the teacher; this chapter presents papers on stages of teacher development, initial teacher training and continuing professional development. Chapter 4 addresses issues of teacher responsibility and the variation encountered in specific cultural contexts; several papers here describe the realities of teaching in the transitional world. In Chapter 5 we turn our attention to the English language itself, specifically to its structure and lexis. Chapter 6 addresses questions related to the use of reading texts in the classroom and critical thinking instruction, while Chapter 7 focuses on the productive skills of speaking and writing. Chapter 8 explores aspects of English for Specific and Academic Purposes, while Chapter 9 addresses another specific area of ELT, that of teaching young learners. Chapter 10 brings together a number of papers describing the use of technology both inside and outside the classroom, and the focus of Chapter 11 is on methods of testing and evaluation. Finally, the papers in Chapter 12 all describe the use of stories in some form, from picture stories for young children to Shakespeare for ESP students.

Unfortunately, despite the increase in the number of pages and the elimination of chapter introductions, not all papers submitted could be included, and a number of deserving submissions have had to be excluded. I hope the writers of these submissions will be encouraged to seek alternative forums in which to publish their work.

Of course, the preparation of a volume of this magnitude is never the work of one person, and there are a number of people whose contribution to *Selections* has been invaluable. All submissions are read 'blind' (in other words, with identifying details removed) by an editorial committee consisting of experts in various aspects of ELT; the editorial committee members are Siân Morgan, Sandie Mourão and Amos Paran. Their feedback was extremely helpful to me when making difficult decisions about what to include. I would also like to thank our copyeditor Simon Murison-Bowie and our designer and typesetter Keith Rigley for bringing their remarkable talent to these pages. My biggest thanks, however, go to my predecessor, Briony Beaven. As the new editor of *Selections*, I have worked closely with Briony for over a year now, and I am grateful for her ongoing support and quick responses to my frequent questions.

Finally, I would like to express my appreciation to all presenters who took the time to send me their reports. It was a privilege to read all of your submissions, and I very much hope to meet many of you in person at a future IATEFL event.

I hope you will enjoy reading this volume, and I will see you in Brighton!

Tania Pattison
Editor, *IATEFL Conference Selections*
Email: cseditor@iatefl.org

1 Conference reviews

1.1 Whodunnit: following in the footsteps of Agatha Christie

Sharon Hartle *University of Verona, Italy*

Being originally from Yorkshire myself, I am no stranger to Harrogate, a lovely city with many temptations including Betty's Café and, of course, the historic Royal Baths, with their elegance, reminiscent of a lost world of gentility. Harrogate was also the milieu of genteel detective stories, and Agatha Christie herself was discovered here after her unexplained disappearance in 1926. This air of mystery was, in fact, a feature of the 44th Annual IATEFL Conference, too. Storytelling was one of the threads running through the conference this year, ranging from David Heathfield's memorable evening where people were brought together through stories shared from all round the globe, to Ema Ushioda's thought-provoking anecdotes [see report 2.1], and finally to the wonderful closing plenary where Jan Blake transported us all to a highly charged emotional space, leaving very few dry eyes in the auditorium [see 12.8].

Setting the scene

The first hint of mystery, however, came in an email before the conference even started, when Ellie Broadbridge wrote from IATEFL's Head Office asking for 'Whodunnit' postcards; these were cards that delegates were asked to produce in advance, and which were then sold at the conference to raise money for IATEFL's Wider Membership Individual Scheme. When you buy the postcard, you discover who created it. It might be a plenary speaker, a delegate, or a well-known celebrity from the EFL world like Herbert Puchta, the president of IATEFL. A simple idea in itself, this is typical of many of the creative initiatives that abound at the conference and that, in my view, make it particularly special.

The president kicked it all off with a participant-friendly speech, featuring a scrambled numerical trivia game (which he returned to at the end of the conference to round it all off), where the audience was asked to match statistics to facts, such as the 3,500 cups of tea or coffee drunk at the Cardiff conference or the 3,000 tweets made. There are all sorts of conferences in the world, but IATEFL is an invitation to join in the fun and become part of an interactive, lively community; and whilst it is true that the conference is enormous, with 2,030 delegates and more than 500 speakers this year, it is also very friendly. To take the Agatha Christie theme a bit further, however, it's time to play detective and find out what went on.

Following the clues

An efficient conference goer, like an efficient detective, must be able to follow the clues—or in our case, the well-designed conference programme—deciding quickly what the best line of inquiry might be, but keeping an open mind, too. This year

I decided to focus mainly on technology, and with the help the colour-coded pages of the programme, this was quite easy to do. I arrived on the Tuesday ready for the pre-conference Learning Technologies event on the Wednesday. I followed the scent and quickly found the Learning Technologies SIG, by listening to cries of 'Anybody got an iPod charge lead?'

Whodunnit?

The aim of the detective is to find out 'whodunnit', and in this case 'whodunnit' means 'who or what inspired me'. As far as technology is concerned, one key area was Twitter, which I had resisted in the past, taking the line that it was simply a lot of meaningless 'twitter', as the name implies. I learned from Graham Stanley [see 10.9], however, that this is far from true and went straight to my laptop to increase my network of friends, becoming part of this giant extended staffroom almost instantaneously. Dave Willis was as inspiring as ever with his wise words on language itself. The Interactive Language Fair was a successful new innovation, too, giving delegates the chance to get a taste of varied different presentations; and, of course, there was the chance to see one of the many videos of sessions available on the Harrogate Online site.

Reaching a verdict

A lovely setting, food for thought, networking and afternoon teas ... the list could go on forever, but I'm afraid you must excuse me as I have to go and tweet about what a memorable conference it was. See you next year.

Email: sharon.hartle@univr.it

1.2 Waters and workshops in Harrogate

Ken Lackman *Freelance, Toronto, Canada*

Harrogate is one of my favourite IATEFL conference sites. The town was once a popular destination for the British and European aristocracy who came for the healing powers of the mineral-rich waters. The focal point of this migration was the Turkish-style Baths and the adjacent Winter Garden, into which one descended via one of the two semicircular staircases. With the decline of the aristocracy after World War I, there came a decline in the spa towns they frequented; however, Harrogate managed to pick up the slack by converting itself into a venue for conferences. The extensive conference centre is only seconds away from the building that housed the Turkish Baths, the heart of the old spa town. And although the entrance hall to the Baths is now a Chinese restaurant, one is still able to descend into the former Winter Garden for needed relief provided by their healing waters. These modern healing waters do not contain sulphur and iron, but an intoxicating mixture of hops, barley malt and yeast.

All a collection of friends or colleagues needs to do before entering any of the numerous pubs and restaurants within crawling distance of the conference centre is to find some topics for discussion. One way to accomplish that is to attend any of the numerous sessions outlined in the 200-page IATEFL conference programme. The great thing about IATEFL is that you can choose to focus on virtually any aspect or area of English language teaching, and you are bound to find a multitude of relevant workshops and presentations. My focus at this conference was methodology, for even though we are supposedly in a post-method world, I still think insights on how to teach are important.

I come all the way from Canada and pay my own ticket to IATEFL because I believe it's the best way to keep up with what is happening in my field. And what seems to be happening this year is what was happening last year also. Into the abyss left by the decline of method fall little bits and pieces of all the old methods, no matter when they were officially pronounced as deceased. This was summed up brilliantly in an entertaining presentation by Scott Thornbury, in which he gave a brief overview of the history of language teaching methodology and then presented all those bits that we need to select from when deciding how to structure and/or present our lessons. Another highlight for me was the debate that broke out between Anthony Bruton and Dave Willis. The latter just happened to be in attendance when the former delivered a talk suggesting that PPP was perhaps more conducive to language acquisition than task-based learning. Going back even further than PPP, Gloria Sampaio's workshop dealt with the benefits of translating whole texts. It was perhaps fitting that the last session I attended, part of an excellent drama symposium, had Eugene Schaefer presenting a teaching method developed in 1977, which seemed heavily influenced by Krashen and Community Language Learning.

With everything old becoming new again, I came away with only one definitive conclusion about language teaching methodology—that, regardless of the method employed, learners need ample opportunities to work with language. And this brings me to my only criticism of the Harrogate conference. I believe that participants presented with new ideas are not that different from language learners: to effectively process the ideas, we need to work with them. Yet it seemed that numerous sessions that could have easily involved some interaction were presented as talks with little or no chance for discussion, debate or other means of working with ideas. Sometimes a token interactive task was employed at the beginning of a session or in the middle, seemingly to justify the presentation's designation as a workshop. In stark contrast to this, a session on giving praise to students allowed frequent discussion and debate, even debate between the two presenters (Philip Nathan and Sylvie Donna). As a result, I left the session pondering issues that had been raised in the interactive portions of the presentation.

A few other participants I spoke to also felt that there could have been more 'true' workshops, yet one said that he often appreciated sessions where he could just sit back and be entertained, especially after a long day. So, after a long and worthwhile conference, one could ask for no better entertainment than Jan Blake's terrific closing plenary on storytelling [see 12.8]—a dynamic conclusion to another wonderful conference.

Email: klackman@kenlackman.com

1.3 Perspectives old and new: coming home to IATEFL

Fiona Aish and **Jo Tomlinson** *Target English, London, UK*

Fiona: Returning to the conference after a three-year absence, I was not disappointed. Old friendships were rekindled and new ones made, confirming the great networking opportunities available to all who brave the hordes of IATEFL.

As usual, the sessions were innumerable and wide ranging in focus, ensuring that all tastes and interests were catered for. Sometimes the event can feel overwhelming: What session should I go to? How do I know the speaker will be good? Why are two sessions I am interested in scheduled at the same time? When am I going to fit in lunch? The decisions can make you dizzy! I attended a lot of sessions and noticed that, compared to three years ago, there seemed to be much more interest in English in higher education contexts, a buzz about Web 2.0 technology and a push from all the tests currently available to students of English. For me, some of the most thought-provoking sessions were those given by speakers from African nations describing the challenges they face and how the teaching of English is responding to their social and economic changes.

This year I was impressed by the jobs market area; the jobs being advertised were from the four corners of the globe and served as a reminder that the bulk of the EFL world is outside the UK. Personally, I would like the jobs market to expand to include volunteer work, internship opportunities and teacher networks as a way to link and share all our expertise.

The new formats of sessions this year were experimental and bold but unfortunately did not always work. Colleagues reported favourably on the Interactive Language Fair on Sunday morning, but the symposiums held at the same time were not well attended; this was a shame because the one I attended on EAP Speaking Skills was excellent.

Finally, the entertainment. The Majestic Hotel in Harrogate is a beautiful setting for a few drinks with friends old and new and the *Pecha Kucha* evening event was nothing short of fantastic—IATEFL's got talent!

Jo: This was my first IATEFL conference. I had heard great things about the event—a massive networking opportunity, a wealth of mind-expanding ideas, and the chance to see EFL royalty in the flesh (I think I stood about three metres away from Scott Thornbury)—and I was not disappointed.

I was particularly impressed by IATEFL's online presence. Conference snippets were being tweeted by the second, the forums were well populated, and overseas audiences could catch up on sessions via the internet. Many sessions looked at using technology in teaching, certainly the topic *du jour*. Some of these sessions looked at the wonder of the web, but I think looking at the practical teaching applications of this wonder could have been much more beneficial in some talks, remembering that technology should be a means to the end of teaching, and not the end itself.

I can honestly say I felt like a new student at a language school. Eyes agog, conference programme clutched desperately in clammy hand, spinning on my heels to find

Harewood 2 before the start of the approaching session. I would have benefited from an induction! I did manage to find the correct rooms in time to see some really inspirational sessions; Sam McCarter's IELTS session was fascinating, and the symposium on Teaching Academic Writing [see 7.4] gave great practical insight, even though woefully under-attended.

Overall, the conference really was a massive and impressive event. I shall certainly be going again. (I will try to assume some experienced bravado in year two.) I am very encouraged that a conference centre so large can be filled with language fans like myself. I've come home!

Email: fiona@target-english.co.uk
jo@target-english.co.uk

2 The learner: motivation, identity and autonomy

2.1 Plenary: Socialising students' motivation and autonomy in the English-language classroom

Ema Ushioda *Centre for Applied Linguistics, University of Warwick, Coventry, UK*

Introduction

As a Japanese person born and brought up in an English-speaking environment in Ireland, I have long been interested in the interplay between self-perceptions, language, culture, identity and motivation. Over the past fifteen years or so, my research interests have focused on the interactions between language learning motivation and autonomy. Specifically, I have drawn on insights from autonomy theory to illuminate the analysis of motivation, particularly from a sociocultural theoretical perspective, and to develop our understanding of how we as teachers can socialise optimal forms of motivation in our language classrooms (for example, Ushioda 1996, 2003, 2007, 2008). Motivation has traditionally been regarded as something that teachers 'do' or 'give' to learners through a variety of motivational tricks and strategies. Yet, for effective and autonomous language learning and language use to take place, motivation needs to come *from within* and be *internally regulated* rather than externally regulated by teachers, parents or other social forces. However, social processes are pivotal in mediating the healthy internal growth and self-regulation of motivation. Understanding this complex interplay is vitally important if we want to help our students develop and express their own motivation and enable them to sustain and regulate their motivation. In this plenary paper, I will explore some key theoretical concepts that can illuminate this relationship between internal and external processes and discuss their implications for classroom practice.

Internally driven motivation

I will begin by exploring concepts of internally driven motivation. Some years ago (Ushioda 1996), I became known to have pushed the argument that the internally driven motivation that underpins autonomy is defined as *intrinsic motivation*. Intrinsic motivation means doing something as an end in itself, for its own self-sustaining pleasurable rewards of enjoyment, interest, challenge, or skill and knowledge development. It is usually contrasted with *extrinsic motivation*, which means doing something as a means to some separable outcome such as gaining a qualification, getting a job, pleasing the teacher or avoiding punishment. I still believe that intrinsic motivation represents an optimal kind of internally driven motivation. After all, there is a great deal of research evidence to suggest that intrinsic motivation promotes high-quality learning, since intrinsically motivated learners are deeply concerned to learn things well, in a manner that is intrinsically satisfying and that arouses a sense of optimal challenge appropriate to their current level of skill and competence. (See, for example, the collection of studies in Deci and Ryan 2002.) However, it seems unrealistic to expect language learners to achieve and maintain a steady state of high intrinsic motivation when faced with the realities of institutionalised language learning, such as exams, boring textbooks or heavy coursework demands.

Moreover, extrinsic motivation is not necessarily an undesirable form of motivation. While some forms of extrinsic motivation may be externally regulated by teachers (the 'carrot-and-stick' approach), we need to recognise that there are forms of extrinsic motivation that are *internally regulated* by learners themselves. In most educational and career development contexts, we strongly value certain types of extrinsic goal, such as obtaining a qualification, getting into a good university, securing a job or achieving promotion. Thus, as van Lier (1996) puts it, motivational factors intrinsic to the learning process (enjoyment, challenge, skill development) and those extrinsic to the learning process (personal goals and aspirations) are best viewed as working in concert with one another. At bottom, what is crucially important is not whether motivation is intrinsic or extrinsic but whether it is *internalised and self-determined* (emanating from within the learner), or whether it is *externally regulated* by others (for example, teachers, negative peer pressures, curriculum demands, parents). (For further discussion, see Ushioda 2008.)

How do we promote motivation from within?

A key practical question, then, is how do we promote this motivation from within? After all, anything we as teachers do to try to motivate our learners runs the risk of backfiring and communicating the message that motivation is something *we* control and regulate (by dispensing rewards and incentives, or threats and punishments), instead of enabling learners' own motivation to grow and develop from within. In fact, quite a lot of research evidence shows that using rewards, incentives, praise and other methods of controlling behaviour not only fosters unhealthy teacher-dependent forms of extrinsic motivation, but can also undermine any intrinsic motivation students may have, since it takes away their perceptions of their own sense of control and self-determination. (See, for example, Eisenberger and Cameron 1996; Lepper and Greene 1978.)

What can we do instead to enable students' own motivation to grow and develop, especially beyond any initial interest and enthusiasm they may have? How can we get learners to *want* to do what they may not necessarily want to do (such as hard work), without resorting to external forms of motivational regulation and coercion? How can we get them to *want* to do not just the things they like doing (like free conversation or language games) but also the things they have to do (like learning vocabulary and grammar, reading difficult texts, doing boring exercises)?

The key, it would seem, lies in orchestrating the social learning environment in such a way that students will *want* to participate and thus want to learn. In this connection, Riley (2003) reminds us of that wonderful illustrative episode in Mark Twain's novel *Tom Sawyer*, where Tom has been given the chore of painting his Aunt Polly's garden fence and faces the taunts of his friends who are out playing and enjoying themselves. Yet Tom craftily engineers the situation so that his friends end up *wanting* to help, through the simple ploy of making the painting task seem as attractive, valued and interesting as possible. In short, even a dull and tedious task can be turned into a motivating one if looked at from a different perspective. What is important is not the nature of the task itself, but how the activity of engaging in the task is constructed through people's interactions, and how motivation develops through this *dynamic of social participation*. As Good and Brophy (1997) emphasise, motivation develops as a result of interactions among persons, tasks and the larger environmental context. Motivation is not a process of spontaneous combustion. It does not simply materialise within the individual but is socially formed and distributed, developing through participation and involvement in experience.

Of course, there is a critical dividing line between orchestrating social participation in experience and wilfully manipulating the behaviour of others to serve one's own ends (as in Tom Sawyer's case). Clearly I am not advocating that we as teachers should seek to manipulate the motivation and behaviour of our learners. Equally clearly, on the other hand, it is our pedagogical responsibility as teachers to create a learning environment where students will want to learn and participate. As I argue here, we can achieve this by orchestrating the social learning environment and learning experiences in ways that enable and promote interaction, participation and involvement and thus motivation from within. Returning to our question of what we as teachers can do to socialise students' motivation from within and their motivation to engage in tasks that call for hard work and effort, we need to think in terms of this dynamic of social participation and involvement, rather than simply trying to control or regulate their motivation from outside.

Socialising motivation through promoting participation and autonomy

As I have discussed elsewhere (Ushioda 2007, 2008), one theoretical tradition that can illuminate this process is Vygotskian sociocultural theory. Vygotsky (1978) developed a sociocultural theory of mind, and its central principle is that higher-order cognitive functions are internalised from social interaction with more competent others. For example, the young child learns how to do jigsaw puzzles through the social experience of doing jigsaw puzzles with older siblings or caregivers. Learning is a socially mediated process. Bronson (2000) explains how this principle of socially mediated learning applies also to the *socialisation of motivation* for culturally constructed goals and activities. This process of motivational socialisation takes places through the child's participation in activities in a particular social setting. Thinking, wanting and doing are shared and jointly constructed in the interactions between children and members of the surrounding sociocultural setting, or we might say between learners and the surrounding social learning environment. Gradually, children (learners) internalise these culturally valued patterns of thinking and doing, and they also internalise culturally valued goals and intentions (i.e. motivation). Thus, being motivated means participating in particular cultural systems of activity, and endorsing and internalising their rules, goals and values so that they become part of our own motivation and value system. For example, when we play tennis or chess, we do not simply make up our own rules at the expense of our opponent. Instead, we derive our pleasure and motivation from exercising our skills within the rules of the game in which we socially participate.

Enabling full participation in the social setting entails enabling people to make meaningful choices and decisions within that setting, so that they experience a sense of personal control or autonomy. Within the field of language teaching, the classic story that illustrates this intimate connection between motivation and autonomy is Leni Dam's (1995) well-known account of how she became involved in learner autonomy. As she writes, her engagement in classroom practices to promote autonomy came about through sheer desperation to find ways of dealing with unmotivated teenage learners:

> In order to survive I felt I had to change my usual teacher role. I tried to involve the pupils—or rather I forced them to be involved—in the decisions concerning, for example, the choice of classroom activities and learning materials. I soon realized that giving the learners a share of responsibility for planning and conducting teaching–learning activities caused them to be actively involved and led to better learning. (Dam 1995: 2)

As Deci and Flaste (1996) explain, from a psychological point of view, involving people in making choices and decisions not only engenders willingness, it also instils a sense of responsibility, since people become responsible for the choices and decisions they make and their outcomes. Developing this sense of responsibility is critical in promoting motivational growth and, in particular, motivational self-regulation. Put simply, an important aspect of motivational self-regulation is our willingness to deal with less-pleasurable tasks which are nevertheless necessary and important in regulating our lives, such as paying our taxes or going to the dentist. In essence, we need to take responsibility for accepting and internalising these regulatory aspects of life if we also want the freedom to enjoy life's pleasures. In this respect, in the education field, there is considerable research evidence to suggest that students' readiness to internalise curricular goals and values depends to a large extent on the degree to which the social learning environment supports their sense of autonomy and involves them in some of the decision-making processes that shape their learning (for example, Ryan, Connell and Grolnick 1992). In short, by promoting autonomy we may facilitate the alignment of individual student motivation with the broader goals and values of the educational process. Moreover, we may socialise students' willingness to take responsibility for regulating their motivation and learning behaviour in line with inevitable constraints and demands.

Autonomy, motivation and identities

Thus far I have discussed general principles in socialising students' motivation from within through promoting autonomy, particularly in terms of enabling participation and involving students in making choices and decisions, and taking responsibility for their learning. In the remainder of this paper, I would like to focus on another key aspect of autonomy theory and practice which has a significant bearing on motivation—specifically, the emphasis given to individual identity and self-expression. The arguments I sketch here draw on more detailed discussions I have developed elsewhere (Ushioda 2009, forthcoming)

While theories of language motivation and associated pedagogies have largely focused on abstract models and concepts and on learners as theoretical bundles of variables, as Riley (2003) observes, a key characteristic of writing on autonomy is its concern with the learner as a fully rounded person, with a social identity, situated in a particular context. In language classrooms that seek to promote autonomous learning, it seems that this concern is translated into pedagogical practices which encourage students to develop and express their own identities through the language they are learning—that is, to be and become themselves so that, as Little (2004: 106) puts it, 'what they learn becomes part of what they are'.

This is vividly demonstrated in Legenhausen's (1999, 2000) comparative analysis of German and Danish children learning English. His study constituted part of a longitudinal programme of research comparing the English-language development of students from traditional textbook-based communicative classrooms in German *gymnasium* and comprehensive schools, and students socialised in a more autonomous learning environment in a Danish comprehensive school. Comparing free conversation practice among pairs of students from the two contexts, Legenhausen shows that students in traditional communicative classrooms seems unable or unwilling to 'speak as themselves' (1999: 181) when invited to converse in English with one another:

S: How old are you?
A: I'm twelve years old. And you?
S: Eleven.
A: Ehm. Do you live in a house or in a flat?
S: I live in a house in Olfen.
A: I live in a flat in Olfen, too. (..) Ehm, eh.
S: What's your telephone number?
A: My telephone number is three five seven five, and what's your tele/ telephone number?
S: My telephone number is ehm three two two two (..)
A: Ah, ah, do you like school?
S: Yes, sometimes.

(Legenhausen 2000: 48–9)

Invariably, they fall back instead on memorised routines and content from textbook dialogues, such as asking one another how old they are, where they live and what their telephone number is. Moreover, their conversations do not follow the development of natural conversations where interlocutors build on one another's turns organically but follow a rigid question–answer structure. In short, these children behave as *language learners* practising vocabulary and structures, instead of *speaking as themselves as people* and expressing their own meanings and identities.

In sharp contrast, students socialised in the autonomous learning environment engage their own motivation, personal interests and identities in their conversations:

C: What shall we talk about?
M: I don't know. What do you think?
C: Ah, we could talk about yesterday.
M: Ok.

C: [What did you?]
M: [What did you?] (laughing)
M: What did you do?
C: Well, I went home from school, and I write (..) some some music for my music group.
M: Yeah.
C: We shall play here Friday, after school, we have (..) borrowed a a room with drums and guitars, and so (..) we're going to (..) record a tape, with our songs.
M: How many are you in your group?

(Legenhausen 2000: 49)

Furthermore, as Legenhausen demonstrates through analysis of turn-taking structures, interactional moves and Gricean principles, these autonomous learners' conversations develop in a far more natural and organic fashion than the pseudo-communication practised by students socialised in traditional communicative class-rooms.

So what happens to *motivation* when students are encouraged to 'speak as themselves' and to express and engage their own identities through the language they are learning? A study by Richards (2006) sheds interesting light on the moti-vational dimension. Richards applies Zimmerman's (1998) model of discoursal and social identities to the analysis of language classroom talk, in an effort to explore whether 'real conversations' are possible in this institutionalised setting. Following Zimmerman, Richards makes a distinction between three aspects of identity:

- *situated identities* explicitly conferred by the particular context of communication (for example, doctor or patient identity in the context of a health clinic; teacher or student identity in the context of a classroom);
- *discourse identities*, as participants orient themselves to different discourse roles in the developing interaction (for example, initiator, listener, questioner);
- *transportable identities* which are latent or implicit but can be invoked during the interaction (for example, during an English lesson a teacher may allude to the fact that she is a mother of two or an avid science fiction fan).

In his paper, Richards undertakes detailed conversational analyses of samples of classroom talk between teachers and students in different language classrooms and shows very convincingly the powerful motivational impact of invoking and orienting to *students' own transportable identities* in the talk. The stretches of talk where such episodes happen indicate a high level of personal involvement, effort and investment in the talk from students. This contrasts with traditional teacher–student talk where students are invariably positioned as language learners who are merely practising or demonstrating knowledge of the language, rather than engaging their own identities and speaking as themselves through this language.

In short, to the extent that we as teachers invoke and orient to our students' transportable identities in the classroom and engage with them as *people* rather than as simply language learners; to the extent that we encourage and create opportunities for them to speak as themselves and engage and express their own meanings, interests and identities through the medium of the target language; the more likely that students will feel involved and motivated to communicate and thus to engage themselves in the process of learning and using the target language.

Of course, this argument does not represent anything really new. This notion of engaging our students' identities is something that experienced language teachers have always intuitively known and is something that has often found its way into the language teacher training literature in the shape of buzzwords like *learner-centred teaching, authentic communication, personalisation* and so on. Without wishing to sound too provocative, I believe that this is a case where practice leads, and where motivation theory has simply lagged behind and is only now catching up with what effective teachers have long been doing in their classrooms. In short, this paper represents an attempt to analyse and theorise such practice.

Current perspectives: motivation as value-based and identity-oriented

As I indicated earlier, a basic limitation of L2 motivation theory to date is that it has been primarily concerned with abstract models and concepts and with learners as theoretical bundles of variables. This abstract and depersonalised approach has been true also for the motivation literature in general educational psychology, which for some 40 years or more has revolved around the central concept of *achievement*, building on the early classic model of achievement motivation developed by John Atkinson (1964), and the associated concepts of need for achievement, achievement orientation, expectancy of success, fear of failure, self-efficacy, attributions and so on. However, it seems that theories of motivation in education are now beginning to shift away from achievement-oriented frameworks towards value-based and identity-oriented frameworks. There is now a growing body of opinion that motivation theories in education should be informed by identity theories, as evidenced in a recent special issue of the journal *Educational Psychologist* edited by Kaplan and Flum (2009).

Of course, at a very general level, it seems a rather obvious thing to say that motivation and identity are linked in this way, i.e. that there is an intimate connection between our goal-directed behaviours and the identities we pursue; between the activities we value and engage in and the social groups we want to identify with; between what we do and the kind of person we see ourselves as or want to become. However, as Kaplan and Flum (2009) point out, it is only recently that motivation researchers have begun to explore these connections and to re-theorise motivation in terms of value-based and identity-oriented frameworks.

In the L2 motivation field too, we have begun to re-theorise language learning motivation in relation to concepts of self and identity, particularly one's aspirations towards certain kinds of linguistic or cultural identity, or towards valued personal or professional identities which are defined in part by proficiency in particular languages. (For a recent collection of theoretical and empirical papers, see Dörnyei and Ushioda 2009.) These ideas have been developed in particular by Dörnyei (2005, 2009) in his recent model of the L2 Motivational Self System, in which he proposes the concepts of *ideal* and *ought-to L2 selves*—that is, visions of L2-related possible future selves to which we aspire and which thus motivate us to learn the L2.

As these concepts of possible future selves imply, and as Kaplan and Flum (2009) also explain, by linking motivation with identity goals and identity formation we bring into focus long-term developmental processes and personal trajectories which contribute to and are shaped by current situated motivational processes. Students' engagement in school, their choices, struggles and negotiations, are clearly affected by and in turn influence who they think they are, who they think they want to be, and who they actually become. As Brophy (2009) emphasises, this perspective on the developmental trajectories of motivation and identity underlines the critical importance of *socialisation* in promoting motivation towards adaptive values and identities and away from those which are less desirable. The identity perspective on motivation thus brings into sharp relief the socially mediated nature of motivation as emergent through the complex interactions of social, individual and contextual processes. (For further discussion, see Ushioda 2009.) As Brophy (2009) comments, identities grow and change, partly in response to encouragement or pressure from the culture at large, or from socialisers, peers and significant others in one's social circle; and these emerging motivational dispositions and identities can solidify and develop into core values and more long-term stable identities.

In terms of my arguments in this paper, there is clearly an important message here. Classroom practices that promote autonomy encourage students to speak as themselves, express their own preferred identities, participate actively, explore and exploit opportunities, make choices and decisions, negotiate, take responsibility, share experiences with one another, evaluate these experiences, and self-regulate their learning and their motivation. Such practices are more likely to contribute to socialising and consolidating adaptive values, identities and motivational trajectories than classroom practices that seek to regulate students' learning behaviours and motivation in a controlled way. Thus, by promoting autonomy and motivating learners to speak as themselves now, we may enable them to fulfil their potential to be the persons they want to become (or grow to value), and to use the language to do the things they want (or grow to value), in a healthy and adaptive way that is internally consistent with their own motivation and sense of self (Ushioda forthcoming).

Email: e.ushioda@warwick.ac.uk

References

Atkinson, J. W. 1964. *An Introduction to Motivation.* Princeton, N.J.: Van Nostrand.

Bronson, M. 2000. *Self-Regulation in Early Childhood. Nature and Nurture.* New York: Guildford Press.

Brophy, J. E. 2009. 'Connecting with the big picture'. *Educational Psychologist* 44/2: 147–57.

Dam, L. 1995. *Learner Autonomy 3: From Theory to Classroom Practice.* Dublin: Authentik.

Deci, E. L. and R. Flaste. 1996. *Why We Do What We Do: Understanding Self-Motivation.* New York: Penguin.

Deci, E. L. and R. M. Ryan (eds.). 2002. *Handbook of Self-Determination Research.* Rochester, N.Y.: University of Rochester Press.

Dörnyei, Z. 2005. *The Psychology of the Language Learner: Individual Differences in Second Language Acquisition.* Mahwah, N.J.: Lawrence Erlbaum.

Dörnyei, Z. 2009. 'The L2 Motivational Self System' in Z. Dörnyei and E. Ushioda (eds.). *Motivation, Language Identity and the L2 Self.* Bristol: Multilingual Matters.

Dörnyei, Z. and E. Ushioda (eds.). 2009. *Motivation, Language Identity and the L2 Self.* Bristol: Multilingual Matters.

Good, T. L. and J. E. Brophy. 1997. *Looking in Classrooms.* New York: Longman.

Eisenberger, R. and J. Cameron. 1996. 'Detrimental effects of reward: Reality or myth?' *American Psychologist* 51: 1153–66.

Kaplan, A. and H. Flum. 2009. 'Motivation and identity: The relations of action and development in educational contexts—An introduction to the special issue'. *Educational Psychologist* 44/2: 73–7.

Legenhausen, L. 1999. 'Autonomous and traditional learners compared: The impact of classroom culture on attitudes and communicative behaviour' in C. Edelhoff and R. Weskamp (eds.). *Autonomes Fremdsprachenlernen.* Ismaning: Hueber.

Legenhausen, L. 2000. 'Focus on learning rather than teaching—with what results?' in D. Little, L. Dam and J. Timmer (eds.). *Focus on Learning Rather Than Teaching: Why and How?* Dublin: Trinity College, Centre for Language and Communication Studies.

Lepper, M. and D. Greene (eds.). 1978. *The Hidden Costs of Reward: New Perspectives on the Psychology of Human Motivation.* Hillsdale, N.J.: Lawrence Erlbaum.

Little, D. 2004. 'Democracy, discourse and learner autonomy in the foreign language classroom'. *Utbildning & Demokrati* 13/3: 105–26.

Richards, K. 2006. ' "Being the teacher": Identity and classroom conversation'. *Applied Linguistics* 27/1: 51–77.

Riley, P. 2003. 'Drawing the threads together' in D. Little, J. Ridley and E. Ushioda (eds.). *Learner Autonomy in the Foreign Language Classroom: Teacher, Learner, Curriculum and Assessment.* Dublin: Authentik.

Ryan, R. M., J. P. Connell and W. S. Grolnick. 1992. 'When achievement is not intrinsically motivated: A theory of internalization and self-regulation in school' in A. Boggiano and T. S. Pittman (eds.). *Achievement and Motivation: A Social-Developmental Perspective.* Cambridge: Cambridge University Press.

Ushioda, E. 1996. *Learner Autonomy 5: The Role of Motivation.* Dublin: Authentik.

Ushioda, E. 2003. 'Motivation as a socially mediated process' in D. Little, J. Ridley and E. Ushioda (eds.). *Learner Autonomy in the Foreign Language Classroom: Teacher, Learner, Curriculum and Assessment.* Dublin: Authentik.

Ushioda, E. 2007. 'Motivation, autonomy and sociocultural theory' in P. Benson (ed.). *Learner Autonomy 8: Teacher and Learner Perspectives.* Dublin: Authentik.

Ushioda, E. 2008. 'Motivation and good language learners' in C. Griffiths (ed.). *Lessons from Good Language Learners.* Cambridge: Cambridge University Press.

Ushioda, E. 2009. 'A person-in-context relational view of emergent motivation, self and identity' in Z. Dörnyei and E. Ushioda (eds.). *Motivation, Language Identity and the L2 Self.* Bristol: Multilingual Matters.

Ushioda, E. forthcoming. 'Motivating learners to speak as themselves' in T. Lamb, G. Murray and X. Gao (eds.). *Identity, Motivation and Autonomy: Exploring the Links.* Bristol: Multilingual Matters.

van Lier, L. 1996. *Interaction in the Language Curriculum: Awareness, Autonomy and Authenticity.* Harlow: Longman.

Vygotsky, L. S. 1978. *Mind in Society: The Development of Higher Order Psychological Processes.* Cambridge, Mass.: Harvard University Press.

Zimmerman, D. H. 1998. 'Discoursal identities and social identities' in C. Antaki and S. Widdicombe (eds.). *Identities in Talk.* London: Sage.

2.2 Learner identity: does Meredith really want to sound like me?

Stuart Perrin *Queen Mary, University of London, UK*

Introduction

Language learners have complex multiple identities, and these identities play an important role in accessing the English-speaking communities that the learners wish to belong to, both real and imagined. Norton (2000) suggests that existing theories of motivation do not engage fully with the complexities of the relationship between language learners and the target language, and that motivation is better understood through the concept of investment. Investment links a learner's identity with his/her commitment to learn the target language, where investment in the target language is 'also investment in a learner's own identity' (Norton 2000: 11). Society is not equal; the linguistic communities that discourse is placed in are not standardised and are often places of conflict, with power relationships constructed (and co-constructed) from an individual level up to national and international levels. Identity is influenced and constructed by and within this potpourri of discourses. Language plays an important role in negotiating a sense of self, acting as a gatekeeper in terms of gaining or being denied access to social networks that allow language learners the chance to speak.

The study of Meredith

Meredith was an English language student from Beijing who had come to England to improve her English and study on a pre-master's university preparation course before starting a master's degree in Maritime Law. She came to England with a good level of English and was successful in passing an English language exam to continue her postgraduate studies. The study of Meredith was part of a larger research project that looked at the relationship between constructed language learning environments and language students' identities as learners through a case study of Chinese EFL students in London.

During the study, the importance of acquiring an 'English' accent was a recurring theme with Meredith, highlighted by her sense of failure if she returned to China with a 'Chinese' accent. She wanted to acquire a 'perfect' English accent, where 'perfect' meant 'Received Pronunciation' or 'educated native speaker' (ENS) (Jenkins 2006: 82). One recurring theme was that Meredith felt that for Chinese people generally, pronunciation was important, as was sounding 'correct', highlighted by her belief that having a 'Chinese' accent would be seen as a sign of low proficiency.

Interpretation

Kanno and Norton describe a need to understand investment in second language learning in terms of 'the context of future affiliations and identifications, rather than prevailing sets of relationships' (2003: 244). Meredith's language goals, therefore, needed to match the language expectations of her future imagined community; if these goals were not met, this could mean exclusion, with a resultant loss of status and symbolic power. Meredith's desire to acquire a 'perfect' English accent, therefore, needs to be understood in terms of what this would mean to her once she returned to China, and the potential consequences of being seen as having a 'Chinese' English accent.

London as an English language learning environment was seen by Meredith as important as it added further status in terms of her learning of English. However, being in London also increased the possibilities for exposure to forms of English that would challenge her idea of 'perfect' English pronunciation. Meredith seemed to overcome this by creating a dual 'London', one that was real and consisted of everyday exchanges, and one that was imagined and constructed by her. Meredith was thus able to withdraw from contact with the 'real' English-speaking community, maintaining only surface relations, which enabled her to preserve an 'unreal' image of London and Englishness and not challenge her own ideas of what constitutes proper English. As a result, Meredith was able to keep a sense of direction towards her future imagined community as well as preserve the image of the ideal language that she wished to attain.

Conclusions

Meredith's perceptions of English, or what she perceived to be 'correct' English, were in many respects a result of the status and resultant power that she believed this would provide. Meredith, along with other members of her future imagined community, was claiming ownership to the variety of English that she felt she was expected to learn, thus enabling access to that community élite, and rejecting other varieties that did not meet her criteria as being ENS standard as 'not for them'. This relationship of language and power as demonstrated by Meredith in her rejection of what she imagined as 'non-perfect' English, clearly has implications for ELT practitioners as they need to somehow take into account the perceived need of learners to aspire to levels of imagined native-speaker accuracy.

Email: s.perrin@qmul.ac.uk

References

Jenkins, J. 2006. 'English pronunciation and second language speaker identity' in T. Omoniyi and G. White (eds.). *The Sociolinguistics of Identity.* London: Continuum.

Kanno, Y. and B. Norton. 2003. 'Imagined communities and educational possibilities: Introduction'. *Journal of Language, Identity and Education* 2/4: 241–9.

Norton, B. 2000. *Identity and Language Learning: Gender, Ethnicity and Educational Change.* Harlow: Pearson Education Limited.

2.3 Motivation revisited: when in Britain, do as the Britons do?

Mikio Iguchi *University of Warwick, Coventry, UK*

Background

Integrativeness has been deemed the cornerstone of L2 motivation, which reflects a learner's interest in learning the L2 in order to integrate with a tangible target-language community (Gardner 2001). However, this concept has been questioned in contexts where a target-language community is absent or vague for L2 learners. The UK, in which the present research was undertaken, may appear to offer learners favourable opportunities to experience actual integration into a local Anglophone community. However, this assumption does need to be examined.

L2 learning in a target-language community results in the creation of a new cultural-ethnic identity for learners in adjusting and adapting to a new culture. Such 'hybrid identities' of L2 users has recently started to gain favour within academia. Thus, I set out two research questions to explore the motivation and identity of eight native Japanese speakers (hereafter referred to as 'NJS') who live in the UK:

1 How do the NJSs weigh Gardner's integrativeness as they use English in the UK?
2 What is the NJSs' self-perceived identity in the UK?

Research methodology

The focus is on the interpretation of the participants' lived experience in the UK from a hermeneutical perspective rooted in social constructivism. The following data collection methods were used: semi-structured interviews, participant observations, participant diaries, and research diaries. The eight NJS participants (two postgraduate students and six immigrants) were all brought up in Japan. It was a prerequisite that the NJSs had stayed, or intended to stay, in the UK for at least a year.

On integrativeness

In general, the participants felt an affinity with people with whom they could empathise. Common conversation topics draw interlocutors closer, and their ethnicities or languages are not the only driving force. Naomi (a homemaker, 10 years in the UK, married to a British husband) stated that she felt affinity when there was mutual understanding. She felt that her non-Japanese friends living in Japan were closer friends than local Japanese in Japan because she could understand the hardships and loneliness they felt while living abroad. It can be inferred that in daily conversation contexts, we need empathy with others in order to become closer.

On cultural-ethnic identity

All the participants believed that their cultural-ethnic identities were Japanese rather than British. Karen (a homemaker, 11 years in the UK, married to a British husband) reported that she had had no time to think about her cultural-ethnic identity until her children started going to school. She gradually started realising how attractive

Japanese culture was by practising the tea ceremony and *kimono* (Japanese dressmaking) with Japanese friends. The more she realised that there were no Japanese things around her in the UK, the more she missed them.

Spencer-Oatey (2007) suggests that an identity can be located in the spectrum between 'core' and 'periphery' and that it is a subconscious self-perception which emerges like an anti-virus software when threatened. Karen's most valued identity was that of 'mother'. Her cultural-ethnic identity shifted from 'periphery' towards 'core' when she found she had more time on her own. Thus, when she realised how much she missed her ethnic heritage, she longed for it.

However, this does not mean that the participants separated from the British community and consolidated their cultural-ethnic identity. Regarding their attitude towards Japanese culture, they perceived themselves somewhat differently from Japanese people in Japan.

Conclusion

Integrativeness was not the driving force behind the participants' desire to learn or use English in the UK. The current research does not deny the existence of integrativeness, but it implies that integrativeness is not the core value for these participants, since they were living in the UK as 'Japanese' in a 'mosaic' rather than assimilating into British society, as implied by the 'melting pot' analogy. The participants were not driven closer to others just because of their ethnicity or language, but because of empathy derived from commonalities. The participants' self-perceived cultural-ethnic identity was 'Japanese' which was latent when secure but emergent when threatened, thus shifting between the 'periphery' and the 'core', in search of local acceptance.

Email: mickey73wwjd@m2.gyao.ne.jp

References

Gardner, R.C. 2001. 'Integrative motivation and second language acquisition' in Z. Dörnyei and R. Schmidt (eds.). *Motivation and Second Language Acquisition.* Honolulu: University of Hawaii Press.

Spencer-Oatey, H. 2007. 'Theories of identity and the analysis of face'. *Journal of Pragmatics* 39/4: 639–56.

2.4 Implications of research on measuring language learner autonomy

Fumiko Murase and **David Hall** *Macquarie University, Sydney, Australia*

Introduction

Learner autonomy has been widely recognised as multidimensional and defined in terms of its different aspects, such as 'technical', 'psychological', and 'political' (Benson 1997). The fact that learner autonomy is not a single-function construct makes it difficult to understand what it really is. This study aimed at clarifying the seemingly complex nature of learner autonomy by investigating the interrelationships among the sub-constructs that together make up the construct, since such interrelationships are often neglected. Legenhausen (2007: 18), for example, claims:

> Although she [Oxford 2003] claims [...] to have come up with a more 'systematic model of L2 learner autonomy', the four suggested 'perspectives' she proposes lack one essential ingredient of a model: the interrelationships between the various components are not indicated.

Besides, there is little empirical research investigating these interrelationships (Benson 2001).

The study

The study was conducted by analysing the data collected through a questionnaire, the 'Measuring Instrument for Language Learner Autonomy' (MILLA), which was developed to measure the degree of Japanese university students' autonomy as EFL learners from multidimensional perspectives of learner autonomy. Based on the literature review, learner autonomy was operationalised as consisting of four main sub-constructs: technical, psychological, political-philosophical and socio-cultural autonomy, all of which were covered in the MILLA. The paper-based questionnaire consisted of 113 items on a five-point Likert scale and was written in Japanese. The participants were 1517 Japanese students from 18 different universities in Japan.

Data analysis

The data were analysed statistically, using both exploratory and confirmatory factor analysis (EFA/CFA), and the latter was conducted using structural equation modelling (SEM). Firstly, a model of each sub-construct (for example, technical autonomy) was specified on the basis of its hypothesised relationships among both latent (non-observable, theoretical) and observed (or observable) variables. The model was then tested using SEM to investigate the level of fit of the model. If the hypothesised model did not show an acceptable level of fit, alternative models were re-specified based on the results of EFA with different number of factors, and then CFA was conducted on the re-specified models using SEM to examine their level of model fit. The model which showed both the best fit and most theoretically justifiable structure was selected as the final model of that particular sub-construct. The procedures of data analysis are illustrated in Figure 2.4.1.

After a model of each sub-construct was confirmed, a 'combined model' that incorporated the hypothesised interrelationships among the four sub-constructs were specified and the model was tested using SEM in order to validate the hypothesised structure and investigate the correlational values.

Findings

The results indicated that there were significant correlations between all the pairs of sub-constructs. The correlational value of each pair is shown in Figure 2.4.2.

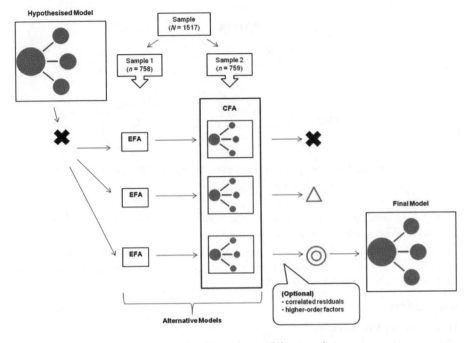

Figure 2.4.1: Procedures of data analysis

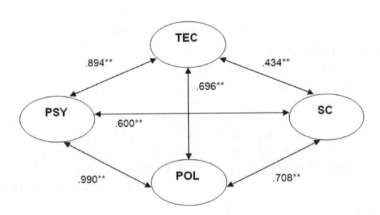

Figure 2.4.2: Correlations between different aspects of learner autonomy (n = 1517)

TEC = technical; PSY = psychological; POL = political-philosophical; SC = socio-cultural. The coefficient next to the arrow indicates the estimated correlation between each pair. ** $p < .001$

However, the results showed that the fit of the model was statistically unacceptable. Therefore, the combined model was re-specified by considering the extremely

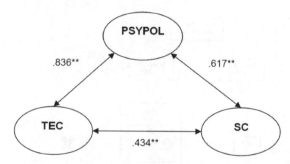

Figure 2.4.3: Correlations between sub-constructs of learner autonomy
*(n = 1517). ** p < .001*

highly correlated pair (i.e. PSY and POL) as a single sub-construct (labelled as PSYPOL). The results are shown in Figure 2.4.3.

The modified model was found to be acceptable and achieved an acceptable level of model fit. The results also indicated that there were statistically significant correlations among the three sub-constructs.

Implications

Implications for theories

This study showed that there were significant correlations among the different aspects of autonomy, which can be seen as empirical evidence to support the suggestions in the literature. It also indicated that the construct of autonomy was multidimensional and that there were three main sub-constructs of autonomy.

Implications for practice

How could our findings be used by teachers to effectively promote their students' autonomy? We would suggest that teachers should be aware of the multidimensional nature of the construct and incorporate the multi-perspectives into their practices so that they can effectively help their students develop all different aspects of autonomy in a balanced way. For example, they should not focus heavily on strategy training, focusing only on the technical aspect of autonomy, but incorporate other aspects such as raising students' awareness (i.e. psychological autonomy).

Email: fumikomurase@gmail.com

References

Benson, P. 1997. 'The philosophy and politics of learner autonomy' in P. Benson and P. Voller (eds.). *Autonomy and Independence in Language Learning.* London: Longman.

Benson, P. 2001. *Teaching and Researching Autonomy in Language Learning.* London: Pearson Education.

Legenhausen, L. 2007. 'Classroom research in autonomous language learning'. *Independence* 42: 17–20.

2.5 How autonomous are my students?

Anja Burkert *University of Graz, Austria*

Introduction

In my presentation I reported on the findings and pedagogical implications of a small-scale interview study which I conducted with a first-semester grammar class in the English Department of Graz University. The purpose of my research was to find out where my students stood in terms of autonomy after attending my three-hour class for a whole semester (i.e. around three months). In this class, I had introduced some aspects of learner autonomy such as learner diaries, peer-reviewing sessions and collaborative group work.

Methodology

The research questions for my semi-structured interviews were as follows:

1 Are my students able to stand back from their learning process and think in a reflective manner about their learning?
2 Are my students aware of themselves as language learners?
3 Are my students able to benefit from group work and peer-reviewing sessions?
4 Are my students aware of their own responsibility as learners, or do they primarily rely on the teacher?

I conducted 13 interviews, including two pilot interviews, which lasted around 20 minutes each. In order to generate data relevant to my four research questions, I asked around 12 questions concerning the keeping of the learner diary, the students' awareness of their strengths and weaknesses as language learners, their beliefs and attitudes in relation to group work and peer-reviewing of home assignments, and finally their stance on the distribution of responsibility among teacher and learners. To analyse the data, I used qualitative content analysis.

Findings

Research question 1: ability to reflect on their learning

As the Austrian school system does not seem to particularly foster the development of learner autonomy, first-semester students tend to need support in learning how to learn in(ter)dependently. The university certainly expects students to be able and willing to take charge of, and responsibility for, their own learning. However, as the number of students in the language classes is quite high and contact hours limited, it is often difficult to determine the exact needs of individual students in this respect.

I therefore decided, as a first step, to promote reflectivity and awareness of language learning in my classes by introducing learner diaries. In these diaries, students had to answer a set of specific questions after each class (*What* did we do today? *How* did we do it? *Why* did we do it? Good/bad points? Suggestions for changes?). In my interviews, I found that my students seemed able—at least to some extent—to think in a reflective manner about their learning, but that they still needed a lot of practice.

Research question 2: awareness of themselves as language learners

Here I found out that not all of my students appeared to be aware of their strengths and weaknesses and only few students seemed to check their progress or set themselves learning goals.

Research question 3: ability to benefit from collaboration with their peers

I found out that my students seem to think that group work can enhance language learning and seem to be able to benefit from peer-reviewing sessions. They also seem to have no problem accepting feedback from their peers.

Research question 4: awareness of responsibility for their own learning

Here I found out that my students seemed to consider both teachers and learners responsible for the success of a lesson, and that they expected the teacher to be a sort-of guide.

Pedagogical implications of findings and conclusion

I have gained valuable insights from my interview study for my own teaching. I have learned, for example, that keeping learner diaries definitely promotes students' ability to reflect on their learning. I will, therefore, continue to have students keep learner diaries, but I will alter the questions slightly to put more focus on students' learning instead of my teaching. I have further decided to encourage students to use their learner diaries also to reflect on their progress and to set learning goals for themselves. In addition, I will, in future, introduce in my classes self-assessment tasks and progress checks. Finally, I intend to enhance group work, but also to ensure that students document the outcome of their collaboration.

To conclude, I would like to quote one student whose remark showed me that I am on the right track: 'I really enjoyed your classes because it was not just sitting and writing; it was really working.'

Email: anja.burkert@aon.at

2.6 Toasting the future of Independent Learning Centres

Kerstin Dofs *Christchurch Polytechnic Institute of Technology, Christchurch, New Zealand* and **Moira Hobbs** *Unitec, Auckland, New Zealand*

Introduction

While Independent Learning Centres (ILCs) and their equivalents (Self-Access Centres, Language Learning Centres, Self-Directed Learning Centres) have been developing over several decades in tertiary institutions worldwide, many in New Zealand are now undergoing yet another 'restructuring' process. There are several reasons for this. Firstly, the guiding principle for this combination of philosophical and locational shifts directed by senior management stems from the concept of amalgamating various student-oriented functions such as Course Information, Libraries,

Information and Academic Literacies including IT, Academic Support and Pastoral Care services, into one shared space, called a Student Learning Centre, Library Commons or Hub. Secondly, another main force behind these changes is financial restraints—both from within the institution (for example, required economic returns, staff–student ratios, staffing allocations and workload, faculty funding formulae for research, etc.) and from external factors (for example, changing funding mechanisms and overall governmental financial support for students and research, and the global recession affecting enrolments and student travel).

In the current environment, many ILCs are being forced to re-think their management and survival strategies. This research project aims to offer some 'good practice' guidelines for the successful development of existing and planned ILCs. One of the goals is to assist with the development of autonomous learning initiatives, as this seems to be an important focus of many centres, i.e. enabling students to make their own study decisions and control their future learning—*what* they do, and *when, how* and *where* they do it, including self-assessment and evaluation of their learning.

Although this project focuses on ILCs within the English as Speakers of Other Languages (ESOL) context in New Zealand, the findings are equally applicable to institutions not having a discrete language school yet hosting students who need English language and/or general academic literacy support anywhere in the world.

Background

This study follows a number of research projects and pilot studies done by the researchers, resulting in improvements in three main areas: increased utilisation of the ILC; improved learning support for students, teachers and ILC staff; and raised awareness of effective learning strategies. The current study is also informed by research into setting up and managing ILCs (Gardner and Miller 1999), practices for advising (Mozzon-McPherson 2001) and assisting students to develop learning strategies, and discussions about autonomous learning and ways of measuring its success (Pemberton *et al.* 2009).

Our study to date includes data from seven universities and polytechnics throughout the country. Observations and interviews of key personnel have been conducted in order to collate useful models and ideas for a 'Good Practice in ILCs' brochure, which will be made available to all institutions.

Findings

The main themes and issues emerging so far fall into five broad categories:

1 The institutional philosophical and guiding principles of senior management which inform decisions about autonomy and ILCs, and where they sit physically within the institute.
2 ILC staff reporting lines, academic status and workload.
3 How and where ILCs are publicised and used, and how materials are resourced and displayed.
4 Learner activities, for example, speaking opportunities and learner involvement in the Centre.

5 An identified need for a national support network which could link with a global forum for international validation and standardisation of ILCs proposed by David Gardner (Hong Kong) and Marina Chavez-Sanchez (Mexico).

Future directions

The researchers plan to visit more ILCs to get a broader picture of what services are currently available and what pertinent issues have arisen; to re-establish a network amongst practitioners, based on the defunct Self-Access Centre Special Interest Group (SACSIG); and to create some form of a virtual Community of Practice, with the overall aim of leading to new and improved ILCs and student results in terms of success and retention.

Both researchers are also refining new specialist roles of paid Academic Tutorial Assistants or Learning Facilitators within their Centres and/or in the classrooms and computer/language labs. The scaffolding provided by these staff members may involve appointments within timetabled classes or simply drop-in sessions, either one-to-one or in small groups, sometimes utilising a 'learn by teaching' technique.

As many people involved in language teaching and learning know, people are like snowflakes—each having a unique shape and structure—so each individual has his/her own combination of cultural and educational backgrounds, learning experiences and learning styles, living and working situations, personal aspirations and abilities in both the cognitive and meta-cognitive domains, and self-identity and learner beliefs. Therefore, personalised autonomous learning approaches with appropriate scaffolding bodes well for the recognition and resourcing of ILCs in the future.

Email: dofsk@cpit.ac.nz

mhobbs@unitec.ac.nz

References

Gardner, D. and L. Miller. 1999. *Establishing Self-Access: From Theory to Practice.* Cambridge: Cambridge University Press.

Mozzon-McPherson, M. and R. Vismans (eds.). 2001. *Beyond Language Teaching Towards Language Advising.* London: CILT.

Pemberton, R., S. Toogood and A. Barfield (eds.). 2009. *Maintaining Control: Autonomy and Language Learning.* Hong Kong: Hong Kong University Press.

2.7 If it isn't in your body, you haven't learned it

Juliet du Mont *Freelance, Cape Town, South Africa*

Why use movement in English language teaching?

The mention of movement in the context of learning a language still tends to raise an eyebrow, even though over the past decade there has been an increase in research on movement and its link to learning (Stevens-Smith 2004). Research has not only suggested that movement activates and builds the neurons and 'wiring' necessary for learning, but it has also uncovered a connection to an area in the brain involved in memory, attention and spatial perception which shows that movement and learning are processed in the same area of the brain (Jenson 2000).

Learning involves internalisation of information. In language learning one way of assisting this process may arguably be by incorporating activities using the kinaesthetic sense in combination with those employing the visual and aural, by having recourse to what may be referred to as 'muscle memory' through total body involvement.

Findings from my recent research project 'Teacher and student perceptions of a kinaesthetic approach to English language teaching' revealed that teachers and students alike perceived a kinaesthetic approach to learning English as helpful, both from the point of view of improving memorisation and of creating a learning-receptive state through relaxing, focusing and bonding students; however, they also felt the need for specific training with regard to how to create movement activities for a specific language goal and how to apply them in the classroom.

The focus of this workshop was therefore to discuss what is involved in creating movement-based language tasks and for participants to create task-associated movement activities for use as review, drills, practice, storytelling or as passive intake of new language.

First movement activity: the icebreaker

Participants were asked to quickly introduce themselves around the room by miming an activity that they enjoy, for example playing tennis, followed by giving their name. The person to whom they were introducing themselves would then mimic the mimed activity and repeat the name of the person associated with it. The roles were then reversed. The aim of the icebreaker was twofold: to individualise a name by adding personal information, and to make that information more memorable by committing it to 'muscle memory' in a physical act of learning.

Participants were then asked to form small groups to answer the following question: 'What issues should you concern yourself with when creating movement activities?' Together we created the following list:

- specific language goal/matching movement task,
- class profile/level,
- cultural appropriateness,
- constraints—noise, available space,
- timing/duration of the movement activity,
- clarity of instructions to learners,
- how to evaluate the activity.

Second movement activity: the warmer

With these recommendations in mind, participants considered the functions of a warmer: to bond, focus or relax learners on arrival in class, to provide a 'wake-up call' during a class by providing a different dynamic, or to function as a lead-in to a new topic. In groups, participants created warmers which included writing a word or phrase on a partner's back to review vocabulary; using a physical warm-up to teach new vocabulary; and drilling phrasal verbs, for example, through the use of commands given by learners to each other to perform certain actions.

Two broad categories of movement task had emerged from my research. The first was what I call *pedestrian* movement tasks where movement is an additive rather than an end in itself— for example, student use of the whiteboard. In this case, movement is used to enliven a task or energise learners but is optional. Secondly, there are tasks I have defined as MELT (movement *essential* to language task) accomplished through movement as an end in itself, as in acting out verbs of locomotion. Together we discussed what kinds of language goals and matching movement tasks may fall into each category.

Focusing on the second category (MELT), we examined some of the inherent advantages: it is fun; it is good for memorising; it is especially good for elementary classes, as the emphasis is on understanding rather than production; and teacher talking time is minimised. On the other hand, the issue of shyness was raised and the possibility of unruly classes, particularly in the case of teens. Recommendations included the importance of explaining to learners *why* we use movement.

Third movement activity: creating a MELT movement task

Participants were given a choice of various contexts for creating a MELT movement task: information-gathering, phrasal verbs, drills, review, Total Physical Response, idioms and storytelling. The favoured context was acting out an idiom, which naturally provided a very lively ending to the workshop!

Email: julietdumont@hotmail.com

References

Jenson, E. 2000. *Teaching with the Body in Mind*. San Diego, Calif.: The Brain Store.

Stevens-Smith, D. 2004. 'Movement and learning: A valuable connection'. *Reston* 18/1: 10–12.

2.8 Symposium on the good language learner

Convenor: Carol Griffiths *Yeditepe University, Istanbul, Turkey and AIS St. Helens, Auckland, New Zealand* with
Andrew D. Cohen *University of Minnesota, Minneapolis, USA*
Sarah Mercer *University of Graz, Austria* and
Bonnie Tsai *Pilgrims, Canterbury, UK*

Introduction

Since its first appearance in the applied linguistics literature around 35 years ago, the 'good language learner' has generated a great deal of controversy which continues to this day. Nevertheless, the underlying logic remains that if we want to know how to do something well (be it music, maths, sport or language), we should look at those who have already demonstrated competence.

Research has investigated the relationships between good language learning and many other variables, including age, aptitude, gender, autonomy, strategies, motivation, style, personality and culture. (See for example, Griffiths 2008.) But many questions remain, three of which will be addressed here.

Question 1: What are the belief systems of highly successful language learners?

This was the question posed by **Sarah Mercer**. Much of the research investigating good language learners (and, by implication, also unsuccessful learners) has focused largely on their learning strategies or styles, with less attention being paid to other learner characteristics. A recent collection of papers has broadened perspectives by including contributions which consider a wide variety of factors, but research into the beliefs of expert learners remains scant, despite the widespread recognition of the importance of learner beliefs in guiding learner behaviours and the ways in which learners interpret their experiences (White 2008).

In order to further investigate this important question, a study of the belief systems of two expert tertiary-level EFL learners was conducted in Austria. Qualitative data were generated with the students in two extended interviews and were analysed employing a grounded theory approach. The study focused on three sets of beliefs: (1) beliefs about the nature of language learning; (2) mindsets; and (3) self-concept. The study attempted to indicate some of the complexity and interrelatedness of learners' beliefs, as well as the close connection between learners' beliefs and their personal language learning history.

Considering the two learners' histories, one more education-based and one more experience-based, it was shown how these learners had developed two very different sets of beliefs. These findings raise various questions about current understandings of beliefs. For example, might it be more appropriate to consider the suitability of a learner's beliefs for an individual, a context and a particular learning purpose, rather than categorising sets of beliefs as being fundamentally 'positive' or 'negative' per se? What are the interrelations between, and relative effects of, socio-cultural, educational and personal contexts on belief development? And to what extent it is possible to make generalisations about the beliefs of good language learners?

Question 2: What does it take for an adult learner to achieve and maintain multilingual abilities?

Andrew D. Cohen addressed this question. In a globalising world, it is increasingly necessary to achieve long-term success in three or more non-native languages. 'Success' in this case may mean being able to use the language as the vehicle of communication in a university course; being able to write professional papers in the language; having control of second language pragmatics, pronunciation and grammar; having people think your second language pronunciation is native or nearly so; having the second language vocabulary trip off your tongue relatively effortlessly; being able to read and critique doctoral dissertations in the second language; or taking an active part in an academic meeting conducted entirely through the second language.

Dabbling in a variety of languages may not be all that difficult. You say a few words or phrases in the target language, and the addressee perhaps acknowledges you warmly for the effort. But then you would be hard-pressed to do anything more substantive with the language, so you quickly switch back to your first language or another language with which you are more comfortable. Often we reach a stage where little remains of what once existed when we were high school or university students fulfilling our language requirement. What does it take to get really good in a second language so that the skills remain for a lifetime—being good enough, for example, to successfully teach a university-level course using that language?

Similarity across languages helps since it potentially reduces interference, but if the languages are dissimilar, it helps for them to have an alphabetic or syllabic script, be morphologically complex, and if genetically unrelated, then at least share areal features, i.e. those that arise from languages being in contact with other as opposed to being derived from the same source language (personal communication from Michael Erard, see Erard forthcoming).

It also helps to have innate ability, such as neural hardware so that your brain allows you to 'pick up' a language after childhood and to monitor yourself effectively ('executive function'). (Personal communication from neurolinguist, Loraine Obler). Talent at retaining language, especially vocabulary, is necessary, as well as an ability to perform your knowledge, attending not only to the gestalt, but to the nitty-gritty details.

The successful multilingual will have a better-developed ability to learn languages (a robust strategy repertoire and an ability to cater to style preferences); will have an identity as a language learner and high motivation—a sense of mission about learning languages (Erard forthcoming); and will be willing to devote lots of hours of hard work to memorising vocabulary, working through the grammar and practising the language in numerous ways.

It helps to be in a context where the second language is needed and where use of that language is socially and materially rewarded, whether the language is purposely selected or is determined by circumstance. A need for the language is crucial; if you don't use your language skills (listening, speaking, reading and writing), you lose them.

Question 3: Is creativity the X factor in the language learning process?

Finally, **Bonnie Tsai** looked at this issue. According to Pugliese (2010), creativity can be seen in such qualities as curiosity, experimentation, sense of adventure, playfulness and intuition. These are qualities essential to the good language learner, and the learner who has these qualities has a head start in learning a language. These are the people who will succeed regardless of the teaching approach or the abundance of material.

Creativity is about having 'mindful thinking' skills, which bring about genuine understanding. This occurs when students are able to take information and skills they have learned in school or other settings and apply them flexibly and appropriately in a new and—at least somewhat—unanticipated setting. Simply put, this definition describes what happens when students understand, when they are able to go beyond simple recall and computation. Students who possess genuine understanding are able to synthesise what they have learned and use their understanding in a context that may be unique to them.

Thinking about creativity in relation to understanding in this way changes the role of the learner. Good language learners make connections across disciplines. In all probability, they will find themselves searching in unexpected corners for more varied information and hopefully talking about and sharing ideas with other students who have different interests and strengths. When students learn to work and share together in the classroom, creativity is generated from this co-operative spirit where everyone contributes knowledge and skills to produce something of real value.

Conclusion

As these three questions demonstrate, there are still many variables relating to good language learners which remain to be further investigated. Answers discussed here suggest that good language learners have varied belief systems, that they have a degree of aptitude, and that they are motivated and creative. It is important that teachers are aware of the characteristics of good language learners if they are to facilitate the process of successful language learning.

Email: carolgriffiths@gmail.com

adcohen@umn.edu

sarah.mercer@uni-graz.at

tsaibonnie@hotmail.com

References

Erard, M. Forthcoming. *Babble No More.* New York: Free Press/Simon and Schuster.

Griffiths, C. (ed.). 2008. *Lessons from Good Language Learners.* Cambridge: Cambridge University Press.

Pugliese, C. 2010. *Being Creative.* London: Delta Teacher Development Series.

White, C. 2008. 'Beliefs and good language learners' in C. Griffiths (ed.). *Lessons from Good Language Learners.* Cambridge: Cambridge University Press.

3 Teacher training and development

3.1 Plenary: The professional life cycles of teachers

Tessa Woodward *Hilderstone College, Broadstairs and Pilgrims, Canterbury, UK*

Introduction

We are very used to cycles and phases in the natural world. We watch the seasons go by and repeat. We know the ages of humankind from watching our families: baby, child, teenager, adult, middle age, old age and second childhood. We use phases in our own thinking too. We see, for example, in the life of groups, first the 'forming' stage, then the 'norming', 'storming' and 'performing' stages (Tuckman 1965). Perhaps there is even a 'mourning' stage as a group breaks up and we feel bereft for a while. Although we are used to experiencing and dreaming up phases, we may be less familiar with the idea of professional life cycles or stages. This is what my plenary was about.

There are many models of teacher career stages available to us. Steffy and Wolfe (2001) present a framework for career development and a wonderful professional wish list, which goes from 'Novice' to 'Apprentice', 'Professional', 'Expert', 'Distinguished' and 'Emeritus'. Some models are linear, some cyclical. Some blur the lines between phases, others are sharp and clear. They are all useful as catalysts for thinking and understanding our own professional lives and those of our friends and colleagues.

I chose four main influences on my own talk. I will introduce them to you in turn, and you can follow them up via the reading references at the end. The first person I want to mention is Jennifer Jarvis, who was Senior Lecturer in Education, TESOL at the University of Leeds and is now retired. Teachers came to Jennifer from Pakistan, Slovakia, Tanzania and many other countries. As she wanted the courses they took to be maximally relevant and useful to them, she used questionnaires and discussion to find out how teachers saw their own career development and needs (Jarvis 1991). In this, she found the work of Michael Huberman (1985, 1989) very helpful, and she told me about it. Huberman was interested in how teachers saw their careers, depending on the number of years they had been in the job; his research included interviews with teachers whose years of teaching experience ranged from one to forty.

Patricia J. Sikes, when at the Institute of Education, University of Warwick, used biographical and narrative approaches to follow teachers from their probationary year to retirement. She wanted to know how secondary school teachers perceived and adapted to their own ageing, their growing old themselves (Sikes 1985). Thus, so far, we have one researcher interested in the number of years a teacher is in the job and another interested in the age of the teacher. Finally, Erik Erikson, a controversial psychoanalyst in the USA in the 1950s and '60s, believed that all of us, no matter what job we are in, go through eight main life stages, each with its own challenges, crises and opportunities (Erikson 1959, Gardner 1999).

In my talk, I used the work of Huberman as a basis and threaded insights from Sikes and Erikson through the talk as appropriate. I also used some video clips from *Teachers' TV* to illustrate various themes that emerged in the research. I told quite a few jokes, and I commented on the less academic, but nevertheless very interesting, work of others. I am sorry to say that for those non-reproduceable aspects, 'You just had to be there!'

The reasons why I chose this topic for my plenary were fourfold. First, a plenary can save listeners time. It can help them to get to know, in just one short hour, an interesting corner of the literature. Second, it can then alert participants to reading which can be followed up later, if something catches their interest and imagination. Third, professional life cycle research can also give us all a perspective on our own career development and on that of our colleagues and friends. Finally, there are also implications arising from it for those with a teacher-training function.

Huberman's study

Starting with Michael Huberman's research, I explained that he worked in the Geneva canton of Switzerland in a school system that he described as monolithic, homogenous and with a strong bureaucracy. He gave two reasons for his research. His first motive was reckless curiosity: he found the initial research questions absolutely irresistible! There were questions like, 'How do teachers view their younger and older peers?', 'Is burnout an extensive phenomenon?' and 'Are there times when significant numbers of teachers think seriously of leaving the profession?' He said his second motive was more mischievous: he wanted to look at some phenomena which were taken for granted by those school officials in Geneva who thought they knew a lot about different 'types' of teachers, even though the evidential basis for their preconceptions was pretty soft!

So, in his study, he interviewed 160 teachers of all subjects, women and men, all working at the secondary level; each teacher underwent five hours of interviews divided into two sessions. From the results, Huberman felt we could plot trends in teachers' careers—roughly related to the number of years of teaching, but not fixed to these in individual cases. He reminds us to handle the identification of phases and sequences very gingerly, as descriptive rather than normative. In other words, the themes that emerged are fairly typical, but this doesn't suggest it is the way things *should* be.

The years and the phases

In the hours of interviews, in answer to open-ended questions and in responses to flash cards and checklists, the teachers in the Huberman study carved up their careers into phases or stages and came up with names for them based on the dominant themes and issues for each stage. Table 3.1.1 provides some notes on a schematic model of successive themes presented by Huberman. (See Huberman 1989 for the original.)

Years of teaching	Emerging themes	
1–3	Career entry: Survival and Discovery	
4–6	Stabilisation	
7–18	Experimentation/Activism	Reassessment/Self-doubt
19–30	Serenity/Relational Distance	Conservatism
31–40	Disengagement: Serene or Bitter	

Table 3.1.1: Themes in the professional life cycles of teachers, as presented by Huberman (1989)

In the plenary I flashed up each year band, one by one, together with its theme or themes. I then explained the themes using quotations from the teachers in the Swiss study. I also showed related video clips from *Teachers' TV*, and I referred to other informal studies and to insights from Sikes, Erikson, and my own experience.

So, for example, for the year band 1–3, I talked about the painful beginnings implied by the theme 'survival'. I mentioned the reality shock many starter teachers feel when they land in the complex environment of the real classroom with all its different student reactions, quite different from the ideal impression gained from their training. At this time, beginner teachers are often preparing for hours every night and may feel as if they are drowning. I showed a short video clip of some Newly Qualified Teachers (NQTs) who had no idea how they were going to make it to the Christmas holidays! I mentioned Sikes' work with probationary-year teachers, some of whom felt very insecure. This insecurity sometimes showed in rather formal behaviour at work. I mentioned Erikson's 'Young Adult' life stage where the challenge is 'intimacy' versus 'isolation'. Beginner teachers may start off wanting to be a friend or like an older brother or sister to their students; they may thus be disappointed when their students don't even see them as real people. I quoted some beginner teachers who said things like, 'I feel a bit of a fraud. Sometimes in class I look around to see where the teacher is, and then I realise it's supposed to be me! And I wonder, am I up to this?'

In the same year band 1–3, the more positive theme of 'discovery' comes up. This is where a young teacher feels the thrill of having her/his own class and her/his own students for the very first time and experiences the professional pleasure of being a peer among colleagues.

In the year band 4–6, the possible theme of 'stabilisation' emerges. This has to do with making a commitment to teaching and having freedom for the first time from constant direct supervision. At this point a teacher may be finding his/her feet and developing a rudimentary repertoire of routines.

Years 7–18 are associated with a number of themes. 'Experimentation' occurs when teachers play with the sorts of things within their classroom over which they have control, such as the use of new technology, rearrangement of the furniture, different pupil groupings, and so on. The teacher is concerned about increasing his/

her impact within the classroom. Teachers may now be actively trying to forget what they learned in their training! They have become more interested in the pedagogy (or 'how') than the content (or 'what') of teaching.

This experimentation phase may lead teachers to become more aware of the institutional barriers constraining their impact. Some teachers need to get past or beyond the walls of their own institution and thus become 'activists'. They may start going to conferences or co-ordinating projects, editing newsletters or learning how different parts of their institution relate. They may be very interested in professional development opportunities.

Less positive themes, from a teacher's point of view, in the 7–18 year band are 'reassessment' and 'self-doubt'. The reassessment can be mild if the teacher simply feels a numbing sense of routine. It can be a mid-career crisis where the teacher wonders what on earth he/she is doing in the teaching profession. It may be even more serious and represent a full-blown existential crisis. We move here into the territory of words like 'stale', 'disenchanted' or 'burnt out'. At this point, I played a very touching video clip of a teacher who was asking for help. Teaching had completely taken over her life. Her partner was finding their joint child care difficult, and the teacher herself was complaining of being constantly tired and stressed. She felt she was getting ill more than other people. She said she would just like to feel calmer; she wanted to avoid feeling that if something unexpected came up, it was a complete disaster and as if the whole world had fallen apart.

As a reaction to the video, we paused for a while to consider what would consti-tute resolution or non-resolution of this phase of possible 'stagnation' and possible 'generation', to use Erikson's terms. Non-resolution could be staying in the profession but continuing to feel bad. Resolution could involve quitting, going part-time, taking on new responsibilities such as mentoring, or something apparently simple such as finding a new hobby.

The year band 19–30 throws up the possible themes of 'serenity', 'relational dis-tance' and 'conservatism'. Teachers who owned up to the feeling of 'serenity' admitted that perhaps they were a bit more mechanical in class; on the other hand, they were more self-accepting and had more natural authority, so discipline was easier. As our students stay relentlessly young (especially if we teach young people), we grow, in relational terms, further and further away from them as we get older. The least pleas-ant path mentioned is perhaps 'conservatism'. This implies resistance to innovation ('I don't want to know about Twitter or Facebook!') and a general feeling that 'The older I get, the better I was!'

By the years 31–40, one question we could ask is, 'What is it that helps people to stay in teaching that long?' We have the possibility, from the studies so far, of either 'serene' or 'bitter disengagement'. With serene disengagement comes a reflective acceptance of one's own mortality, a task not made easy by that fact that, at this stage, even one's department head may be younger than one's own youngest child! The 'bit-terness' referred to involves feelings of dejection, anger, cynicism, or a sense of wasted effort. By this stage, it is not just the children you teach who may think you are 'past it'; maybe even the younger teachers in the same staffroom are beginning to feel this. There is pressure on you to cede your place.

And so, in this way, I built up with teacher quotations and video images, memories and jokes, models and explanations, a picture of each year band and its emergent themes. After doing this with both the positive and pleasant themes such as 'discovery' and 'stabilisation', and with the more painful ones such as 'self-doubt' and 'bitter disengagement', I asked the assembled audience if they recognised themselves or any of their colleagues in any of this. The auditorium was full of nodding heads and I heard lots of 'yeses' around the room. There is an intuitive gut-level feeling that this model rings true. I think it is because it is not a model made by a top-down, external theorist; the year stages, the themes, the quotations I used had all emerged from the teachers themselves during interviews and narrative enquiries.

For some, Huberman says, the career trajectory may be linear. But for many others there are plateaux and regressions, dead ends and spurts and discontinuities. We may stabilise early or not at all, or we may stabilise only to destabilise again later on when an unexpected career challenge or change throws us back into 'survival' mode.

At this stage, I did offer a caveat or caution. Citing Todd Nelson on ageism, I reminded people that the pervasive, and apparently innocuous and well-intentioned, belief that older workers *should* retire in their late 50s or early 60s may be seen by those who wish to continue working as 'dripping with ageism' (2002: 174). Disengagement theories, says Nelson, state that '... ageing individuals loosen ties through lessened social interaction and withdraw' but that 'mounting evidence actually suggests that a large percentage of older workers would prefer to stay in the workplace' (pages 174–175). Confirmation of this comes not just from the experience of my own friends but also from that of several people who attended the 'Question and Answer' session later in the day. Teachers there remarked on the employment law in the UK (that states that a worker can be compulsorily retired at 65) and how it was used against them to force them to retire before they were ready—or, in one case, to put pressure on them to continue with the same workload but now to be paid at an hourly (lower) rate than their previous salary! Shortly before the conference, too, I noticed a report from the conference of the National Union of Teachers in the UK stating that older teachers were angry at the pressure to give up work whether or not they felt ready to do so.

Implications

Once I had worked through the year bands and the emergent themes and had added Nelson's caveat, I suggested that we look at the implications of this research for ourselves personally and for those who have a teacher-training function.

I suggested that one implication for ourselves is that, whatever we are going through at the moment in terms of theme, be it survival, serenity or burnout, the chances are strong that we are not the only ones going through it! This, in itself, can be a helpful thought, for we may blame ourselves too often when we are swept by strong feelings at work. Another implication helps us as we look around at our colleagues and at our fellow participants at conferences, at people who by their dress, actions, questions and conversation show themselves to be very different in their concerns from ourselves. Having familiarised ourselves with the work on professional life cycles, we should realise that they may be undergoing a different theme from us.

We may, for example, be experiencing the activist theme while they are in more of an experimentation mood. In short, knowing about this work should help us to have more compassion for others in our professional community.

As for those of us who are mentors, teacher trainers, teacher educators, directors of study—who have a teacher training function regardless of what we may be called—what are the implications for us? Let's go back to Huberman for a minute here. His study attempted to predict later phases from earlier ones. He wanted to see if it was possible to tell from earlier phases who, for example, would later on be serene or who would feel rather bitter. It proved very difficult to soothsay in this way, but there was one suggestive predictor:

> Teachers who steered clear of reforms or other multiple-classroom innovations but who invested consistently in classroom-level experiments ... what they called 'tinkering' with new materials, different pupil groupings, small changes in grading systems ... were more likely to be satisfied later on in their careers than most others and far more likely than peers who had been heavily involved in schoolwide or districtwide projects ...

And thus ...

> Tending one's own private garden, pedagogically speaking, seems to have more pay-off in the long haul than land reform, although the latter is perceived as stimulating and enriching while it's happening.
>
> (Huberman 1989: 51)

As teacher trainers then, we should not scorn the working teacher's search for tips and recipes, for ideas that will aid his or her pedagogical tinkering. Classroom-level experiments allow us teachers to make decisions about those things over which we have control. This sense of control and this creative tinkering may lead to a feeling of serenity later on in our career.

We thus need, as teacher trainers, to find creative and satisfying responses to all the year bands and all the themes emerging for the teachers we work with, as well, of course, as for our own themes.

Given Nelson's earlier caveat, we may need to add an extra thought here, too. As a profession, we have thought a fair amount about supporting young or starter teachers as they go through their reality shock. We have put a little thought into preventing burnout. Should we also turn our attention to the 'Veterans', those who have been in the classroom for 24 years or more? Can we make sure that their skills and energy are not lost? Can school managers, teacher trainers and colleagues come up with ideas that mean teachers do not become over-routinised and do not disengage bitterly after a few or many years? Can we listen to and respond to those teachers who resist the expectation that they should retire because they are not ready to do so?

I hope that the work I introduced during the plenary and which I hint at for you now, gentle reader, and which you may feel curious enough to read about in time, will imbue all of us in this wonderful professional community of ours with a sense of compassion and understanding for ourselves and our colleagues.

Email: tessaw@hilderstone.ac.uk

References

Erikson, E. 1959. 'The problem of ego identity' as cited in H. Gardner. 1999.

H. Gardner. 1999. 'The enigma of Erik Erikson'. *The New York Review of Books* June 24, 1999.

Huberman, M. 1985. 'What knowledge is of most worth to teachers? A knowledge–use perspective'. *Teaching and Teacher Education* 1/3: 252–62.

Huberman, M. 1989. 'The professional life cycle of teachers'. *Teachers' College Record* 91/1: 31–57.

Jarvis, J. 1991. 'Perspectives on the inservice training needs of NNS teachers of English to young learners'. *The Teacher Trainer* 5/1: 4–9.

Nelson, T. D. 2002. *Ageism: Stereotyping and Prejudice against Older Persons.* Cambridge, Mass.: MIT Press.

Sikes, P. 1985, 'The life cycle of the teacher' in S. J. Ball and I. F. Goodson (eds.). *Teachers' Lives and Careers.* London: Falmer Press.

Steffy, B. E. and M. P. Wolfe. 2001. 'A life-cycle model for career teachers'. *Kappa Delta Pi Record* 38/1: 16–19.

Teachers TV. http://www.teachers.tv/

Tuckman, B. 1965. 'Developmental sequences in small groups'. *Psychological Bulletin* 63: 384–99.

3.2 Professional pathways for teacher trainers and educators

Tim Phillips *The British Council, Manchester, UK*

This talk focused on themes in the development of ELT teacher trainers, using feedback from local teacher trainers who have worked on British Council training programmes in countries around the world. It identified three characteristic stages of development: (1) a beginning stage; (2) a developmental stage; and (3) a mature stage.

The beginning stage

Initial steps into teacher training are not necessarily accompanied by any formal training. Experienced teachers often begin by running short INSET sessions and are encouraged by the following factors: confidence in their abilities as teachers; the feeling that they have something to offer teachers; the encouragement of other colleagues; existing engagement in their own professional development; the ability to articulate their work; and opportunities to try training. One encouragement for new trainers is that the experience helps them in their own teaching: teacher training is invigorating because it enables teachers to see their own instruction in a different light by reflecting on it. Beginning-stage trainers are often modest about their contribution:

- I think if one has to become a teacher trainer, one must always have in mind that everyone has something to teach at any given time to someone.

This stage is often characterised by sporadic training opportunities; some trainers do not seek to do more than this.

The developmental stage

Trainers who do continue often find little in the way of formal training and few opportunities to gain formal qualifications; many trainers in the second stage of development stress the importance of working with colleagues in a supportive community in which the less experienced can learn from the more experienced. They also start to develop their own materials:

- We used to use materials developed by other trainers ... Now, I explore the topic on my own and then decide on which ideas to focus on. It helps me feel more comfortable and confident during my sessions.

  However, there can be considerable stress in the trainer role:

- Now it's my third year of teacher training ... Yes, it's more difficult than teaching ... sometimes it's rather time-consuming and requires a lot of research in search of necessary materials for my sessions ... This way I am still learning myself! Also, I like working with my younger colleagues, feeling that I contribute to their professional growth and development ...

  As they progress, some trainers also recognise that their approach changes from a focus on the content of the training to a focus on the teachers involved and their needs.

The mature stage

At the mature stage, there is confidence and satisfaction in the achievements of being a teacher trainer. There is also an understanding of the need to remain up-to-date with issues relevant to teachers. Some stress the importance of returning to the classroom to remain close to the issues faced by teachers. Over time, the need to respond to changing contexts becomes noticeable, as does the usefulness of extended and detailed study and reflection. However, many experienced teacher trainers find that it can be difficult to find training opportunities:

- I really enjoyed my time as teacher trainer for the project, and am sorry it finished. I have few opportunities now to work as a trainer.

  There is often a lack of paid work:

- I wanted to be a trainer more, but there's not a full-time opportunity. I want to help teachers and now work as an administrator for the local education committee.

  Others find that classroom teaching lures them back:

- After my work training with the British Council, I worked with a private teacher-training institution. It was very challenging, but now I feel I want to go back to teaching.

  While there are opportunities for trainers and educators in teacher-training colleges and in-service training institutions, many trainers rely on fixed-term training projects managed by the British Council and other organisations. This, coupled with the lack of recognised qualifications for teacher trainers and educators, makes it difficult for many to sustain the role.

  Though this is a descriptive presentation about the development of teacher trainers and educators, it does raise some questions about how trainers and educators are supported. More guidance in career pathways could be offered, with recognised qualifications, clear professional standards to aim for, wider CPD opportunities and better rewards, both financial and professional.

Email: tim.phillips@britishcouncil.org

3.3 Practising 'inclusiveness' in teacher training through Critical Cultural Awareness

Padmini Bhuyan (Boruah) *Gauhati University, Guwahati, India*
IATEFL Ray Tongue Scholarship Winner

Background: Critical Cultural Awareness (CCA) and introspection

In teacher-training programmes, the classroom becomes an arena for the interplay of personal, social and professional identities. This aspect of classroom dynamics can be explored as a methodological resource to allow for more inclusive approaches in the language classroom. The methodology calls for trainee ESOL teachers to examine critically their perceptions and responses regarding other cultures as manifested in intercultural communication. Introspection, the goal of which is to gain 'reflexive knowledge of social and cultural practices' (Alred *et al.* 2003: 4), allows teachers to reinvent their pedagogies and move towards a fuller understanding of classroom dynamics.

Demonstration of CCA in practice

Responses to culture

The objective of this workshop was to take ESOL teachers through a series of introspective activities that focused on raising their CCA (Byram and Fleming 1998). In the first activity, the audience looked at a series of office memos that focused on the gradual distortion of a message from the CEO of a company to the office staff. The laughter generated allowed the audience (Indian, British, Israeli, Arab and Korean participants) to realise that shared knowledge (for example, humour in linguistic messages) pervaded cultural and linguistic diversity. Their response was similar not because of their cultural backgrounds, but rather because of their experiences of sub-cultures, such as those played out in offices between superiors and junior staff. From this activity we moved on to evolving understandings of the term 'culture': typical responses being (knowledge of) art, literature, traditions, religion, customs, beliefs and values of individuals; some have surface-level manifestations while others influence our thoughts and actions at a deeper level. The focus of this activity was not on formulating definitions of 'culture'; it simply allowed participants to create a space for various interpretations and to accept the validity of each.

Activities for raising cultural awareness

In the next set of activities, the participants were presented with linguistic material from a particular culture—Indian—and invited to explain the following: (1) the messages behind a set of adverts from popular Indian magazines, and (2) the meanings of a list of expressions from Indian English. The responses of the audience showed their unfamiliarity with this *other* culture as manifested in typical Indian social constructs such as the 'joint family' (three generations of a family living together) or the jargon of the urban Indian youth. The activities encouraged the audience to examine critically their Inter-Cultural Competence (ICC) through their encounters with a different culture and a different variety of English.

Awareness, self-reflection and pedagogy

The discussion following each activity allowed the audience to analyse the interconnectedness of CCA and ICC, and the pedagogical possibilities of using such an approach to develop the CCA of learners in their own teaching contexts. Two pedagogical conclusions were derived from the discussion:

1 Exposure to intercultural experience challenges 'customary modes of perception, thought and feeling' (Alred *et al.* 2003: 4) and leads to self-awareness and self-understanding;

2 Critical awareness generates the linguistic resources to effectively negotiate one's way in different communication situations and to develop intercultural competence.

Critical Cultural Awareness and inclusiveness

How, then, do we *practise* inclusiveness through CCA? Inclusiveness arises from the understanding that the functions of language in one culture may differ from that in another. As demonstrated by the workshop exercises, activities based on the real-life experiences of people from other cultures can be effectively used to expose trainees to manifestations of this otherness. Critical responses to otherness can encourage trainees to accept and allow for different meanings and language behaviour, and make this the basis for developing intercultural competence. For instance, when an Indian declares in conversation that he or she 'passed out' in 2005, it does not refer to their physical condition; it simply means the speaker 'graduated' in that year! Our acceptance of otherness is likely to encourage us to modify our teaching methodologies to include various perspectives and attitudes to the language.

Conclusion

Attitudes to culture and responses to cultural icons, images, linguistic interpretations and values can serve the pedagogical purpose of encouraging critical cultural awareness in the training classroom. The experience of responding critically to events and situations can, in turn, give teachers strategies and tools to situate culture in their familiar classroom contexts and encourage meaningful dialogue. Classroom activities that involve learners' perceptions of themselves and their personalities can serve as sites of language as well as identity development. The teacher-training classroom can thus be used effectively to critically interrogate cultural assumptions and develop intercultural awareness.

Email: padminiboruah@gmail.com

References

Alred, G., M. Byram, and M. Fleming. 2003. 'Introduction' in G. Alred, M. Byram and M. Fleming (eds.), *Intercultural Experience and Education*. Clevedon: Multilingual Matters.

Byram, M. and M. Fleming. 1998. 'Introduction' in M. Byram and M.Fleming (eds.). *Language Learning in Intercultural Perspective*. Cambridge: Cambridge University Press.

3.4 Language classrooms as social spaces

Richard Kiely *UCP Marjon, Plymouth, UK*

This paper examines the social dimensions of language teaching. The analysis is based on two dominant strands in social science research in recent years: *identity*, drawing on the work of Wenger (1998) and the *social value of work*, as set out by Sennett (2008). First, the notion of identity as relational and performative sees all interactions and social encounters as shaped by who we are, and how we want this to contribute to a given social situation. In classrooms, teachers manage people and tasks to ensure participation and engagement. They harness their own identity, personal and professional, to ensure that the social context promotes and supports a sense of contribution and progress. Second, the Sennet view of work as craftsmanship emphasises job satisfaction, which contributes to personal well-being and social esteem. In this view, teaching is something teachers are proud of and feel good about when lessons and classroom interactions work well, and is characterised by mutual feelings of engagement and achievement. The craft of the language teacher is thus essentially social: it involves connecting with each student, and fostering in her or him a sense of purpose, social role and achievement.

The data for this analysis comes from a research study based on a continuing professional development (CPD) programme in a UK further education (FE) college. In this programme, we recorded lessons of participating teachers, identified *critical learning episodes* (CLEs) (Kiely and Davis 2010) which on analysis and discussion raised teachers' awareness of interactions, and thus constituted opportunities for learning. As part of the research process, we created a database of CLEs, captured teachers' reflections on these via emails and journals, recorded and transcribed workshops, and carried out interviews with the teachers towards the end of the programme. These data facilitated two approaches to analysis: a thematic approach, based on shared themes in the views of teachers, and the case study analysis, based on fine-grained analysis of the development of specific CLEs.

Drawing on these theoretical resources and the research project data, we have identified five facets of the holistic, integrated craft of English language teaching:

1 Analytic, cognitive activity (ACA)
2 Learning awareness (LA)
3 Social, affective and cultural factors (SAC)
4 Classroom continuity (CC)
5 Curriculum policy context (CPC)

ACA

Constant planning and
adapting in the classroom,
informed by lesson goals,
student responses,
capacities and personalities

CPC

What the teacher is required
to do, in terms of materials
use, test preparation and
student expectations

LA

Individual trajectories of
learning, related to
challenge of lesson material

CC

Remembering and drawing
on the shared memory and
learning experiences of the
group

SAC

Friendship, respect and
mutuality in the social
space of the classroom

Figure 3.4.1: Facets of English language teaching

In this paper I focus on Facet 3, examining the social dimensions of language classrooms. Teachers talking about their work in general and in relation to specific CLEs routinely referred to the social dimension of classrooms: good atmosphere, good relationships, and mutual respect. They all reflect, as part of the process of becoming experienced, a tendency to emphasise the student rather than the language point, the relationship rather than the lesson plan, the student's engagement and investment rather than immediate correction and uptake.

The analysis of particular episodes illustrates the same orientation to the social. In the 'Scooter' episode, this is evident in three ways. First, to introduce the focus of the lesson—writing a letter of complaint—the teacher tells a story about her daughter's birthday. This elicits a very social response: 'How old is she?' Second, when she is distracted by someone at the door of the classroom, the teacher asks a student to draw a 'scooter', the word she is pre-teaching. She notes later that she did this in part to 'give him a sense of standing in the class'. Third, when further questions about 'scooters' come, the teacher explains their place in UK society, compared to other countries such as Italy. Here she is playing host, explaining how things are in this country.

In these ways, the teacher is constantly performing to make the classroom work as a social space, where people are valued for their social contribution, and where the teacher's professional identity is textured by social and interpersonal considerations. This raises questions of professionalism: is English language teaching a bounded professional activity, or a more general carer role? It also raises issues about how to research teaching and learning in language classrooms: to what extent can we separate the language learning in classrooms from the social strategies and investment which individual teachers have developed to a fine art?

Email: rkiely@marjon.ac.uk

References

Kiely, R. and M. Davis. 2010. 'From transmission to transformation: teacher learning in ESOL'. *Language Teaching Research* 14/3: 277–96

Wenger, E. 1998. *Communities of Practice: Learning, Meaning, and Identity.* Cambridge: Cambridge University Press.

Sennett, R. 2008. *The Craftsman.* London: Penguin.

3.5 The place of imagination in ELT teacher education

Chris Lima *The Open University, Milton Keynes, UK*

A case for imagination

The fundamental reason to carry out a discussion of imagination in teacher education is the writer's firm belief that imagination is not something that is manifest only when teacher trainers use creative material in their sessions, or when they propose tasks which lead participants to employ their own imagination and creativity. Imagination is the core principle that defines the way we see the world, how we understand ourselves and how we act in society. Imagination is what shapes human actions and responses to the self and to others, and it is what enables human beings to communicate and change their world (Bronowsky 1978). Therefore, a discussion of imagination should play an important role in teacher education, since learning to teach engages the learner in a process of 'personal meaning-making' and in the 'participation in and membership of a culture of teachers' (Malderez and Wedell 2007: 14–15), often in socio-historical and cultural contexts that are rarely stable.

The presentation

The workshop started with participants being asked to analyse commonly used metaphors for the language classroom, draw their own metaphors and discuss them in pairs or small groups. Working with metaphors in teacher education has multiple functions. It helps us to create images that represent the way we see things, clarify the nature of our constructed images, and reframe our existing metaphors in alternative ways by comparing and contrasting them with other possible images for the same concept. Creating metaphors demands the engagement of the imagination, for only imagination can allow us to visualise one thing in terms of another and make us conceive the idea of the classroom as a garden or a stage.

The following activity explored the fictional lives of teachers in films. If used mindfully, fictional accounts can provide teacher trainers with a 'safe ground' for the exploration of teaching/learning concepts, beliefs and feelings without exposing participants too much. If *all* stories have mythical, mimetic, cathartic, phronetic (i.e. coming from the teacher's own experience and knowledge) and ethical functions (Kearney 2002), fictional narratives may be as useful for triggering analysis and reflection on teaching/learning beliefs as teachers' biographies potentially are.

These activities were followed by a short presentation on the status of imagination in Western philosophical thinking throughout history and how these ways of seeing imagination have influenced ELT teacher education models. This was followed by a brief discussion on how philosophical and historical understandings of imagination influence the way we conceive the sort of knowledge EFL teachers should have, and how imagination interacts with reflective practices and educational change processes.

Imagination in teacher education

The workshop did not propose the use of creative tasks in order to give teachers practice in adopting and managing the same sorts of activities in their own lessons. It did not propose the use of creative tasks in order to convince teachers that imagination is important for their learners. It advocated that the main reason for adopting an imaginative approach to teacher education is to help teachers to use the power of their own imaginations to make the necessary connections between the different areas of teaching knowledge, and to visualise a big picture of ELT education.

What we need in teacher education is a way of thinking that helps teachers and teacher trainers to explore the possibilities their imaginations open to them in the processes of constructing knowledge, initiating and managing change and developing as professionals. It was proposed that practical ways of implementing a more imaginative approach to teacher education would include a discussion of the role of imagination in teacher-education programmes as well as tasks using metaphors, narratives (biographical/fictional), poetry and drama, visual arts, music and virtual worlds, both in initial teacher training and in continuing professional development programmes.

Email: chrislima90@yahoo.co.uk

References

Bronowsky, J. 1978. *The Origins of Knowledge and Imagination*. New Haven, Conn.: Yale University Press.

Kearney, R. 2002. *On Stories*. London: Routledge.

Malderez, A. and M. Wedell. 2007. *Teaching Teachers: Processes and Practices*. London: Continuum.

3.6 'Do you have that as well?' Teacher stories and teacher trainer stories: sharing and learning

Briony Beaven *Freelance, Munich, Germany*

Introduction

In my workshop I firstly presented a rationale for regarding teachers' and teacher trainers' stories as a means of professional development for both groups, drawing on research into the role of narrative in various strands of educational thought. Participants then tried out professional storytelling, exploring the potential of this way of understanding experience, and defining their first impressions. Finally, I reported briefly on three storytelling mini-projects.

Background and rationale

Insights from different areas of educational research and theory have led to the acceptance of teacher storytelling as a valid mode of professional learning. Bruner (1991) points to the specificity of narratives, their rootedness in time, their potential for accrual and the fact that narratives usually describe the unusual, rather than the quotidian, thus making them memorable and powerful tools for learning. Teacher knowledge perspectives suggest that stories from the classroom can capture the complexity of this knowledge and enable teachers to create a coherent view of unpredictable classroom reality. The literature of communities of practice emphasises active engagement in informal communities and a shared repertoire of stories as ways of learning. It also hypothesises that it is easier to understand the meaning of somebody else's personal experience than to absorb an abstract idea. Reflective practice favours the idea of exploring personal experience for professional, storied learning and reminds us that stories need both tellers and listeners; that experience is both personal and social. Clandinin and Connelly (1995) posit a hierarchical educational landscape where teachers are expected to heed 'experts' and in which many teacher stories are mere 'cover' stories, told by teachers who feel obliged to try and shape their experience to others' expectations. On such a landscape there is a need for safe havens where teachers can cultivate authentic relationships and tell their real stories of classroom practice. More recently, modern technology has been employed in order to extend the range and location of teacher storytelling (Kervin and Mantei 2008).

Storytelling

After the theoretical introduction participants were invited to tell their stories in groups. Before the session they had received a short text asking them to prepare an informal story on one of the following subjects:

- how and why you became a teacher of English/teacher trainer;
- something funny/successful/disappointing that happened in your classroom/training room;
- how a colleague/colleagues have helped you be a better or more confident teacher/ teacher trainer;
- how you juggle your personal and professional life;
- a person/course/book that has inspired your teaching/training;
- any other kind of story that relates to your work as an English teacher/teacher trainer.

Groups worked with enthusiasm on the storytelling task and afterwards reported largely positive feelings. The audience raised a number of pertinent and interesting questions, to which I propose to return in another article. They were:

1 What are the similarities and differences between teacher storytelling and cooperative development?
2 How can teachers be prepared for storytelling, especially in contexts where teachers' own English language skills are limited or where language improvement is a main focus of professional development?
3 What kind of learning results from participation in a teacher storytelling group?

4 What variations on storytelling can be introduced to avoid staleness and repetition after the group has met several times?

Project report

I reported on three storytelling groups, firstly a small group of teacher trainers and then two groups of teachers. Comments from the teacher trainers indicated that they had expected to reflect and learn through telling their stories, and all three included a coda with an evaluative comment, articulating what they had learned from telling and listening to the stories. Teachers noted that the storytelling group had made them feel more 'comfortable' with their colleagues, that barriers between teachers quickly came down and that vertical exchanges, in which very experienced and novice teachers told each other their stories, were regarded as particularly helpful. Furthermore, participation in the group had in some instances provided an impulse for new actions, such as keeping a teaching diary, and storytelling had proved fruitful in a different way from reflective writing: 'In telling the story I reflect on my teaching differently from just noting my thoughts about the last lesson'.

Conclusion

Storytelling validates personal, practical knowledge, and makes teaching a joint enterprise rather than a lone (and lonely?) occupation. It fosters a sense of community, deepens and enriches reflective practice, and according to the teachers in my project, is enjoyable! Further practical work and research are planned.

Email: brionybeaven@t-online.de

References

Bruner, J. 1991. 'The narrative construction of reality'. *Critical Inquiry* 18/1: 1–21.

Clandinin, D. J. and F. M. Connolly. 1995. *Teachers' Professional Knowledge Landscapes*. New York and London: Teachers College.

Kervin, L. and J. Mantei. 2008. 'Taking iPods into the field to capture and share teacher wisdom stories' in *Hello! Where are You in the Landscape of Educational Technology? Proceedings ascilite Melbourne 2008*. (Retrieved from http://www.ascilite.org.au/conferences/melbourne08/procs/kervin.pdf.)

3.7 Video teaching practice: creating authentic materials for initial teacher training

Helen Emery *University of Essex, Colchester, UK*

The project

This project arose out of a need for authentic video-based materials for 'Teaching Practice' (TP): two practical teacher-training modules which are taken by MA TEFL students at the University of Essex. In particular, there was a need for videos showing non-native English-speaking teachers (NNESTs). Most commercially produced videos for teacher-training purposes show experienced native speaker teachers conducting model lessons. Their classes never show learners' reluctance to speak or participate in the lesson; the teacher never faces problems that he/she can't deal with adequately (and which provide excellent opportunities for class discussion later); and, in the words of my students, they are 'not always useful when you are learning to be a teacher'. It was with this in mind that the project: 'Teaching Practice on-line: Creating a resource bank of authentic EFL teaching video materials' evolved. The project was set up with dual aims:

1   To amass a bank of authentic video-based teacher-training materials, and to design accompanying worksheets which could be used in class or as self-access materials.
2   To compare teachers' attitudes towards commercial videos and authentic home-made ones which showed NNESTs teaching. In order to carry out this evaluation, teachers were shown a range of videos, both commercially produced and home-made, during TP modules. Both types of videos had accompanying worksheets.

Practicalities of the filming

Filming student teachers whilst on TP was by far the most time-consuming part of the project. The aim was to film every TP session, but for practical reasons this wasn't always possible. In the end, out of 36 hours of teaching, 24 hours of filming were obtained. Of this, only 14 teaching sessions were considered good enough to use, and these were edited down to 10–20 minutes each. The 14 clips were selected on the basis of the teaching techniques they showed, teachers' use of language and the content of lessons being taught. Worksheets were then designed to accompany these clips so that they could be used either in class by the teacher, or individually by students as self-access materials.

Designing the accompanying worksheets

The goal of the worksheets was to provide opportunities for student teachers to focus on the reality of teaching a lesson, including analysis of the events that take place during it. Therefore, the worksheets had to contain questions that did not merely assess comprehension, but which required students to analyse why a teacher may have done something, decide whether his/her course of action was appropriate and, if not, suggest how it might have been done differently. Woodward (1992) suggests that trainers use structured discussions in their teaching as these can help to build on previous experiences of group members, and at the same time, introduce new ideas to the group. Figure 3.7.1 gives a sample worksheet that was designed to accompany a lesson on tourism from Doff and Jones (2000). Structured discussion in this case revolved around the teachers' questioning techniques, elicitation of vocabulary, deviation from the lesson plan and use of supplementary materials.

Using the videos as self-access materials

Most of the student teachers reported watching the videos in their own time; however, few had used the accompanying worksheets in this way. This was slightly disappointing as the main aim of the project was to develop video-based materials for teacher training, and the worksheets were an important part of this training. Watching a video clip without guidance is not in itself a particularly useful task, especially for

1	How does Agna open the lesson? What 'warm-up' questions does she ask?
2	How does she introduce the topic?
3	Agna elicits several words and phrases during the lesson. What are they? Are there any that she had difficulty in eliciting?
4	What other means of explanation for new words does she use? (for example, mime, gesture, drawing …?)
5	Questioning: Is there any S–S questioning, or S–T questioning? Or is it all T–S?
6	Does the teacher deviate from the lesson plan at all? If so, why is this?
7	Does she use additional materials or tasks that are not in the course book? Can you think of any possible tasks that she might have included to support the learning in this lesson?
8	What pair work tasks does she set up? How does she monitor pair work? Can you think of another way to monitor pair work?
9	The teacher asks the students: 'What is dangerous?' What did she mean by this question? Can you think of a better way of asking it?

Figure 3.7.1: Worksheet to accompany Agna's lesson (Language in Use, Pre-intermediate, Unit 22: Around the World)

trainee teachers who have perhaps not had much experience of teaching themselves. Various reasons were given for teachers' reluctance to use the worksheets, the main one being the time factor: it takes twice as long to watch a video and fill out a work-sheet as it does to watch a video alone. As most of the teachers watched the video clips in the university's computer labs, time constraints were important to them.

Project evaluation

On completion, the project was evaluated through a questionnaire which contained a range of open-ended and fixed-response items. One hundred per cent of teachers responded that the project videos (showing NNESTs) had helped them develop their teaching skills, and 71 per cent said they had benefited more from the project videos than the commercial videos they had also watched in class. The video clips and accompanying worksheets have been uploaded to the university's intranet and will be stored there for a period of five years, so they can be used by future generations of trainee teachers.

Note

Further details of the project can be viewed at http://www.essex.ac.uk/ltu/funding/projects.shtm.

Email: hemery@essex.ac.uk

References

Doff, A. and C. Jones. 2000. *Language in Use, Pre-Intermediate*. Cambridge: Cambridge University Press.
Woodward, T. 1992. *Ways of Training*. Harlow: Longman.

3.8 E-development for primary teachers in the Black Sea region

Suzanne Mordue *British Council, Istanbul, Turkey*

The starting point

The introduction of languages into the primary curriculum in Turkey highlighted both the importance of English and the lack of qualified professionals to teach the subject for this age group. As a result, the government was forced to continue accepting short-term teaching certificates as a qualification for English teachers, although these had been phased out in other subject areas in 1998.

In-service training was unable to bridge the gap as the training offered was a 'drop in the teaching ocean': each teacher could only be guaranteed a week's training *every 30 years*. When offered training, teachers were often disappointed to find a lecture style used and a focus on teaching theory that they saw as irrelevant to their day-to-day teaching needs.

As the British Council already had a strong working relationship with the Ministry of Education, we decided to develop a project to support the need for appropriate training, which could reach the 30,000 primary teachers working in 80 cities across Turkey. It was clear that such a large number of teachers could only be reached online, and we decided to develop a blended-learning course. With the growth in internet usage, this was a realistic aim in Turkey, and we chose Moodle as our virtual learning environment.

Piloting

To add an observation element to the online learning experience, a local primary school teacher was filmed using some of the teaching techniques discussed on the course. I would recommend this for anyone setting up online teacher training as it has become the most popular element of the course. Anecdotal evidence suggests that, in many schools, peer observation is not practical because of the long working hours of teachers.

The initial pilot project highlighted how ambitious we were in setting up the online component with 60 participants! With hindsight, we realise that a maximum cohort of 25 participants is more workable for the tutor. An independent evaluation showed us the importance of socialisation to the success of online courses. We added Plenary and Social forums where off-course topics could be discussed to create a wider sense of community. We could also clearly see that we needed to expand the geographical scope of our training in the next stage.

With support from the Ministry of Education, 14 teachers from nine cities in Turkey were trained to be face-to-face and online trainers for this course. In 2009 these facilitators trained over 400 teachers across Turkey. Again, many lessons were learned from this next step. We set up a section of our Moodle platform as a trainer's resource kit with detailed supporting documents, and we included a 'coffee shop' where the facilitators could share ideas and chat about their courses. Creating this interaction between the moderators has been one of the most successful approaches we have taken, as this takes the place of 'staffroom chat'. We also produced checklists of the tasks for all modules, so that the tutors could record the information quickly and see at a glance which participants were keeping up with their workload. As many online tutors will have discovered, moderating a course can be very time consuming unless support mechanisms are in place.

Getting to know our neighbours

Mixing online groups so that teachers were meeting participants who were not on their face-to-face course led to more productive discussion; when we expanded the English Teacher Training Online (ETTO) project into other countries, this approach became even more beneficial. We started to work with project managers in Armenia, Azerbaijan, Georgia and Ukraine. For historical reasons the political relationship between some of these countries is strained, so this project was important from a cultural relations point of view. Many teachers made friends with their 'neighbours' for the first time; as the similarities of their teaching situations quickly began to emerge, bonds were forged. We found that teachers who had struggled to find training in the past—for example, those in smaller cities such as Batumi in Georgia—were the most appreciative.

With the only prerequisite being internet connectivity, online education can break down barriers and also bring much-needed resources. As online educators, we should be reaching out in this way. One of the participants, Elif Arpacı, says it best:

> I just thank you for giving me the chance to improve my career. In my hometown I don't have anything to do apart from participating in some seminars. With the help of this online course I could participate and learn lots of things.

Email: suzanne.mordue@britishcouncil.org.tr

3.9 Harnessing reflection and Continuing Professional Development

Seamus Harkin *British Council, Colombo, Sri Lanka* and **Wasantha Yapa** *Regional English Support Centre, Mahiyangana, Sri Lanka*

Journal writing provided an essential link between the training room and the classroom for 220 novice teachers on an initial training programme in Uva Province in Sri Lanka. Comments from these journal entries led to the development of a simple innovation, the *Teacher Journal*.

Regional English Support Centres

Uva Province is a remote area of Sri Lanka, high in the hill country. It suffers from an acute shortage of primary English teachers and was struggling to meet central government targets. The Chief Governor invited the British Council to conduct a training programme for new graduates from a range of disciplines who had been appointed as English language teachers.

The network of 30 Regional English Support Centres (RESCs), resource and training centres, is one of Sri Lanka's lesser-known gems. It was natural for the British Council to draw on the expertise and local knowledge of the trainers in Uva's four RESCs, who became mentors on this nine-month preparation course.

The training programme

Teachers attended one-week training blocks interspersed with three-week teaching blocks. During the teaching blocks there were only very occasional observations by mentors owing to both the remoteness of the schools and the limited resources available. It was essential to accelerate the development of the reflective capacity within these trainees so that they could effectively carry out classroom-based assignments and tasks independently. The introduction of journal writing at an early stage was the main tool used for this. We aimed to help the teachers to consciously make links between the professional knowledge they gained from the training blocks and their personal, practical knowledge from the classroom so that they were better able to make sense of the training and apply it in the classroom. The journals also became the main means of communication between the mentors and teachers.

Teachers' concerns

The 16 mentors read and commented on these journals; while discussing the contents together, they noticed three main areas of concern being expressed:

1 Teachers were worried about the progress they were making without the mentor present to guide and discuss lessons; there was no perception of progress.
2 Teachers wanted access to resources so that they could try out ideas from the training course. They also felt isolated in the field and missed the joint preparation of micro-teaching and discussion of ideas.
3 The teachers wanted to continue improving their own language skills.

The *Teacher Journal*

In response to these concerns, we developed the *Teacher Journal*. It comprises five sections:

1 **Diary:** this is similar to an organiser and contains weekly planners, important dates and contact information.
2 **Reflections:** this encourages teachers to continue to make journal entries beyond the course.
3 **Development:** this section contains a range of tools and suggestions for Continuing Professional Development.
4 **Resources:** this provides information about sources of materials and channels of support as well as a bank of low-resource, low-tech classroom activities.
5 **Notes:** this can be used as a notebook by teachers.

We included guidance on getting the most from the *Teacher Journal* in the latter part of the course and have followed up with teachers to find out how teachers use it and how useful they find it. During the session at IATEFL, we watched interviews of teachers who have been using the *Teacher Journal*. Malkanthi Amarapala told us that writing reflections helped her analyse why her learners seemed to understand in lessons but did not perform well in evaluation, and helped her to plan how to deal with the problem. J Hemantha explained why he found the resources section so useful as a way to add variety in his lessons. Finally, Duminda Jayasinghe showed us the portfolio he has started compiling and explained that other teachers at his school are doing the same. He said it helped to measure his improvement.

We received useful suggestions from participants at IATEFL on making the *Teacher Journal* more effective by providing space and guidance for teachers to add their own evaluation and ideas in the resources section, and we have incorporated these into the *Teacher Journal*.

We concluded by acknowledging that the *Teacher Journal* does not actually contain anything new, but that it has been received very positively by teachers in India and Sri Lanka and is providing useful tools and is helping to foster continuous development.

Email: sgharkin@hotmail.com
yaparesc@gmail.com

3.10 Monitoring large-scale teacher development projects

Alan S. Mackenzie *British Council East Asia, New Delhi, India*

Why monitor?

Monitoring large-scale ELT projects is essential to enable project managers to accurately assess changes happening as a result of training, to represent training programme outcomes accurately to stakeholders, and to ensure that the change project is on track.

Monitoring throughout the project lifetime ensures that what is happening is what is supposed to happen. It focuses on the processes of development to ensure project outcomes are achieved. By forming a constant framework for information flow through the project, monitoring not only generates data for evaluation, but also enables action to be taken to ensure the project progresses as planned.

Evaluation processes are often prioritised over monitoring. This can be damaging in that it focuses too much on results and not enough on the processes that achieve them. Over-focus on evaluation can also happen when finding evidence to illustrate project results is considered only as an afterthought. This leaves it too late to build in monitoring processes, and the opportunity to use monitoring data to take action during the lifetime of the development process is lost (Markee 1997).

An ideal monitoring framework

Looking at the whole project cycle from initiation through implementation to institutionalisation (Fullan 1989), I created an ideal framework for project monitoring

Level	Description	Key question to answer
1	Reaction	Did trainees like it?
2	Learning	Did they learn anything?
3	Behaviour	Could they use what they learned?
4	Results	Did they change their workplace behaviour?

Table 3.10.1: Kirkpatrick's four-level model of evaluating teacher response to training (after Kirkpatrick 1998; see also Fullan 1989)

and evaluation with Kirkpatrick levels (Table 3.10.1) on one axis and project stages ('before', 'during', 'immediately after', '2–3 months after' and '1–2 years after') on the other.

The Kirkpatrick levels build on one another from the shallowest response (reaction) to the deepest (results). Within this grid are questions, based on the four levels that need to be asked at each of the project stages for each of the project components. I constructed a flowchart of all the processes that could be monitored for all the stages of the project cycle including suggested tools to use at each stage. During the presentation, I talked through two parts of this ideal framework to demonstrate its usefulness in identifying what tools and processes can be used to monitor the forms of impact the course is having. Unfortunately this is too large to fully reproduce here, so a sample framework for 2–3 months after the course is included in Figure 3.10.2.

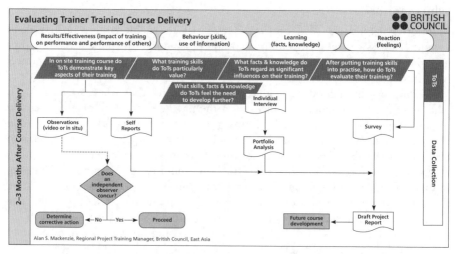

Figure 3.10.1: Ensuring implementation: monitoring 2–3 months after training (ToTs = trainers of teachers)

All attendees at the presentation received copies of the full framework. If you would like one, please contact me at the email address below.

Planning considerations

Frequently, monitoring and evaluation are not budgeted for in project plans—an oversight which can prevent any real, meaningful impact being measured. Poorly thought-through monitoring plans can be overly bureaucratic, generate too much data to be efficiently processed, or generate the wrong kind of data to make any useful decisions about the project. Unsystematic data collection, or cherry-picking of the best data that only shows where the project worked, can lead to biased representations of the project and inaccurate reporting to stakeholders of teacher development needs. Plans featuring little or no monitoring prevent learning from taking place throughout the project cycle which decreases the likelihood of current and future project success.

Very few projects will be able to monitor all of the steps in the process outlined in the framework and managers need to be selective. The main factors to consider are as follows: budget constraints; political issues; time constraints; educational culture; personnel availability; and other context factors (availability of information; ability of the individuals within the system to provide the information; willingness of the individuals within the system to cooperate).

Conclusion

Without monitoring programmes, we have little evidence that our training programmes are having the desired impact. End-of-course questionnaires are not evidence of change in the classroom. Only longer-term monitoring focused on deeper levels of change is likely to provide the evidence we need to prove to our stakeholders that our training programmes work, given preparation, time, support and manageable processes.

Including key education ministry personnel in the analysis, design, monitoring and evaluation of the training program based on this framework can help us to increase buy-in. This can open opportunities for looking at improving performance management systems and identifying opportunities for integrating training and learned behaviours into the workplace more systematically.

Email: alan.mackenzie@in.britishcouncil.org

References

Fullan, M. 1989. *Implementing Educational Change: What we Know.* World Bank. (Retrieved 16 June 2010 from http://www-wds.worldbank.org/external/default/WDSContentServer/WDSP/IB/1989/07/01/000009265_3960929042553/Rendered/PDF/multi_page.pdf.)

Kirkpatrick, D. 1998. *Evaluating Training Programmes: The Four Levels.* San Francisco: Berrett-Koehler Publishers Inc.

Markee, N. 1997. *Managing Curricular Innovation.* Cambridge: Cambridge University Press.

4 The global educator: challenges and opportunities

4.1 The expatriate teacher of English

Susan Barduhn *SIT Graduate Institute, Brattleboro, Vermont, USA*

Why do those of us in the ELT profession not only go to live in other countries but continue moving on to new ones? And what has been our influence on the spread of English and on trends in teacher training? I was fortunate to receive over 200 responses to such questions from Americans, Britons and respondents of seven other nationalities. The respondents needed to have lived outside their country of origin for at least six years and in at least two different countries. I looked upon this research as a puzzle, and my starting point was cultural identity.

Cultural identity

Singer (1987) depicts cultural identity in terms of *perceptual groups* and *identity groups.* Perceptual groups consist of individuals who perceive the world in similar ways, but who are not a group because they do not communicate these perceptions among themselves. Once they do, they become an identity group. I wanted to find out in what ways teachers who choose to live outside their countries of origin are an identity group.

One feature I considered was cultural marginality. There is a Sanskrit word, '*antevasin*', which means 'one who lives at the borders'. It originally referred to people who chose to leave the safety of their homes and venture out to the edge of the forest where the spirits dwelt, in order to uncover the answers to the sacred in their lives. In *Eat, Pray, Love*, Elizabeth Gilbert describes it as 'living on that shimmering line between your old thinking and your new understanding' (2007: 203). Bennett (1993) considers marginality in terms of *encapsulated marginality* and *constructive marginality.* Encapsulated marginals are persons who allow the dominant groups to *ascribe* their identity. Constructive marginals are persons with *avowed* identities, not dependent on particular group affiliations, who are capable of moving among all communities. They can be described as being conscious of choice, intrigued by complexity, and never *not* at home wherever they go. These distinctions helped me decide on the questions to ask in my survey.

Overview of results

My starting point was wondering what motivated expatriate teachers to go and live in each country. I compiled a list of 19 reasons and asked the respondents to choose all that applied for each country. The top three choices for each year, in this order, are shown in Table 4.1.1.

I compiled another list of 19 descriptors of personality and skills, and this was the order of their top eight choices: I am curious; I am self-reliant; I have a willingness to communicate; I like helping others; I have empathy; I am perceptive; I am

1st Country	Travel, adventure, Peace Corps
2nd Country	Professional development, culture, love of teaching
3rd Country	Love of teaching, professional development, career advancement
4th Country	Career advancement, economic reasons, professional development
5th Country	Professional development, career advancement, economic reasons
6th Country	Family, attracted to change and risk, professional development
7th Country	Love of teaching, professional development, attracted to change and risk
8th Country	Looking for greener pastures, attracted to change and risk, personal development

Table 4.1.1: Reasons for moving countries

self-motivated; and I have a strong sense of self. The three factors that were rated the lowest were: the ability to let go; to manage stress; and to access supports.

I asked who the respondents' closest friends were in each country, and the majority answer was other expatriate language teachers. I asked about language learning and discovered that the respondents tended to reach a very high level in the language of their first foreign country, but that this happened rarely in subsequent countries. When asked what the primary reason was (or would be) for returning to their country of origin, one reason stood out: family.

Many wrote of the gratitude they felt towards having been able to live such interesting lives. Foreign countries became part of them, like rings on a tree, stretching them and expanding their humanity and tolerance, including towards their country of origin. They developed professionally through being able to experience different contexts and then use this knowledge of multiple contexts in their teaching, thereby expanding their students' worldviews.

Expatriate teachers have created a huge community of teachers around the world and have contributed to the spread and popularity of professional teacher organisations. Regarding the spread of English, one respondent spoke of serving a need more than creating it, and another wrote that if English were a drug, expatriate teachers would be the dealers. The phenomenon of expatriate English teachers could be considered a historical, cultural movement.

Email: susan.barduhn@sit.edu

References

Bennett, J. 1993. 'Cultural marginality: identity issues in intercultural training' in R. M. Paige (ed.). *Education for the Intercultural Experience*. Yarmouth, ME: Intercultural Press.

Gilbert, E. 2007. Eat, Pray, Love. New York: Penguin.

Singer, M. 1987. *Intercultural Communication: A Perceptual Approach*. Prentice Hall.

4.2 Self-evaluation of the critical global educator

Maureen Ellis *The Open University, Milton Keynes, UK*

The session began with a quick look at Oxfam's definition of a global citizen. Oxfam's website and extremely helpful publications define and describe the knowledge, skills, attitudes and participation expected of someone 'outraged by social injustice'. Further resources can be accessed by searching for 'cosmopolitanism' or the 'global dimension'. We considered the Department for Education and Skills' eight key concepts of global citizenship: social justice, conflict resolution, interdependence, diversity, human rights, sustainable development, values and perceptions.

In my research into the personal and professional development of the critical global educator, I am struck by the wealth of critical theory, which is unfortunately not drawn upon sufficiently in our understandings of 'critical'. As methodology, a critical realist perspective in philosophy reveals the false dichotomies of fact and value, theory and practice, and other binary divisions, and the need for dialectical thinking. Such an understanding enables us to identify the spaces for individual and collective agency in a transformational model of social activity, rather than simplistic contradictions of structure and agency. Those present agreed that their own opportunities for academic study had led to an enhanced appreciation of the empowering role of theory in their lives, and our discussion confirmed that theory and practice need to be integrated like body and blood, in a holy communion, both at individual and collective levels. Making teachers' beliefs explicit provides a foundation for critical appreciation of academic theory. A truly communicative 'community of practice' may thus be inspired or converted, have new life breathed into a 'community of praxis'.

My pilot surveys, interviews and focus group discussions, with over 400 postgraduate teachers and around 100 more practitioners, have shown a high degree of responsibility and enthusiasm for the teacher's role in conveying a global perspective, particularly linked to disciplinary knowledge and expertise. Despite not being aware of institutional or curricular requirements, or of the statutory position of the global dimension in the British National Curriculum, teachers participated enthusiastically in listing topics within their disciplines which offered scope for addressing global issues.

Another finding was the important role of language and the crucial need for time, if teachers are to personalise and situate their understanding of these policy statements, whether at the level of UN millennium development goals, or in national directives and guidelines. As teachers of language, we are in a strong position to see the genre chains which link global policy, through national educational and curricular documents, to classroom textbooks, online teaching materials down to classroom discourse—and to identify the scope for change at each recontextualisation. Frequently powers and controls at each juncture effectively divert, dilute or diffuse the original intentions and impact of reforms, 'domesticating' and sanitising the original progressive spirit. Eco calls for critical 'semiotic guerrilla warfare' (1976). Freire (1993) insisted on honest dialectical teacher–taught relationships.

We shared experiences of what had first made us think 'global', and which events, incidents or individuals had led to our 'critical' stance. We looked at three tools I've

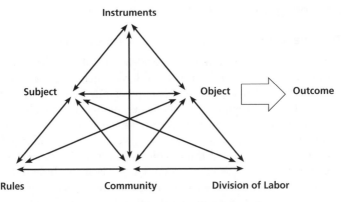

Figure 4.2.1: The CHAT framework
(http://www.edu.helsinki.fi/activity/pages/chatanddwr/chat/)

begun to use in talking to teachers about their lives, work and professional development: timelines, a triangular framework called CHAT (see Figure 4.2.1), and a Ladder of Empowerment. CHAT, or socio-cultural, historical, activity theory, presents an individual's learning within the complex picture of personal motivation or Objectives; the Rules, constraints and affordances within which she works; the Tools or resources, strategies, or technology she deploys to achieve her goals; the Community/-ies she operates with; and the Division of Labour, or who does what, who has what power, whether for financial or policy-making decisions.

Finally, we looked briefly at Rocha's Ladder of Empowerment (1997), which stages personal development through five phases, from Individual, to Embedded, through Mediated, and Socio-Political, to Political Empowerment. My research so far has shown that while as teachers we are happy to talk of 'agency', 'informed engagement', and 'participation', we shy away from the word 'political', revealing how effectively our personal power to make a difference has been neutralised. It is interesting to see how a society can prevent certain discourses by making them 'impolite', thus stripping away the personal passion we bring to our work, which most certainly involves our deepest values.

Unfortunately we did not have time to consider the ELT implications of a global dimension specifically, which is something I had covered at last year's IATEFL conference.

If you believe you are a critical global educator, I would be very happy to hear from you, and to discuss your definition and experience of this very pertinent concept.

Email: t.ellis2@ukonline.co.uk

References

Eco, U. 1976. *A Theory of Semiotics*. London: Macmillan.

Freire, P. 1993. *Pedagogy of the Oppressed*. Middlesex: Penguin.

Rocha, E. 1997. 'A ladder of empowerment'. *Journal of Planning Education and Research* 17: 31.

4.3 I don't 'do' politics … do I?

Danny Whitehead *British Council, Kinshasa, Democratic Republic of Congo*

'Politics' is more than electioneering, or considerations of right/left theory. Politics concerns principles of power and status at all levels, including the classroom. The process and materials of language teaching are inherently political, with concerns of linguistic imperialism or creeping Anglophone hegemony reinforced by content-light textbooks pushing the cult of celebrity and assuming (depositing) western assumptions of life and lifestyle. As English language teachers, we can't avoid 'doing' politics.

But this isn't necessarily a bad thing. Politics is a 'real' subject which motivates learners: it is relevant, and it stimulates cognitive involvement. Indeed, the L2 classroom is an ideal environment for encountering challenging issues, as ELT has great potential to create counter-hegemonic discourses. A longitudinal study in the Democratic Republic of the Congo explored this potential, with the teaching of seven key precepts (with suggested activities), which I call 'The Teacher's Manifesto'.

The Teacher's Manifesto

1 *I will try to use critical praxis in my lessons.* 'Critical praxis' is teaching practice which recognises the power of English, but which seeks to subvert it or use it for the creation of new identities and counter-hegemonic discourses (developed from Gramsci 1975).

2 *I will help my learners to explore who they are, who they want to be, and how English will help them get there.*

Activities

- Learners critically assess positive and negative factors in their lives in individual extensive writing, uncorrected for accuracy.
- Learners imagine what their 'best possible self' is, considering who they want to be in the future and what their aspirations and goals are; they complete a piece of open, extensive writing describing this self. Learners may use multiple media if they wish. These texts should not be corrected.
- Learners consider what role (if any) English will have in their 'best possible self', and create realistic ideas of developmental pathways (adapted from Sheldon and Lyubomirsky 2006).
- To activate motivation, learners choose and research a role model from their mother culture, focusing on values and successes.

3 *I will explore challenging issues in the classroom, ensuring that the environment is supportive.*

Activities

Moving away from the traditional self-access focus on closed activities, Tomlinson's (1998) 'access-self' activities encourage reflection and reduce anxiety: tasks are open ended, they engage the learners personally as human beings, and they stimulate both left- and right-brain activity. Post-reading tasks elicit holistic responses, and feedback is provided through commentaries and suggested answers rather than through an answer sheet. Follow-up activities (possibly involving other learners) are encouraged (Tomlinson 1998: 322–3).

4   *I will encourage my learners' pride in their L1, and I will use this positively in the classroom.*

Activities

- Learners and teachers negotiate the choice of texts for classroom study, ensuring a mixture of L1 and L2 texts. ELT activities can be stimulated by L1 texts, too!
- Learners think of proverbs and idioms in their L1, then attempt to translate them into English. Translation is first 'word for word', followed by a semantic translation of meaning, exploring the richness of the L1 and its value.
- Learners compare grammatical structures in English and the L1 and question whether structural differences lead to difference in thought.

5   *I will raise learners' awareness of embedded cultural hegemony in texts.*

Activities

- Learners critically explore the meaning and symbolism of pictures and images in textbooks.
- Learners compare newspapers in their L1 and English, or online news texts, or news texts in other media, examining the choice of news and the representation of different groups.
- Learners assess the accents chosen in listening texts and their relevance.
- Learners examine artistic representations of different groups in popular culture and create their own multimedia representations of self and other.

6   *I will encourage language mixing and the development of learners' spontaneous grammar.*

Activities

- Learners examine real examples of language mixing and examine why particular languages were chosen in each case.
- Learners experiment with language mixing.
- After learners have practiced 'fun' activities, language mixing is encouraged in extensive writing to show developing complex identities

7   *I will not 'do nothing', because that in itself is political.* Learners are political beings, just as classrooms are political spaces. Choosing to 'do nothing', to continue without further thought and with existing materials, is a political choice which perpetuates the problem.

The research in DRC indicated the development of complex language identities, and of emergent and empowering spontaneous grammars. Interestingly, participants in Harrogate reciprocally questioned the ethics of using (or depositing) the manifesto in non-native English speaking teachers; this should be examined in further research.

Email: danny.whitehead@hotmail.com

References

Gramsci, A. (ed. V. Gerratana). 1975. *Quaderni del Carcere*. Turin: Einaudi.

Sheldon, K. and S. Lyubomirsky. 2006. 'How to increase and sustain positive emotion: the effects of expressing gratitude and visualizing best possible selves'. *Journal of Positive Psychology* 1/2: 73–82.

Tomlinson, B. 1998. 'Access-self materials' in B. Tomlinson (ed.). *Materials Development in Language Teaching*. Cambridge: Cambridge University Press.

4.4 Korea opportunities: access all areas!

Maria K. Norton *British Council, Seoul, Republic of Korea*

The Bus Project in Korea

The Bus Project in South Korea was a three-year programme that took English out of the metropolis and into rural areas. As the programme drew to a close, there were some useful stories to share. Successes and learning points will shape this article, describing activity geared towards supporting teacher development and engaging students. A corollary theme of this article is Corporate Social Responsibility (CSR) and I will illustrate how the CSR agenda of a large insurance company, PCA Life, was matched to the core values of the British Council and the educational objectives of stakeholders of English teaching in Korea.

English in Korea

Increased demand for English in South Korea has pushed market growth in all but the remotest of locations. The Bus Project went that extra mile and travelled to rural areas, reaching almost 30,000 learners aged 8–13. Through this project British Council Korea gave free English lessons in small country schools and orphanages (SOS Children's Villages). We worked with approximately 1,200 local teachers, providing training workshops and peer observations to help them in their desire to better meet learner needs. Whilst the British Council may seem well placed with its network of resources, there were significant challenges, not least the proliferation of American English, and research findings revealing that the UK was virtually unknown in Korea. Therein lay one objective of our collaboration: to share knowledge and expertise about the UK with teachers and learners. The in-school teacher training sessions and lessons in state schools correlated to the Korean national curriculum; the peer observations, however, needed careful management as the observation form was in English and school principals and other staff were keen to turn this into Korean to ensure wider participation.

The bus

The bus was equipped with five activity zones displaying aspects of British culture and staffed by a British Council teacher. This teacher soon became overwhelmed with visitors wanting to communicate in Korean, so a Korean helper was employed. They were soon translating training workshops too, and occasionally all the staff of the host school would participate in the event. As Freire and Araujo Freire have pointed out, one should 'include security people, cafeteria personnel and custodians' as people who contribute to ongoing educational development (1992: 14). The bus was copied in one region—emulation being the highest form of praise?

Corporate Social Responsibility

Corporate Social Responsibility (CSR) is defined as follows:

> a voluntary approach that a business enterprise takes to meet or exceed stakeholder expectations by integrating social, ethical, and environmental concerns together with the usual measures of revenue, profit, and legal obligation.
>
> (dictionary.bnet.com 2010)

CSR, then, can constitute a platform from which to deliver projects of value to the environment(s) we operate in, and indeed, working with PCA Life (a.k.a. Prudential) proved beneficial. The benefits obtained were not only of an in-kind nature (their staffing of the bus as it toured Korea), but also of a financial nature. PCA Life gave us a generous budget to provide a wide-reaching service that otherwise would have been beyond our reach. The partnership helped to promote the work of both PCA Life Korea and the British Council and contributed to PCA Life being named Korean Social Benefactor 2007 by the Chamber of Commerce.

Success factors

With Bill Lyles at the helm of PCA Life, the Bus Project became well established; he claimed it was 'wonderful to be paired with the British Council'. However, true to the literature on CSR, when the CEO changed, so did the momentum. As Williams and Aguilera postulate, the likelihood of CSR success is 'shaped by the managers' individual ethical perspective and their organizational culture' (2006: 12). Mr Lyles' commitment was sadly contrasted by the subsequent CEO's focus on other interests and so the British Council team had to work harder at maintaining communication channels with PCA Life and their audiences. Keeping momentum required regular status updates across teams, as well as efforts to engender sustainability by getting fresh blood involved and responding to stakeholder feedback.

Conclusion

The Bus Project in Korea succeeded both internally in the form of increased staff pride and a strengthened desire to contribute, and externally in the form of teachers' and learners' eagerness to engage further with the British Council. The seal of approval of the Korean Social Benefactor 2007 award bestowed to PCA Life also gave this partnership a significant endorsement and has encouraged us to seek further corporate partnerships.

Email: maria.norton@britishcouncil.co.kr

References

Bnet dictionary. 2010. http://dictionary.bnet.com/definition/Corporate+Social+Responsibility. html.

Freire, P. and A. M. Araujo Freire. 1992. *Pedagogy of Hope: Reliving Pedagogy of the Oppressed.* New York: Continuum.

Williams, C. A. and R.V. Aguilera. 2006. 'Corporate Social Responsibility in a comparative perspective'. University of Illinois at Urbana–Champaign. (Retrieved 18 June 2010 from http://www.icaew.com/index.cfm?route=127637.)

4.5 The Hornby Scholars' panel presentation: ELT in transition: teachers' voices from around the world

Convenor: Shelagh Rixon *University of Warwick, Coventry, UK, with*
The Hornby Scholars at IATEFL 2010

The Resources Group: Kalyan Chattopadhyay *India*; Emma Evele *Cameroon*; Natalya Eydelman *Russia*; Nerissa Lomeda *Philippines*; Diego Fernando Macias *Colombia*; Abeer Mohammed *Sudan*; Sayed Abdullah Mousavi *Afghanistan*; Turganaly Zhanadilov *Kazakhstan*

The Teacher Empowerment Group: Laura Aza *Argentina*; Carla Castelar *Brazil*; Guillermo Reyes Chavarría *Mexico*; Ramanujam Meganathan *India*; Kondwani Kelvin Mkandawire *Malawi*; Hossain-Ahmed Mohammed *Bangladesh*; Florence Muluh *Cameroon*; Abdulmalik Ofemile *Nigeria*

The A. S. Hornby Educational Trust, in cooperation with the British Council, provides a number of scholarships each year for study in the UK at the master's level. Scholars are supported in the UK by Tim Phillips, Hornby Progammes Manager of the British Council, and by Penny Trigg, Teacher Networks Consultant. Hornby Scholars are English language teachers and teacher educators from transitional or developing countries around the world who have been making a difference and who are expected to go on doing so. A joint presentation by Hornby Scholars has become a tradition at the IATEFL Annual Conference. What follows is a summary of a session to which everyone in the group of sixteen Hornby Scholars contributed, providing information on their contexts, supplying visual material or using their IT skills to help design the PowerPoint used by the speakers. This year the Scholars shared perspectives and insights from their different contexts on two themes: Resources and Teacher Empowerment.

The Resources Group

The Resources Group mainly addressed the issues of low resources, although there were also representatives of high-resource contexts in which IT resources were very highly developed. These presented their own problems concerning how best to utilise resources. In low-resource contexts, classroom difficulties stemmed from conditions such as large numbers of students in class; cramped classrooms; poor classroom environments or even a lack of classrooms; insufficient teaching resources; schools attended by different populations of pupils in two or even three shifts; and untrained or insufficiently trained teachers. The umbrella question was 'How do we teach when all we've got is chalk?' and the group's answer was 'Use creativity!' The examples demonstrated included the following:

'Spellbound'

'Spellbound', a set of hand-made cards and foldable sheets to practise sound–spelling rules in English, was demonstrated by its developer, **Emma Evele** of Cameroon. It serves both as a class teaching aid and as a focal point for teacher education: once teachers get the idea they can create their own resources along the same lines.

'Big Books'

Nerissa Lomeda of the Philippines showed not only how teacher-made 'Big Books' helped to solve the problems of a lack of individual pupil materials in large classes, but also how 'Big Books' have very powerful pedagogical benefits of their own. They can be designed to cover topics that are interesting to the children and adjusted to their level; also, from a teacher's point of view, they can be designed to be value laden and 'heavy with the lesson for the day'. A story might contain repeated examples of a sound–letter correspondence, for example.

Low-cost resources

Diego Fernando Macias of Colombia shared his work on low-cost resources, a focal point of much of his teacher training. He demonstrated outcomes with photographs taken on return visits to schools some time after his original training sessions. Teachers in crowded and under-resourced classrooms were seen making direct use of the classroom environment in various ways: using students' personal items as teaching props or, in a lesson on giving directions, treating the layout of the classroom as if it were the streets of a town. Teachers involved groups of children in making posters to illustrate language, topics, activities or cultural aspects of their English learning. The students benefited from the process of creating the posters and the posters then became a resource which could be used again with other students. Paper-bag puppets were used to present dialogues or to act as characters in a story. Some puppets even became a favourite 'mascot' character in class, acting sometimes as a teacher substitute for interactions.

Turganaly Zhanadilov from Kazakhstan described his government's plans to move the educational system in his country closer to the higher-resources situation found in some institutions in Russia and India, as represented by **Natalya Eydelman** and **Kalyan Chattopadhyay** respectively. (These Scholars gave solo talks on their contexts in other sessions at the conference and so did not speak at this presentation; for their talks, see **7.8** and **10.4**.)

The Resources Group's overall message was this: 'Wherever we are in the continuum of low-to-high resources, we can make big things happen in our classes.'

The Teacher Empowerment Group

The Teacher Empowerment Group saw empowerment not only as a way of helping to overcome the difficulties encountered by teachers in many under-resourced contexts but also as a way to make the teacher an agent of dynamic change.

For many teachers, teaching is nothing but a source of employment, a means to get out of the house or a job imposed by family traditions. In some contexts, teachers' morale is undermined by a society which trivialises the teaching profession. This is particularly evident in countries where the ever-increasing demand for teachers of English outstrips the number of qualified candidates available. The tenet that 'any graduate can teach English' leads to mass recruitment of graduates who are not competent users of the English language and who have to grapple with language proficiency as well as with pedagogy. They need and deserve support.

Even trained English teachers find theories learnt on their courses inadequate for the realities of the classroom, and there are few continuing professional development opportunities for teachers. Where CPD is available, the cost is usually borne by the teachers themselves. Teachers in some contexts have to present papers, carry out research, get higher qualifications, and have good annual appraisals in order to be promoted. However, no adequate provision is made by the educational authorities to help teachers attain these goals.

The group members expressed their belief that professional teachers' associations are the solution. They can provide structures through which teachers may become empowered and develop self-efficacy. There are vibrant teachers' associations in Brazil, Cameroon, India, Mexico, Nigeria, Bangladesh and Argentina; these enrich the teaching experience by means of regular workshops, seminars, conferences and networking. Some associations, such as those in Brazil, Bangladesh and Cameroon, produce journals; these reach out to teachers cut off by geographical distance and poor communication systems and allow developing teachers to publish their ideas.

We heard personal testimonies from **Carla Castelar** from Brazil and **Florence Muluh** from Cameroon of the transformative impact that membership of their associations had had on their lives and careers. Both felt that they owed their current status as Hornby Scholars to their experiences with their teachers' associations. Carla described how BRAZ–TESOL opened many doors for her. She started in the association by sharing some work in the regional chapter; this led to an invitation to publish an article about what she had presented; and later she was offered a scholarship to follow a course in Texas, the results of which she then shared with colleagues. Her central message was that sharing ideas was essential. Florence started as someone who went into teaching just to be sure of a job. She found her teacher training an easy experience and enjoyed learning theories of language learning and teaching. However, her first day in the classroom was a catastrophe as the realities of the situation hit her: 146 noisy students who spoke 75 different languages and had no textbooks! After two months of dejection and sleepless nights she attended the first seminar of a newly created teachers' association in the region and returned with a wealth of coping strategies. From then she went from strength to strength. She has since been very active in the teachers' association, having taken on official roles within it, created divisional branches and run workshops of her own.

The link between the two themes of the Hornby presentation was clear—the need for teachers to be creative and proactive in order to serve learners in the best possible ways in circumstances which do not always make teaching and learning English an easy matter.

Email: S.Rixon@warwick.ac.uk

4.6 Teaching English in large multicultural classes: a narrative enquiry

Prem Bahadur Phyak *Department of English Education, Tribhuvan University, Nepal*

IATEFL Gill Sturtridge First-time Speaker Scholarship Winner

Introduction

As Nepal is a multicultural country, the majority of schools have students from different cultures. These students have distinct values, beliefs and identities which influence their way of learning. If their culture is not discussed in the classroom, they feel alienated; moreover, members of different cultures do not always interact effectively in pair and group work. Drawing upon the perspectives of three teachers who have been teaching English in large Nepalese classrooms for a decade, I aim to discuss how local culture can be a source for teaching English in large multicultural classes.

Culture in ELT

Since native speakers of English around the globe are outnumbered by non-native speakers, learners of English need to be able to communicate not only with native speakers but also with non-native speakers from different cultural backgrounds.

Holliday (1994) argues that not all teaching methods work in all contexts. Diverse socio-cultural milieus play a role, and the notion of 'method' does not take into consideration socio-cultural factors like family background, motivation, individual differences and learning styles, which have an important impact on language learning. For example, the communicative and the task-based methods, which are effective in the resourceful contexts of the UK and USA, may not be effective in under-resourced and large-class contexts. Similarly, the particular texts presented in textbooks may not be relevant in all contexts. This suggests that there is a need to use context-appropriate texts, activities and methods. To this end, the use of local culture may be an important tool for teaching English.

Local culture in teaching English: teachers' views from Nepal

Three English teachers in Nepal—Rabi, Birat and Mohan (pseudonyms)—argue that the use of local culture not only motivates students to interact but also help to preserve their beliefs, values and identities. In this regard, Rabi argues:

> Textbook passages, photographs, videos on local culture can be incorporated. They reflect our linguistic and cultural diversity … Students grow up in their culture, and use English to communicate with other cultures.

We see that the use of local culture promotes diversity. Similarly, Birat says that the students in large classes interact with each other when local cultures are discussed in the classroom. He further suggests, 'By using local culture, we can merge English into our local life'. Likewise, Mohan says:

If we don't care [about] constructivism in social learning, we can never bring change in any language teaching. When there is a lesson about *Chandinaach, Rodi, Kouda, Maruni* [cultures of different ethnic groups in Nepal] and so on, students will construct ideas themselves in a language.

The above discussion suggests that intercultural competence, the ability to negotiate with people from diverse cultural backgrounds, should be the goal of teaching English in large multicultural classes. This promotes students' awareness of their own culture and values while learning English by associating it with their social context. With this, I argue that unless we make students aware of their own culture, they may not see the relevance of learning English in their life. This also raises the question of sustainable learning.

Conclusion

Local culture can be a tool to promote interaction in large classes. This also fosters critical language awareness (Fairclough 1992) as students are engaged in the sharing and critical appreciation of various cultures. In this process, they negotiate their identities and beliefs by respecting each others' values. Moreover, the use of local culture promotes cultural sustainability; in other words, it keeps endangered cultures alive (Barfield and Uzarski 2009). Thus, I argue that if students' local cultures are used in the classroom, the students in large multicultural classes will participate actively in classroom interaction. However, as one participant commented, teacher training in using multicultural texts is required for teachers; otherwise, there may be a risk of bias towards one or two dominant cultures. Likewise, teachers and textbook writers should scrutinise whether the language used in the textbook represents local cultures.

Email: pphyak@gmail.com

References

Barfield, S. C. and J. Uzarski. 2009. 'Integrating indigenous cultures into English language teaching'. *English Teaching Forum* 1: 2–9.

Fairclough, N. (ed.). 1992. *Critical Language Awareness.* London: Longman.

Holliday, A. 1994. *Appropriate Methodology and Social Context.* Cambridge: Cambridge University Press.

4.7 Challenging themes: radio English for teachers and learners

Thelma Umeh *British Council, Kano, Nigeria* and **Paul Woods** *British Council, Gaborone, Botswana*

Context

There are approximately 11.4 million English language teachers and 1.1 billion English language learners in the world today. Of these, 750,000 teachers and 100 million learners are in sub-Saharan Africa, where internet connectivity is still patchy and generally unaffordable for teachers and learners. As the British Council wanted to reach many more learners and teachers using its limited resources, we had to explore different channels to reach our target audiences at a distance; these channels included radio, newspapers and mobile phones.

Why radio?

You may say, 'Radio is old hat. It's all been done before by BBC English'. True, radio has been around for a long time, but there are still very good reasons for using it, especially in Africa. Widely available in developing countries, radio is accessible, it provides a cost-effective way of reaching audiences in countries with low levels of school attendance, and it gives high impact for relatively low levels of investment.

A Nigerian case study

In Nigeria we adapted for radio the British Council's *Language Improvement for Teachers* product (originally designed for face-to-face delivery). The course was very clearly defined, but it had a skeletal nature which needed to be filled out. To do this, two consultants were employed to adapt the global product content. ELT experts collaborated with radio producers and presenters to develop a suitable script prior to the actual production of the programmes.

Challenges included finding experienced personnel to work with, getting a national radio station to partner with us, keeping the partner on board, generating additional content, and securing sponsorship for the programmes. We secured a three-year partnership with the national radio network, and the programmes were broadcast on Federal Radio at 7.00 p.m. once a week to an estimated audience of five million, rising to eight million by the end of the series. (Many of these listeners were not teachers of English!)

Teaching English Radio

Teaching English Radio is a series of twelve 15-minute radio programmes we have developed at the global level; these are aimed at teachers of English working in schools in developing countries where large classes, a lack of resources and few training opportunities are a reality. The programmes provide advice and training on teaching English at a very basic level and include clips from over 20 different countries, from Afghanistan to Angola.

The objective of the series is to motivate teachers and provide a catalyst to improve morale, encourage learner-centred strategies and make learning more effective. We have produced supporting notes for teachers, and the programmes are designed to be very flexible: they can be re-packaged and delivered via podcasts, or adapted to include a live studio audience and questions from listeners.

The topics covered include finding and using resources; using group and pair work in large classes; using English in the classroom; the teaching of new language; teaching listening; and teaching reading. We have also produced a promotional pack for radio stations which includes two data CDs and a booklet outlining the programme content, as well as 10,000 sets of three audio CDs, which can be used on pre- and in-service training courses after the radio programmes have been broadcast. We anticipate the first series will create an insatiable demand for more and have already commissioned a follow-on series, covering topics including how to get the most out of your coursebook; managing different levels in the same class; marking; correcting; setting homework; doing revision; and enjoying English lessons.

Challenges

We'd prefer not to have to pay for airtime and hope to find delivery partners in each country who will broadcast the programmes free of charge. One problem was that it took far longer to produce the first series than we had originally anticipated, mainly due to difficulties in obtaining recordings from countries like Afghanistan.

Learn English Radio

For learners of English, we took a different approach, developing an initial concept, then looking for a strategic funding partner. At the outset, we planned to tackle developmental themes, so we produced a glossy flier and approached a range of potential sponsors such as Coca Cola and Nokia. However, this approach failed to produce the results we had hoped for. We have now widened the scope to include other regions (for example, the Middle East and China) and changed the focus to concentrate on English for work situations. Potentially the audiences are huge and by 2013 we expect to reach up to 20 million listeners in sub-Saharan Africa with our programmes.

Email: rphwoods@gmail.com
thelma.umeh@ng.britishcouncil.org

4.8 Teaching English in difficult circumstances: a new research agenda

Richard Smith *University of Warwick, Coventry, UK*

Introduction

It is now 50 years since Michael West coined the phrase 'teaching in difficult circumstances', referring to the importance of considering classes which consist of:

> over 30 pupils (more usually 40 or even 50), congested on benches [...], ill-graded, with a teacher who perhaps does not speak English very well [...], working in a hot climate. (West 1960: 1)

Most English teaching in the world continues to take place in such contexts, which could thereby be termed 'mainstream' despite being largely ignored in mainstream ELT discourse. Indeed, teacher-training manuals published in the UK after 1960 (particularly, after around 1978) shifted in focus away from large-class teaching at secondary level and towards small-class language school teaching. Similarly, UK-based ELT research continues to focus on relatively well-resourced settings (Rixon and Smith 2010). The current situation, it would seem, is a dysfunctional one—mainstream methodological discourse and research dominate but systematically fail to be oriented towards mainstream ELT worldwide.

Past research

In the area of large-class studies, Shamim (2010) has provided a useful review of past research. Within the Lancaster–Leeds Language Learning in Large Classes Research Project (whose 12 reports were all issued in 1989), there was a concerted attempt to investigate some of the issues raised by teaching in difficult circumstances (henceforth, TiDC); however, this effort was not systematically built upon. The project team defined terms, compiled bibliographies and distributed and analysed questionnaires. In line with this research approach, the findings mainly concerned perceptions of class size and associated problems but did not really explore possible solutions from teachers' perspectives. Concrete, bottom-up proposals for appropriate TiDC methodology are still rare, and scholarship and research are still clearly needed.

A new research agenda

Building on the work of the Lancaster–Leeds project, and taking up where it left off, there is a current need for *scholarship* in the field of TiDC, including updating bibliographies and making existing resources more widely available. As Shamim (2010) indicates, a network has been set up to facilitate such scholarship and sharing of resources and ideas. Termed the 'Teaching English in Large Classes' (TELC) network, its website is at: http://www.warwick.ac.uk/go/telc.

Original *research* into TiDC (including large-class teaching) also needs to be revived, and with this in mind I offer the suggestions below. Starting from, but also departing from previous research, the following are avenues that seem particularly worth exploring:

1   Leaving behind conceptions of small-class teaching as the norm and TiDC as a 'problem', we can start with descriptions of practice, in particular 'good practice' as perceived by participants, allowing 'positives' of TiDC to emerge as well as 'negatives'. Ideally, learners' as well as teachers' perceptions will be accessed.

2   With a new focus on issues of practical concern to teachers themselves, not just 'academic' or policy-oriented issues, there is a need to move beyond discussions of 'how large a large class is' and possible effects of class size on achievement, towards a positive focus on developing appropriate methodology 'from the bottom up', for example through practitioner research.

3   A qualitative, exploratory case study approach might need to be adopted in place of generalization across culturally diverse contexts. At the same time, research needs to be better disseminated and discussed across contexts (for example, through devolved ICT-enabled networking).

4   Explicit account needs to be taken of problems of *doing research* in difficult circumstances, and teacher education experiences in the field can also be usefully disseminated and analysed.

Conclusion

Participants in the TELC network have already become engaged in research of the above kind. For example, two of my PhD students, Mais Ajjan and Harry Kuchah, have been eliciting teachers' and students' views of 'good TiDC practice' in Syria and Cameroon respectively. Network committee members in countries ranging from China to Ethiopia have agreed to engage a number of teachers in providing narratives of successful cases of TiDC.

Anyone involved with TiDC and interested in joining in with our current and intended work is encouraged to make contact. We intend to build gradually, aware that there will be no simple solutions to the challenges posed by teaching and researching in difficult and still, 50 years on from West (1960), under-investigated circumstances.

Email: R.C.Smith@warwick.ac.uk

References

Rixon, S. and R. Smith (eds.). 2010. *Directory of UK ELT Research, 2005–08*. London: The British Council. http://www.teachingenglish.org.uk/elt-research.

Shamim, F. 2010. 'Plenary: Teaching and research English in large classes' in B. Beaven (ed.). *IATEFL 2009: Cardiff Conference Selections*. Canterbury, Kent: IATEFL

West, M. 1960. *Teaching English in Difficult Circumstances*. London: Longmans, Green.

4.9 Managing customer feedback and complaints

Justin Kernot *British Council Middle East, Muscat, Oman*

Traditionally providers of English language courses have sought to gather feedback from students and respond to their comments in various ways; these have included suggestion cards, end-of-course questionnaires, focus groups and customer satisfaction forms. The British Council Middle East has approached customer feedback in a different way. While the centres in the region have continued to collect information, comments and suggestions using some of the methods listed above, they have also recognised the range of cultures and backgrounds of their customers, as well as their customers' preferred mode of communication.

The region is very much one that responds more productively and proactively to human contact and verbal exchange. The British Council has realised that in order to gain more realistic, honest feedback from customers, managers need to focus their attention on recording and responding to feedback provided off-paper, with less formal direction and fewer restrictions. A variety of initiatives have been implemented.

Anecdote circles

One office set up a series of anecdote circles, whereby current and former students were encouraged to come along and share their experiences of studying with the British Council. They were not prompted with questions or provided with scripted starters; they were simply asked to share their positive and negative stories. These tales were sometimes shared in English but, where possible, were recounted in Arabic. This provided more freedom of expression linguistically and minimised anxiety for those participating. The stories revealed key impressions of stages or aspects of their engagement with the teaching centre, from the initial enquiry, placement test and registration for a course, to service in the café, perceptions of lessons and teachers, integration of IT, assessment of their progress and re-registration.

Listening to those in the know

It was also considered invaluable to listen to those in the know, that is, to listen to stories from local staff members who share a common language with the students, and whom students trust. These staff members often hear stories that they do not pass on to complaints managers or record formally. Such tales contribute to a bank of 'real' stories and provide an insight into students' experiences.

Clear direction

Making life easy for a customer is always a positive move. In its Middle East offices the British Council has endeavoured to be transparent about the process by which customers provide comments and feedback. The policy and procedures for commenting on products or service are posted on websites and clearly displayed in public areas. It is important that customers feel comfortable making suggestions or comments, and that they know how to do this. This helps to engender a sense that the organisation recognises the value of its customers and their opinions.

The right staff with the right stuff

Customer service advisors in British Council offices are given opportunities to develop their skills in receiving and responding to comments and dealing with challenging situations through participation in customer service training. Staff members are also recognised for their performance in dealing with customers and are rewarded for excellence in customer care.

Motivation among team members comes not only through the recognition of development needs and performance, but also through recruiting and selecting the right people. The recruitment and selection procedures have been redesigned to place more emphasis on applicants' approaches to customer service situations. This has helped to identify more suitable candidates and, indeed, has led to an increase in staff satisfaction levels among customer service teams across the region.

Regionally, the induction process for new customer service staff has been revamped in the Middle East to provide consistency in customer care. While there had been an assumption that customer service advisors had the skills to manage all kinds of enquiries, situations and customer types, it was evident that they needed support. The induction programme offers training in skills for managing telephone and email enquiries effectively and professionally, and for dealing with conflict.

Recognition and response

In order to ensure customer confidence in the system, the offices introduced an online and hard-copy space for displaying customer comments and the subsequent response from staff. This personal touch has been received positively by students, who feel there is recognition of their opinions and thoughts and that action is taken, a solution found, or an explanation given.

Building relationships is crucial in maintaining honesty, trust and loyalty between teaching operations and students. Managing enquiries, comments and complaints has to be viewed positively and perceived by learners as a means by which the relationship and the people involved can grow.

Email: Justin.kernot@om.britishcouncil.org

4.10 Ideal and reality in coursebook selection

Shu-er Huang *University of Warwick, Coventry, UK*

Introduction

This study looks at the theory and practice of coursebook selection, describing the criteria that teachers actually use when selecting coursebooks in universities of technology in Taiwan, and comparing these with suggestions for teachers which are made in the literature.

There has been little research on the recommendations given within teacher training and in teacher-training manuals regarding coursebook selection. It is, therefore, not clear whether the criteria recommended are actually appropriate for helping teachers select a coursebook for their own learners—indeed, the needs, objectives, backgrounds and preferred styles of learners will differ from context to context, and it is likely that the suggested criteria are not necessarily universally appropriate.

Research focus and design

My research focused on exploring criteria used by Taiwanese teachers to select general English coursebooks for non-English-major students in universities of technology in Taiwan. Nineteen teachers in six selected institutes in Taiwan were interviewed in two phases: at the beginning and at the end of an academic year. Nineteen existing lists of criteria were also reviewed from the literature.

Findings

Taiwanese teachers' selection criteria

Using content analysis, I generated eight categories for Taiwanese teachers' selection criteria. According to teachers, a good coursebook should meet the criteria listed below. (Due to space limitations, only the two most common responses are listed here.)

1 **Overall construction**: be carefully graded; provide short reading texts (no longer than half a page).
2 **Ability to meet students' needs**: cater for the four skills; match the vocabulary and grammar level of most of the students.
3 **Ability to meet teachers' needs**: have rich resources and information in the teacher's manual; provide the right amount of content to fit with time available.
4 **Authenticity**: introduce real-life topics; contain reading texts related to real life.
5 **Potential for self-instruction**: contain a CD-ROM for homework and a CD for students to use; be accompanied by online learning materials.

6 **Socio-cultural sensitivity**: introduce foreign cultures; include Taiwanese culture.
7 **Visual design**: have clear page layout; use sufficiently large font size.
8 **Practical concerns**: be of a reasonable price; be part of a complete series of course-books.

Published criteria

I reviewed various published lists of criteria for evaluating materials, beginning in the early 1970s and continuing to the present. Nineteen were selected for in-depth review.

Gaps between Taiwanese teachers' criteria and existing published criteria

Gaps were identified by comparing the published criteria with Taiwanese teachers' criteria as presented above. The main gaps were as follows:

- With respect to overall construction, the literature has little to say about quantity or length, for example, the number of new words per reading text, or the length of reading texts.
- With respect to students' needs, the literature is less specific about considering the interests and needs of students studying in different content areas; about containing useful topics for students' future careers; or about meeting students' needs to pass specific exams (for example, the need to match their difficulty level, task types and question patterns).
- With respect to teachers' needs, the literature says little about teacher development needs (for example, the value of materials that provide learning opportunities for teachers); topics which can stimulate teachers to share their knowledge or experiences with students; and the provision of a teacher's manual written by local teachers.
- With respect to self-instruction, the literature needs to be updated due to technological developments. For example, it needs to refer to the availability of CDs, CD-ROMs and online learning materials.
- With respect to cultural issues, the literature is less specific about the importance of cultural issues, both in relation to contents of texts or conversations, and in relation to the introduction of the students' source culture.
- With respect to practical concerns, the literature does not consider such issues as provision of L1 instructions and explanations; recommendations from colleagues or publishers; publishers' demonstrations; the provision of teacher-training courses; the matching of criteria for government-promoted projects; publisher-provided opportunities for other projects; or previous positive student evaluations.

Conclusion

This study explored how Taiwanese EFL teachers evaluate materials. It also reviewed the criteria suggested for such evaluation in the literature. Finally, it investigated the possible gaps between what teachers *actually* consider when evaluating materials and what it is suggested teachers *should* consider. Overall, it is clear: selecting a coursebook needs to be appropriate to local contexts, and existing published criteria may fail to take this need into account.

Email: huangshuer@yahoo.com

4.11 Symposium on materials writing in ELT

Convenor: Amy Lightfoot *Freelance, UK* with
Lívia de Araújo Donnini Rodrigues *Universidade de São Paulo, Brazil*
Rubena St. Louis *Universidad Simon Bolivar, Caracas, Venezuela* and
Martin Barge and **William Tweddle** *Queen Mary, University of London, UK*

Many ELT teachers report that creating materials for use in the classroom is one of their favourite parts of their job. There is no doubt that classroom practitioners have a vital role as materials writers as we understand our students' specific needs, interests and abilities. In this symposium we explored these in the context of three materials-writing projects, and discussed some general tips and ideas for improving the materials that we create and use.

The symposium opened with a presentation from **Lívia Donnini** who stated that writing materials for ESL/EFL involves a series of decision-making processes. Defining the syllabus, selecting and/or producing oral and written texts, and designing activities for grammar, vocabulary and skills practice are just some of the decisions a writer has to make. Having experienced different contexts of authorship herself (as a teacher–writer; as a published co-author; and as a specialist professor), one thing has become clear: materials writing is loaded not only with personal and pedagogical values, but also with technical, political and institutional issues that novice writers are not usually aware of when they start a writing project. These forces usually impose questions that should be addressed at the initial stages. A few of these questions are as follows:

Defining autonomy as a teacher and writer

How do we deal with contextual forces without letting go of our own 'personal voice'?

The influence of publishing policies/curriculum on the materials

How do we decide when to give in, when to stand up for the project and when to negotiate changes?

Knowledge of the publication process

How do we avoid making unrealistic choices and having to redo things within a limited time schedule? How do we deal with incompatibilities between the adopted approach and technical or financial limitations? How do we respond to problems that arise, for instance, from copyright issues and graphic production? How do we manage both time and creative resources to deal with several simultaneous demands?

These questions illustrate that materials writing is not a solitary task performed in the quietness of an insulated room. As our discussion showed, our answers to these questions may be very different. However, addressing them may help writers to build their own identity and yet remain open to articulating beliefs, and interpreting and acting upon these sometimes conflicting forces, as Graves (2000) suggests.

We then moved on to discuss a project at the Universidad Simon Bolivar in Venezuela. **Rubena St. Louis** explained how a 48-hour remedial English course was designed for students entering the university's pre-university programme. A needs analysis revealed that students had a low competence in English. Materials were required to cover the basic knowledge needed for them to be successful in their first year of academic study.

Second Language Acquisition theory on learning and cognition, affect and motivation in language learning and research in materials development were considered in the design of the materials. Texts were used as input to cover basic and essential grammar points. There was an emphasis on vocabulary, learning strategies and autonomous learning. Care was taken to ensure that materials were based on achievable objectives and at the students' linguistic and cognitive level. Each lesson had six types of activities:

1 **'What do you think?'**
Learners' involvement with texts through sharing of experiences and opinions.

2 **'Looking at vocabulary'**
Words, images, linked to personal experiences; semantic maps to review and learn new words.

3 **'Working with the dictionary'**
Parts of speech, word structure and dictionary use reviewed.

4 **'Reading' and 'Think about it'**
Reflection and discussion of topics; texts as input for language use.

5 **'Grammar review' and 'Work it out'**
Attention focused on language patterns; formulation and discussion of language hypotheses.

6 **'On your own'**
Activities for students to express what they have learnt.

The materials included a learning styles questionnaire in Spanish, two units of materials in English, a vocabulary supplement with strategies and word lists and a grammar guide with comparisons of the Spanish and English language systems.

A year later, students were asked to what extent they thought that the English course had helped them with the reading programme; 90 per cent considered that it had been useful and 12 per cent believed that their reading comprehension had improved although this had not been the main focus. Overall, 89.9 per cent of these students successfully completed the first reading course.

Our next presentation looked at a relatively new area of materials writing. **Martin Barge** and **William Tweddle** outlined the development of a resource of online self-study materials for students of EAP at Queen Mary, University of London, UK.

This project is underpinned by the QMUL strategic plans, the Language and Learning Unit (LLU) eLearning strategy and the Learning Object Creation (LOC) Tool. The QMUL strategic plans identify increases in students studying at a distance and the need to promote high quality eLearning. In 2009 the LLU identified areas of need in EAP online provision and the materials' authors undertook training at the

University of Southampton in using the LOC Tool, which enables teachers to rapidly create eLearning content.

In addition to the LOC Tool, applications used for materials authoring were Hot Potatoes, Tanida Quizbuilder, RunRev rapid application development tool, Flash and code editors, each according varying degrees of flexibility for the materials' author, from the relatively closed, template-based environments of the LOC Tool and Quizbuilder, to the highly flexible environments of RunRev and Flash. This spectrum of flexibility was matched to the degree of customisation the authors wished to obtain within the different components of the learning material.

A representative sample of materials was presented to illustrate the core content areas available so far: academic writing, grammar and seminar skills. This exemplified materials created with each of the authoring tools above, including learning objects, quizzes and games.

Data collated from the student trialling of materials indicated that the materials meet learners' needs, are appropriately structured, clearly laid out, relevant to students' areas of study, easy to use and navigate, suitable for self-study and provide reliable information and helpful feedback. Student feedback comments also highlighted areas for improvement, such as greater elucidation through the giving of further examples. And there was a clear desire for the materials bank to be expanded.

The materials are currently under further development and are due for official launch at QMUL in September 2010. The presenters and their team are working on improving the accessibility requirements and adapting alternative versions that function without JavaScript and Flash.

Finally, **Amy Lightfoot** shared some tips on writing materials for day-to-day teaching. We started by examining the justification for creating materials, given that it is often a very time-consuming process. There are often opportunities to involve the students in the materials-making process that are sometimes overlooked. For example, for an activity that involves language written on cut-up pieces of paper, we can put the students into groups and do a group dictation. The students are split into groups and then quickly read the items to be written down, preceded by a group number. The groups write only the words that are dictated specifically to them. The students are then regrouped so that they have all of the materials and they do the activity as usual.

The second key point was the belief that personalising materials is one of the key justifications for writing them. Mass-produced materials do not always suit our context and this is a gap that we can fill. For example, sentences on a worksheet can be written to refer to situations and places with which the students are familiar, rather than generic ones. Also, common activities can be adapted to make them more relevant. For example, the much-loved ranking exercise where students prioritise items to take to a desert island can be contextualised according to the students: in the activity 'Survival in Delhi', the students have to rank the items that a visitor to the city should bring with them—an idea that is easily adapted to any context.

We also explored the issue of appearance. Students have reported that the 'look and feel' of materials is just as important as the actual content. This suggests that teachers should pay considerable attention to how their materials appear (as well as proofreading them carefully) if they want their students to value them.

Finally we briefly looked at ways that teachers can collaborate and share their materials. We discussed several websites which offer publishing opportunities. These range from the well known website 'Onestopenglish' to the relative newcomer 'Tagito'.

Email: mail@amylightfoot.co.uk
livpring@usp.br
slrubena2003@yahoo.com or slrubena@usb.ve
m.i.barge@qmul.ac.uk
w.tweddle@qmul.ac.uk

References

Graves, K. 2000. *Designing Language Courses: A Guide for Teachers.* Boston: Heinle and Heinle.

Onestopenglish. http://www.onestopenglish.com.

Tagito. http://www.tagito.com.

5 Grammar, vocabulary and spelling

5.1 Urban myths and English grammar

Peter Grundy

There are undoubtedly plenty of urban myths about English grammar. Although contemporary pedagogic grammars tend to favour descriptions like 'present perfect form' (rather than 'present perfect tense'), there are still many teachers who don't know that 'present' designates a tense and 'perfect' an aspect, or who think there are six (or seven or eight) tenses in English. Besides the need to provide accurate explanations for learners, understanding tense, aspect and modality can help us to develop appropriate methodology.

So with regard to *tense*, there are two tenses in English—non-past (present) and past:

Present	Past	
she [eats]	she *ate*	Tense is only marked on the lexical verb when there are no auxiliaries. When there are auxiliaries, tense is marked on the first auxiliary: she i*s*[n't] eating/ she ha*s*[n't] been eating/she **will** [not] have been eating. (Negation follows the first auxiliary.)
she ha**s** eaten	she ha**d** eaten	
she **is** eating	she *was* eating	
she **is** going to eat	she *was* going to eat	
she *will* eat	she woul**d** eat	

Table 5.1.1: Tenses in English

Comrie's (1976) definition of *aspect* as reflecting the 'internal temporal constituency' of an event is illustrated by aspectual meanings such as the following:

Habitual	she eats/used to eat breakfast every day
Perfective	He's read the paper (and finished reading it)
Iterative	he keeps sneezing
Inchoative	he started to sneeze
Conclusive	he stopped sneezing

Table 5.1.2: Aspectual meanings

Two aspects exhibit productive morphology in English:

- Progressive (*be* + *ing*): she **is** eat**ing**/she *was* eat**ing**
- Perfect (*have* + *en*): she **ha**s eat**en**/she **ha**d eat**en**

Perfect aspect marks a difference between event and reference time:

- Present perfect: *She has eaten and now she's asleep.* (Eating is a past event in an utterance referring to present time.)
- Past perfect: *She had eaten before she fell asleep.* (Eating is an event in the distant past in an utterance referring to a less-distant past time.)

From a methodological point of view the difference between tense and aspect is crucial for the following reasons:

- Aspectual distinctions are often lexically encoded: *know, realise, understand* represent internal temporal distinctions in a single semantic area.
- Cross-linguistically, aspect is (?always) marked closer to the lexical verb than tense and typically influences its meaning. Close your eyes and compare the images you see when you say *he was shot / he was being shot,* and you get the idea.
- It enables us to understand how present perfect and past reference differ and prompts us to provide a sufficient context for this distinction to be inferred by our students:

	Present perfect form	**Past form**
Time of utterance	Present	Present
Time referred to in utterance	Present	Past
Time of event	Past	Past

Table 5.1.3: Present perfect vs. past forms

- the more we know, the easier it is for us to work out what learners mean when they say things like *he don't works, I am eat* versus *I have eat, I did been going,* etc., and the more likely we are to be able to help them to find a more comprehensible way of expressing the meanings they want to communicate.

As well as referring to 'real' events, we can also encode the extent to which an event is likely to come about. Typically, languages do this by means of predicates like *possible* and *likely.* Alongside these predicates, modern English has a set of *modal* auxiliaries which express obligation, permission, prohibition, necessity, possibility, futurity and ability. Many of these auxiliaries can also be used to express epistemic meaning (speaker perspective), and with interesting co-occurrence differences:

Root meaning
- You may hand your assignment in late. (permission)
- *You may be handing your assignment in late.
- You may not hand your assignment in late. (not permitted to hand in late)

Epistemic meaning
- He may hand his assignment in late. (speaker's estimate of likelihood)
- He may be handing his assignment in late. (speaker's estimate of likelihood)
- He may not hand his assignment in late. (speaker's estimate of likelihood of not handing in late)

From a pedagogic point of view, epistemic modality is important because it encodes the speaker's attitude to propositional content (subjectification) and enables us to distinguish two levels in the utterance: the higher-level perspective of the speaker and the lower-level proposition. Control over this function is empowering for learners and is central in both communicative and humanistic approaches.

Email: grundypeter@btinternet.com

Reference

Comrie, B. 1976. *Aspect.* Cambridge: Cambridge University Press.

5.2 English grammar for academic purposes

Maxine Gillway *Language Centre, University of Bristol, UK*

The aim of this session was to swap ideas and experiences on the questions below. The 29 participants wrote answers to these questions at the start, which I will refer to in this report.

Do EAP students need more grammar? If so, why?

Once the definition of grammar was widened to include word and discourse grammar, that is, language as opposed to skills, all 29 participants agreed that it was needed. Ten of the participants mentioned the evidence from students' written errors. Twelve mentions were made of the fact that there is corpus-based evidence that academic language is different. Four people pointed out that we should attempt to meet student expectations. The need was also discussed in terms of purpose, that is, the need to be able to communicate effectively, particularly in writing (nine) and to access academic texts (three). The conclusion was that students do need more, but not more of the same.

What grammar do they need?

It was seen as the teacher's role to help students discover what sort of grammar they need. According to Biber *et al.* (2000: 579), 'Much of the new information in academic text is packaged as modifiers in noun phrases, resulting in a very high density of information.' Twelve of the participants mentioned the need for a focus on noun phrases. Seven participants were in favour of some work on tenses, although according to Biber *et al.*, 80–85 per cent of academic text is in the present tense and 5–10 per cent in the past, with the progressive and perfect aspects being rare. While Swales (2004) points out that the average sentence is 25 words long and multiple clauses are common, there was some feeling among the group that students, especially those entering business, should aim for clarity rather than complexity. I suggested that perhaps we should aim for clarity in their productive grammar but enable them to unpack the complex clauses and phrases in their receptive grammar. However, it was suggested that to become fully fledged members of the discourse community they wish to access, they will have to move towards writing more complex noun phrases. Other common suggestions were text-level grammar (seven), academic functions (eight) and the passive voice (nine).

How should it be delivered?

Term 1	Term 2	Term 3
EFL 1 (verb phrase)	EFL 2 (verb phrase)	ESP 1 (productive)
EAS 1 (functions)	EAS 2 (functions)	ESP 2 (receptive)

Table 5.2.1: An International Foundation Programme

The model in Table 5.2.1 is used on an International Foundation Programme. The productive strand focuses solely on editing and involves work on materials produced from a corpus of student essays, which are available for classroom and online use. Students are also encouraged to keep error logs based on feedback on their own written work. The receptive strand is based on language analysis of topic-based texts but also involves a fun element with games such as 'Delete but complete', where students are challenged to delete parts of a complex academic sentence without destroying the sentence structure, and 'Grow your own', where the challenge is to produce the longest noun phrase. The activities I suggested were in line with the themes that emerged from the participant surveys: in context, discovery based, a mix of independent and classroom work, and a mix of integrated and discrete language activities.

(How) should it be assessed?

It was on this last point that I seemed to diverge from the majority view of the group, with 18 participants stating that grammar is or should be assessed indirectly through the criteria for written or spoken tasks. While this does happen in my courses, grammar is also tested directly for 20 per cent of the grade. In the productive strand, the students are given a timed editing task. This is done using the comment function in Word, which is how they have been given feedback on their writing throughout the course. It was hoped that this would have a positive washback in that it would encourage students to edit their own writing more carefully. In student feedback 90 per cent found the focus on common errors useful. Two participants mentioned the interesting option of self-assessment, which can be done using a Virtual Learning Environment. It was an interesting discussion and I am very glad to have seen other presentations on a similar subject—showing that the E is coming back to EAP, and that we are perhaps moving away from purely skills-driven syllabi.

Email: maxine.gillway@bris.ac.uk

References

Biber, D., S. Johansson, G. Leech, S. Conrad and E. Finegan. 2000. *Longman Grammar of Spoken and Written English*. Harlow: Longman.

Swales, J. M. 2004. 'Towards a working grammar of academic and research speech'. Plenary presentation at 2nd IVACS Conference, Belfast, June 2004. (Retrieved 1 April 2010 from http://micase.elicorpora.info/files/0000/0189/Towards_a_Working_Grammar_Swales.pdf.)

5.3 Grammar, correctness and language evolution: what not to teach? Or: 'Against the tyranny of TEFLspeak'

Martin Parrott *Teacher and writer, London, UK*

This talk/workshop raised questions about the value and the validity of some of the grammar that has become the staple of ELT. I argued that in the need to simplify and standardise grammar in order to teach it, we sometimes lose sight both of the variety within English, and of the changes taking place in how the language is spoken and written. I suggested that we may be in danger of teaching a fossilised version of our language that increasingly ignores the reality of English as it is used.

Participants considered the following sentences and were asked to classify each of them as 'correct', 'incorrect' or 'debateable'. For those they classified as 'debateable', they were asked to add a brief comment.

1	I have seen him yesterday.
2	If I'd have been there, I'd have helped.
3	Thank you but you really didn't need to.
4	Please tell me what should I do.
5	She has been ill for a long time before she died.
6	Can I go to the toilet, please?
7	You left your wallet, innit?
8	She was like, 'what's your problem?'
9	I am visiting there every week.
10	I was sat there for hours.
11	I done it already.
12	Where does he living?
13	She drunk it all.
14	Less people came this time.
15	I so don't agree with you.
16	They was on the table.
17	She come here yesterday.
18	Give me them pens.
19	There's lots of names on the list.
20	It was wrote by Shakespeare.
21	That's an interesting phenomena.

The ensuing discussion was wide ranging and informative. What interested me most was the admission by many of those present that they frequently teach language that they don't use themselves. They also sometimes correct learners for using language that teachers themselves use.

I offered the following as a possible response to the exercise:

	Correct	Incorrect	Debateable
1	I have seen him yesterday.		B
2	If I'd have been there, I'd have helped.		A
3	Thank you but you really didn't need to.		A
4	Please tell me what should I do.		B
5	She has been ill for a long time before she died.	X	
6	Can I go to the toilet, please?		A
7	You left your wallet, innit?		E
8	She was like, 'what's your problem?'		E
9	I am visiting there every week.		B
10	I was sat there for hours.		A
11	I done it already.		D
12	Where does he living?	X	
13	She drunk it all.		C
14	Less people came this time.		A
15	I so don't agree with you.		E
16	They was on the table.		D
17	She come here yesterday.		D
18	Give me them pens.		D
19	There's lots of names on the list.		C
20	It was wrote by Shakespeare.		D
21	That's an interesting phenomena.		A

Key: A: Instances which have always been, or which have become, general use. Frowned upon by some. Warning about conservative examinations? **B**: Used by native speakers to make subtle distinctions. Conflict with useful 'rules of thumb'. **C**: Accepted in general use and arguably now 'standard'. Warning about conservative examinations? **D**: Commonly used but considered 'uneducated'. **E**: In common use among young people. 'Standard English' of the future?

I concluded by affirming what several participants had said: that whether we would teach some of these actively would depend on whom we were teaching and our students' reasons for learning. Learners planning to integrate into sectors of society where these are standard, for example, need to know how English is used in these sectors.

I also pointed out that, as teachers, we need to consider such examples for the following reasons, among others:

- Language is changing, and we need to be sensitive to the changes.
- If we expose our learners to 'real English' and encourage them to be sensitive to what they hear and read, and to use listening and reading as a part of their language learning, we need to be able to respond to their questions confidently and accurately.

- We need to ensure that we do not begin to believe that the simplified models we may teach are, in fact, the language itself.

Email: martinparrott@btinternet.com

5.4 Learning vocabulary from reading-while-listening to an authentic text

Nina Daskalovska *Goce Delcev University, Stip, Republic of Macedonia*

Introduction

During the last two decades there has been an increased interest in the role of reading in vocabulary acquisition. First-language studies have shown that children learn about 3,000 words per year between Grades 3 and 12, while the number of words that can be learned in the classroom could only be a few hundred a year (Nagy and Herman 1987); this leads to the conclusion that most vocabulary is acquired from reading and listening. A number of studies have been carried out to investigate whether there is a connection between reading and vocabulary acquisition; these have confirmed that L1 learners can acquire word meanings incidentally while reading.

Studies in foreign language acquisition have found that foreign language learners can also acquire vocabulary while reading for meaning. This study was designed to examine whether EFL university students can learn vocabulary incidentally from reading-while-listening to an authentic text.

Research questions

1 How much vocabulary can EFL university students learn while reading and listening to an authentic text?
2 Are there any significant differences in acquisition rates between learners with different vocabulary sizes?
3 Are the words that appear more frequently in the text more likely to be learned?

Method

In this study, 18 first-year English major students studying at a university in the Republic of Macedonia read and listened to the first eight chapters of the novel *Pride and Prejudice* by Jane Austen. The pre-tests, the treatment, and the post-test took place during their regular classes. The treatment lasted one hour. Fifty-one words with different frequency in the text were selected as targets. The next day the participants were tested on their receptive knowledge of the target words. In order to establish the vocabulary size of the participants in the study, Nation's (1990) Vocabulary Levels Test was used. The test used for this study was designed in the same way as the Vocabulary Levels Test, and contained 17 blocks of six words, three target words and three distractors. The items in the post-test were in a different order from those in the pre-test.

Results and discussion

	Mean	**Standard deviation**
Pre	26.9	8.52
Post	32.7	8.76
Gain	5.8	6.36

Table 5.4.1: Pre-test to post-test gains

As shown in Table 5.4.1, the pre-test results show that, on average, the students knew 26.9 of the 51 target words, so the number of unknown words for the group as a whole was reduced to 24.1. The average number of words learned was 5.8, or 24 per cent of the target words. A t-test for paired samples (t = 3.85, p<0.01) showed that the difference between the pre-test and the post-test was significantly greater than chance. This study showed that the participants were able to learn one in every four words tested.

The Pearson Product Moment Correlation Coefficient for the correlation between the relative gain scores and the total scores on the Vocabulary Levels Test was very small (–0.01), which suggests that the vocabulary size of the participants in this study did not play any role in the rate of learning the meaning of the unknown words. This may be due to the small number of participants and target words.

This study found some support for the expected correlation between the word frequency in the text and the learning gains. While there was no overall correlation between the relative gains and both the local and global word frequency (r = 0.06), the figures that emerged when the words were split by gains showed that there was a moderate correlation between the relative gains of the first 13 words and their frequency in the text (r = 0.41) and a rather strong correlation with their general frequency in the spoken section of the BNC (r = 0.73).

Conclusion

The results show that university-level students in an EFL context can acquire vocabulary while reading and listening to an authentic text, and that for some learners even two exposures are enough to acquire the meaning of previously unknown words. These findings point to the need for including an extensive reading component in language learning programmes.

Email: nina.daskalovska@yahoo.com

References

Austen, J. 1985. *Pride and Prejudice* (Reprint edition). Harmondsworth: Penguin Classics.

Nagy, W. E. and P. A. Herman. 1987. 'Breadth and depth of vocabulary knowledge: Implications for acquisition and instruction' in M. G. McKeown and M. E. Curtis (eds.). *The Nature of Vocabulary Acquisition*. Hillsdale, N.J.: Lawrence Erlbaum Associates.

Nation, I. S. P. 1990. *Teaching and Learning Vocabulary*. Rowley, Mass.: Newbury House.

5.5 An interdisciplinary data-based academic word list: developing an EAP curriculum

Akira Tajino and **Toshiyuki Kanamaru** *University of Kyoto, Japan*

Introduction

Academic vocabulary is a defining feature of academic skills, including academic writing, and is therefore crucial to academic success in higher education. This paper aims to explore ways in which vocabulary instruction can be incorporated into an EAP curriculum at Kyoto University, a multi-disciplinary research university in Japan. For this purpose, a 10-million-word corpus was developed from academic journal articles in various disciplines. Four types of EAP word lists were compiled which, because of their wide usage, can be used in other EAP courses.

Objectives of English education at Kyoto University

At Kyoto University students are required to take both Liberal Arts General Education English courses and discipline-specific English courses. While the former focus on EGAP and the latter on ESAP, there is a growing realisation that the two should be linked in the curriculum; this is a topic in need of investigation.

Developing an interdisciplinary data-based academic word list

Four types of EAP vocabulary

1　ESAP: vocabulary for students in a particular subject area.
2　EGAP: vocabulary for students regardless of academic discipline.
3　EGAP–A: vocabulary for students in liberal arts and social sciences.
4　EGAP–S: vocabulary for students in sciences.

Steps in developing the Kyoto University academic vocabulary database

1　Each of the ten faculties (Letters, Education, Law, Economics, Integrated Human Studies, Science, Medicine, Pharmaceutical Science, Engineering and Agriculture) nominated English language research journals representative of their specialised fields of study.
2　A database of approximately 10.6 million words was compiled from a selection of 1,700 research papers from 170 journals.
3　Words which were included in West's General Service List (1953) were eliminated from the database so that academic words in each subject area were grouped (i.e. ESAP vocabulary).
4　The database was separated into three categories: words common to both Arts and Sciences (EGAP vocabulary), Arts only (EGAP–A vocabulary) and Sciences only (EGAP–S vocabulary).
5　The database was reduced by range and frequency statistical procedures (i.e. the complementary similarity measure and the harmonic mean) to 2,000 words in each category.
6　University EAP teachers reduced the number of words to a total of 1,110 words by taking into account the needs of the students in the EAP courses.

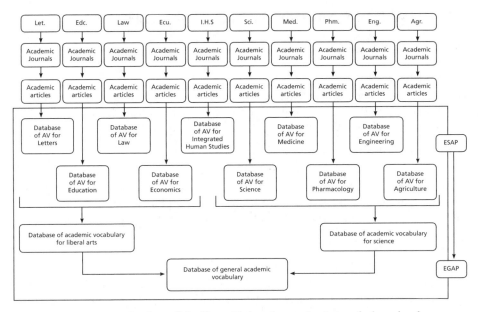

Figure 5.5.1: Outline of the Kyoto University academic vocabulary database

7   The usefulness of the selected words was verified by confirming their use in research journals which were not used to compile the database.

8   A leading dictionary publisher in Japan, *Kenkyusha*, added definitions and example phrases or sentences in English and in Japanese. Discipline- and context-specific meanings or phrases for each word were introduced.

9   EAP teachers reviewed and revised the publisher's work to ascertain that the definitions and examples corresponded to the academic usage of the words.

10 After the first edition of the word list was published, representatives of each faculty were invited to make suggestions for revisions.

Conclusion

As shown above, the database has been developed and validated from both theoretical and pedagogical perspectives. It has been used in a number of ways: for example, one teacher explains how some academic words in science fields such as 'moiety' and 'combustion' were once used in English literature, so that students from both arts and science fields may become more interested in learning academic vocabulary. Future research will focus more on the practical aspects of the database.

Email: akira@tajino.mbox.media.kyoto-u.ac.jp
kanamaru@hi.h.kyoto-u.ac.jp

References

Kyoto Univesity Academic Vocabulary Research Group and Kenkyusha. 2009. *Kyodai Gakujutsu-goi Detabesu Kihon-tango 1110.* Tokyo: Kenkyusha.

West, M. 1953. *A General Service List of English Words.* London: Longman, Green & Co.

5.6 FWAAA!! Fun with acronyms and abbreviations

Mark Bartram *Freelance, Oxford, UK*

Definitions

An acronym is where the first letters of the words in an expression form a new word (for example, 'UNICEF'). An abbreviation or initialism is where the letters are pronounced separately and do not form a word (for example, 'BBC').

Is the distinction important?

Most of the time, probably not. But sometimes an initialism in one language can be an acronym in another, and vice versa. This can cause confusion; for example, a learner might talk about a 'veep', when he means a 'V–I–P'. However, in most cases, the distinction is not important, and in this article, we shall refer only to 'acronyms'.

Why are acronyms important for learners?

1 There are huge numbers of them

There are probably at least half a million, not including technical and scientific ones. What is more, they form part of everyday language, so they are especially relevant for learners living in an English-speaking country. Examples from the UK include 'PTA' (= parent–teacher association), 'MP' (= Member of Parliament) and 'R + R' (= rest and recreation). Newspapers contain hundreds of examples. Many websites which learners have to access (for example, the UK Border Agency site) use them in abundance.

2 New ones are being invented all the time

Learners can be frustrated by what seems to be a conspiracy to baffle them! (One of the functions of acronyms may be to create 'in-groups' and 'out-groups', in the same way that jargon does.) Recently coined acronyms include 'WAGs' (= wives and girl-friends, usually of England footballers), 'ASBO' (= Anti-social Behaviour Order) and 'OTT' (= over the top).

3 They are difficult to understand, both in written and spoken text

When we teach reading strategies, we often encourage learners to guess the meaning of unfamiliar words from the form, for example from affixes or from similarity to a word in their own language. With acronyms, this is not possible. The only ways the learner can access the meaning are as follows:

* Knowing the acronym already! I would encourage much more teaching of acronyms within lexis programmes; in my research for this session, I only found one general English coursebook that included work on acronyms. It seems odd not to teach a lexical area that has more than 500,000 examples.
* Guessing from context. In spoken text, acronyms are particularly hard both to decipher, and then to decode. For example, I recently heard this utterance: 'Well, you wouldn't find it in the OED!' The acronym here [for 'Oxford English Dictionary'] is difficult to decipher, partly because the listener may not be expecting an abbreviation, and partly because of the linking between the vowels; the listener may understand the utterance as a word spelt 'oweedee' or similar.

4 They are difficult to pronounce

Learners may be unsure how to pronounce the letters of the alphabet; they may not know how to link letters in connected speech; and finally, they may not know if the letters need to be pronounced separately or as a single word.

Helping learners

The following are suggested:

1   Teach more acronyms!
2   Encourage learners to find acronyms for themselves, for example, by highlighting them in a newspaper and then researching them in the dictionary or on the web.
3   Encourage learners to decide for themselves if an acronym is worth learning. For example, the acronym 'FSA' (= Financial Services Authority) might be useful for a Business English student, whereas 'BTW' (= by the way) is more appropriate for a teenage texter.
4   Play games with acronyms. One simple game is to give students the definition for a word (for example, 'a person who flies a plane' is a 'pilot'); the students then look for the next acronym in the dictionary after 'pilot', for example, 'PIN' (= personal identification number). They note down the acronym and its meaning and decide whether or not they want/need to remember it.
5   Practise deciphering acronyms in fast speech. Read out some sentences or texts with acronyms. Students must count how many they hear, and/or write them down.
6   Practise guessing from context.
7   Give students the acronym, and they have to say what the letters stand for. This is good for revision, and can be done as a game. Alternatively, give the students the acronym, and tell them to make up the craziest/funniest explanation of what it stands for. Then, show them what the real meaning is.
8   Ask students to work in groups to make up an acronym; groups then create a sentence containing the acronym and challenge another group to guess its meaning from the context.

Email: markjbartram@yahoo.com

5.7 Dictionary skills as a means to develop learner autonomy

Tatyana Ryzhkova *Siberian Federal University, Krasnoyarsk, Russian Federation*

'How do you feel about dictionaries?' This is the question I address at the beginning of every English course to my upper-secondary and university students. Around 70 per cent of the students report feeling reluctant to use a dictionary and only do so when absolutely forced to. There is also a tendency to consult electronic dictionaries rather than traditional paper versions. But the vast majority of students at all levels use dictionaries for one purpose only: to translate from or into English. Other functions of various reference books remain unnoticed and undiscovered though they might help students solve a lot of problems connected with language use and language learning.

Among the most frequent problems are phrasal verbs, words with similar meanings, choice of words best suiting the context, cultural phenomena, and idiomatic language. Often such problems are solved with the help of the teacher who provides the needed information. By doing so the teacher leaves the students unaware of the instrument that an autonomous learner might successfully use in a similar situation. Well-developed dictionary skills add a lot to learner independence and enable learners to provide reliable information about language matters that may have previously demanded their teacher's assistance.

Modern textbooks address this issue by offering activities built on monolingual or bilingual dictionary entries. This adds to learners' understanding of how a dictionary entry is organised. Unfortunately this does not give learners a chance to get acquainted with the organisation of a dictionary as a whole, with all sorts of information a dictionary provides, with the variety of dictionaries and other reference books. One way to fill this gap is through an activity named 'Dictionary race'.

The aim of the activity is to introduce a variety of dictionaries. Experience shows that in order to be effective 'Dictionary race' should take around 90 minutes and present no more than 10 types of reference books. At the beginning the teacher divides the class into three groups and hands out a list of questions. The number of questions depends on the students' level and the time allotted for the activity; 12 to 15 questions are usually sufficient. Possible question types are provided in Table 5.7.1.

No.	Question	Teacher's possible comment
1	Which two of the following verbs can be used in the following sentence: 'In schools today, less emphasis is placed on _____ facts and more thinking for yourself.' *learning/studying/learning by heart/memorizing*	This information can be found in activators. An activator helps learners choose a correct word for a particular context. It also provides information about the difference in meanings between synonymous words. This is one of the biggest problems for learners of languages with very large vocabularies
2	Which word is more often used in English, 'issue' or 'isolation'?	Modern English–English dictionaries provide this information by emphasizing the most frequently used words with font colour, by adding a special icon, or by highlighting them. This information is useful to the learners because it helps them decide which words should be acquired first.
3	When were the legends about King Arthur first told?	Dictionaries of English language and culture are priceless when one needs to understand a cultural or linguistic phenomenon.
4	Which would be better to say, 'big mistake', 'total mistake' or 'huge mistake'?	This information can be obtained in a dictionary of collocations. Learners' English becomes more natural when they try to use collocations in their speech.

Table 5.7.1: Sample questions for 'Dictionary race'

Answers to the questions are only accepted if students can explain how and where they found the necessary information. To make the work of every student more effective it is advisable to ensure the number of dictionaries equals or exceeds the number of students in the class. It is also necessary to ask students to use one dictionary at a time and not to keep it for more than five minutes. When a group finishes, the game is over and the answers are discussed as a class. It is important that during the discussion the class goes through each question and that every student understands where and how the necessary information can be obtained. The teacher can make a comment after each question about the dictionary, focusing on the type of information it provides and on how it can be found. At the end of the session, the students reflect on the value of reference materials for language learners.

Email: ryzhkovatatyana@hotmail.com

5.8 How do you spell ...?

Johanna Stirling *Norwich Institute for Language Education (NILE), Norwich, UK*

What do you think about English spelling?

The workshop started by allowing the audience to air their gut feelings about English spelling and the teaching and learning of it. English spelling was deemed to be 'difficult/challenging', 'crazy', 'confusing', and 'illogical', among other negatives. The most positive was 'complex'. Attitudes to teaching it ranged from 'a nightmare' to the more cheerful 'fun' and 'rewarding'. A couple of people found it 'fun' to learn, but everyone else used negative adjectives.

More than one system

So we then examined why there was so much negativity surrounding English spelling, and I suggested that if we try to fit our complex orthography into a phonological system, then it becomes impossible to justify, let alone teach, many spellings. However, if we see English spelling as a system of systems, in which the phonological sys-

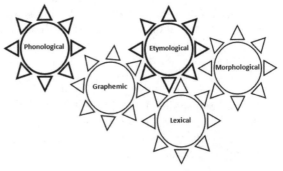

Figure 5.8.1: A system of systems

tem is just one part, it becomes much more teachable. We defined and explored these different systems, represented in Figure 5.8.1.

People spell not only by ear, but also by eye, by hand and by brain. So how do we approach these different systems in teaching?

A cognitive approach

First, we looked at a cognitive approach. By encouraging learners to make links between words they know and ones they have difficulties with, we can help them to see patterns in spelling. Arab learners especially often spell the word 'two' as 'tow', which is a more phonetically logical spelling than that with a silent 'w' in the middle. However, if we show them that the 'tw' links the words with lexically similar ones such as 'twin', 'twelve', 'twenty' and 'between', we provide not only a rationalisation but also a hook to hang the word on.

A visual approach

Good spellers tend to spell visually—they know when a word 'doesn't look right'. We need to help weaker spellers to develop this skill of noticing spelling patterns when they are reading. We looked at an activity based on international football tournaments for noticing vowels. (This is described at http://thespellingblog.blogspot.com/2010/05/world-cup-spelling-noticing-vowels.html.) Another way to encourage learners to notice spelling is to look for words within words. In the workshop we found a surprising number of animals hiding in common words!

Very often when good spellers visualise a word they 'see' the shape of the word and this helps them with the spelling. For example, if there are letters with 'sticks' that rise above the line, such as b, d or h, or letters with 'tails' that drop below the line, like g, j, p or q, then these should stand out and give clues to the spelling. Getting learners to draw around the outline of words is very effective for some students. Also, word shapes can be constructed with Cuisenaire rods: using the ones (white) and twos (red), learners can show where words have 'sticks' or 'tails'. This provides a strong visual image that often stays in the brain longer than the sequence of letters alone does.

A visual–kinaesthetic approach

In the following fun activity, called 'Spelling gym', the visual approach is combined with a kinaesthetic one. Students stand. Tell them that you will say a word which they will all spell together—with their arms. They all put their hands on the front of their own shoulders (arms not crossed). This is the 'neutral' position. When there is a letter with a 'stick' they should all raise both hands above their heads. For a 'tail' they drop hands down to their thighs. For an 'in-line' letter (that is, one with no stick or tail, such as c, e or w) they cross their hands to the opposite shoulders. Between each letter the hands must come back to the 'neutral' position. Now say a word, but before learners move, they close their eyes and try to see the word and notice its spelling. Tell them to open their eyes when they have seen it. Now all say the spelling together making the appropriate arm movements. As learners find themselves visualising a word repeatedly, this should help them to memorise the spelling, as well as improving their ability to visualise clearly.

Multi-sensory learning

The polysystemic nature of English orthography calls for a range of multi-sensory activities like this. There is more to learning phonetically irregular words than just copying a word enough times to remember it for tomorrow's test (but possibly no longer). And it can certainly be more enjoyable, too.

Email: johanna.stirling@gmail.com

6 Reading, critical thinking and reflecting on text

6.1 Making the most of a reading text

Peter Watkins *University of Portsmouth, UK*

Introduction

This talk reported on the outcomes of a very small-scale piece of research. Eighteen teachers were interviewed regarding what they felt constituted a 'reading lesson' and were asked to exemplify their beliefs using texts. In the talk, I proposed that as well as the usual chronological classification of reading sequences into pre-, while- and post-reading tasks (for example, Thornbury and Watkins 2007), a more functional classification was useful, based on how teachers viewed the purpose of the activities they used.

These more functional categories were split into activities that supported comprehension; those that were used as a springboard for other skills work (for example, a reading text may lead into an oral discussion of related issues); and those activities that promoted the study of language as a system. It was the first and last of those categories that were focused on in the talk and will be reported here.

Strategies to support comprehension

Support for comprehension came about through teachers using many familiar procedures. For example, the pre-teaching of key vocabulary allows learners to decode those words rapidly when they read and thus helps to maintain reading speeds and comprehension. Teachers also made use of glossaries so that learners had vocabulary support while reading. These strategies primarily support bottom-up text processing.

Top-down processing was also supported before reading, often through prompts such as 'What do you know about ...?' The more specifically such lead-ins mirror the text content, the more support is given. However, as well as activating content schemata, teachers also activate schemata based on the text type, asking learners about the possible structures of the text genre. This genre-based strategy was used less often by the teachers interviewed.

Prediction activities (based on vocabulary taken from the text, pictures, titles, and so on) were commonly used. However, it would be wrong to categorise them as solely pre-reading activities, as they can be used after sections of text, with learners asked if the text confirmed their expectations or whether they wish to modify predictions for the following sections in light of what they have read.

Teachers used questions of many different sorts to either support or test comprehension. It is beyond the scope of this short report to discuss the differences between these two phenomena, but it was argued that good questions that support comprehension draw the learners' attention to the main messages of the text, while ignoring insignificant details. This is based on the principle that 'In real life we do not process discourse as if it were equally interesting or worthy of being remembered' (Brown 1990: 147). Comprehension-based activities can also be subjective. For example, learners can be asked to indicate which parts of a text they find amusing, surprising, boring, and so on.

Teachers often integrated reading and other skills. For example, a reading text may be used as a prompt for writing a response, or a reading may lead to a role play, and so on, but due to the obvious constraints these were not discussed in the talk at any great length. Instead, we move on to looking at how texts can be used as a way of enhancing awareness of language as a system.

Strategies to support language study

The primary advantage of using texts in this way was considered to be the contextualisation of language and the opportunity to see lexis and grammar used in authentic discourse. The teachers used various well-known teaching activities to focus on lexis and grammar. However, one relatively underused activity in ELT seems to be the study of genre-based text features. For example, learners can be asked to read a text and identify the features of the text that are associated with the genre. This may help in the future with the top-down processing of similar texts.

Several teachers reported using activities that could be grouped as 'restoring damaged text' (such as gap fills, inserting sentences or paragraphs, transposing words in a sentence, and so on). These were seen as particularly useful for students who enjoyed cognitive challenges or as a way of focusing on the form of the text rather than the content if that content was seen as dull and uninspiring.

Conclusion

Comprehension-based activities see reading as a communicative skill. Texts can also be studied as a way of developing linguistic knowledge of genre, vocabulary and grammar.

Email: peter.watkins@port.ac.uk

References

Brown, G. 1990. *Listening to Spoken English*. London: Longman.

Thornbury, S. and P. Watkins. 2007. *The CELTA Course Trainee Book*. Cambridge: Cambridge University Press.

6.2 Teaching reading comprehension through collaborative learning

Esmaeil Momtaz *University of Aberdeen, UK*

Introduction

There is a widespread assumption, supported by some research evidence, that collaborative learning results in better learning. However, limited research has been undertaken of collaborative learning in countries where cultural values and educational traditions could render it less effective than in the West. The author conducted research in Iranian EFL reading comprehension classes in an attempt to answer two research questions:

1 Does collaborative reading lead to greater comprehension of a text than private reading?
2 If so, what aspects of collaborative learning contribute to the higher level of comprehension?

Method and results

A quasi-experimental design was used to answer the first question. The participants, 36 university students, were divided into two classes of equal reading comprehension abilities, as indicated by a pre-test. The intervention consisted of four texts of equal length, comprising two rated in a pilot study as conceptually difficult/linguistically easy, and two rated as conceptually easy/linguistically difficult. The subjects in each class were asked to read the two types of texts for four sessions. Each class read two of the texts collaboratively in small groups and the other two privately. After reading the texts, the subjects were asked to answer in writing ten comprehension questions. Collaborative reading resulted in consistently higher scores than private reading for all four texts, although in one case the difference was not statistically significant.

Qualitative methods were employed to answer the second question. Group interactions during collaborative reading were tape recorded and transcribed, and ten students selected at random from the two classes were interviewed in depth. Using these methods, certain processes of collaborative reading were identified, including brainstorming, paraphrasing, using meta-linguistic utterances, using interaction management utterances and summarising. Other minor processes were also identified such as making positive/negative claim to understand, eliciting confirmation and confirming.

Discussion and conclusions

The results suggest that students who read collaboratively consistently outperform students who read privately. This corroborates Chang's (1995) finding that the average scores of students in cooperative learning were some two points higher than of those in a traditional English reading class. The gains of the collaborative readers can be grouped under the following categories: (1) the increase of student talk; (2) the supportive and communicative learning available; and (3) the interactive processes which stimulate the students' cognitive, linguistic, and social abilities.

In collaborative learning, the students were able to maximise peer interactions which are essential to real learning (Vygotsky 1978). This facilitates such learning activities as mutual corrections, brainstorming, eliciting confirmation, and collective summarising of paragraphs, all of which contribute to developing the students' world and linguistic knowledge. The private readers were deprived of these interactive processes.

Implications and limitations of the study

This study provides evidence that collaborative learning can be effective in developing students' linguistic and world knowledge in EFL reading comprehension classes in

Iranian universities. The linguistic knowledge in this research is interpreted in terms of vocabulary knowledge and knowledge of the grammatical structures. The world knowledge is interpreted in terms of the concepts, and overall purpose or meaning contained in the texts. It should be noted that this study was not precisely a test of the collaborative learning format, neither did it meet the strict definition of collaborative learning. It did, however, investigate in some depth one major principle of collaborative learning, i.e. student interaction.

This study had some limitations. Firstly, the sample was relatively small, being limited to two classes comprising 36 university students. One must be cautious in generalising the results. Future studies on collaborative reading among students in more classes are required before a full picture of the effects of collaborative reading can be achieved. Secondly, students received direct instruction on specific reading comprehension strategies for only one session. As some of the students noted in the interviews, they needed more time for strategy training. Thirdly, the students experienced collaborative reading for only two sessions; they would have benefited from more extensive practice in implementing the reading comprehension strategies.

Email: e.momtaz@abdn.ac.uk

References

Chang, M. 1995. 'Teacher-oriented learning vs. cooperative learning in English reading class'. *Journal of Pingtung Polytechnic Institute* 4: 271–7.

Vygotsky, L.S. 1978. *Mind in Society. The Development of Higher Psychological Processes.* Cambridge, Mass.: Harvard University Press.

6.3 Symposium on critical thinking in English classes

Convenor: Güler Ekincier *Pamukkale University, Denizli, Turkey* with
Mei Lin *and* **Mei-hui Chen** *Newcastle University, UK* and **Hasan Bedir**
University of Çukurova, Adana, Turkey
Danny Norrington-Davies *International House, London, UK* and
Fatma Demiray *Abant Izzet Baysal University, Bolu, Turkey*

Güler Ekincier started the session by describing the position of critical thinking in Turkey. In higher education, students are expected to acquire the four skills: reading, writing, listening and speaking. Critical thinking skills are best fostered through reading; students go through a process in which they are actively engaged with the reading text. They analyse and synthesise the text thoroughly by looking at it from different perspectives, and they evaluate the text through reflecting on their own understanding and by producing their own ideas in response to the text. Ekincier came to the conclusion that although it is obvious that there is a strong relationship between critical thinking and reading, teachers often have a tendency to underestimate the value of critical thinking while teaching reading. This is reflected in the tasks assigned by teachers; the rote memorisation of discrete facts, for example, is not useful. On the other hand, by addressing different cognitive skills in conjunction with critical thinking, instructors can both improve students' reading ability and encourage students to stretch their minds; for example, teachers can ask questions that promote higher-level thinking as an ultimate goal.

While there is a growing interest in developing students' critical and creative thinking skills in the foreign language curriculum, teachers often remain unsure about what thinking skills are, why they should be taught, and how they are best incorporated into existing teaching plans. The next presentation, by **Mei Lin**, **Mei-hui Chen** and **Hasan Bedir**, shed some light on these issues. They talked first about the importance of teaching thinking and gave some examples of thinking skills as specified in a standard language curriculum. The modern language curriculum for secondary schools in England and Wales stipulates instruction on information processing skills, reasoning skills, enquiry skills, creative thinking skills and evaluation skills (DfEE 1999); in addition, primary school children in England are required to be provided with the knowledge which enables them to comprehend, analyse, synthesise and evaluate their experiences (English Language Teaching Curriculum for Primary Education 2006). The presenters focused on higher-order thinking and its relationship with achievement targets and language competence. They applied Bloom's taxonomy of higher- and lower- order thinking to their analysis of the thinking skills implied by the 'can do' statements in the Common European Framework of Reference. The findings suggest that 58 per cent of the 'can do' statements targeted for students at levels B2–C2 require higher-order thinking skills, such as analysis, evaluation and synthesis.

One key question for teachers is how they can encourage and nurture students' higher-order thinking. Lin, Chen and Bedir suggested using questions in class that encourage analysis, evaluation and synthesis (unlike lower-order questions that test knowledge and comprehension). Two activities were introduced as examples of how to develop students' skills in evaluation, reasoning and creativity. One activity used 'five Ws', for example, asking students to elaborate on 'why' a specific travel package was chosen. The other activity asked students to create a story based on four pictures provided. Using quotations from students and transcripts of oral speech produced by the students who had participated in these problem-solving activities, the speakers concluded that incorporating higher-order thinking skills into the EFL classroom can improve students' thinking skills as well as their language competence. The main ingredient is the social-cognitive conflict created by the reasoning involved in the tasks. Listening to others and trying to comment or present their own reasons led to real and purposeful communication. This interactive talk, in turn, provides numerous opportunities for students to think, respond on the spot, and talk. Finally, in considering how thinking and language learning can be assessed, Lin, Chen and Bedir criticised the limitations of standard tests that focus only on critical thinking as independent of language competence; they suggest using alternative techniques, such as rubrics, interviews and classroom data.

In the next presentation, Danny Norrington-Davies focused on using critical thinking with adult ESL learners. His inspiration for this, and for the workshop, came from his recent work writing exam items for the Cambridge TSA (Thinking Skills Assessment) and BMAT (Bio-medical Admissions Test) examinations. Norrington-Davies explained that each exam sets tasks containing a 125-word argument and five multiple choice questions testing the candidates' abilities to identify one of the following: the main conclusion of the argument; a further or unstated conclusion; an assumption; a flaw or weakness; the impact of additional evidence; a principle. Believing this to be something he could use in class, he began to locate texts that could fit this model and started to incorporate them into classes ranging from mid-intermediate to advanced level. Symposium participants were given the opportunity to try out some of the materials he has recently used. These were as follows:

- a letter to an editor. The task involved the students identifying a flaw in the reasoning based on additional evidence;
- a short news report chosen by an IELTS class. The task called for the identification of a conclusion, an assumption, a flaw and one comment supporting the argument;
- a piece of written work from a student in the same IELTS class. The task asked the students to look for a conclusion and to decide whether or not the evidence given supported the conclusion.

The general consensus among the audience was that though the tasks were difficult, they were stimulating and did encourage real thinking and a lot of subsequent debate. Norrington-Davies pointed out that with training in these types of activities, students did get better and more confident.

Lastly, **Fatma Demiray** pointed out that in modern education, critical writing is an important skill and one that many academic departments would like to see improved. Her presentation described her efforts to develop the critical writing skills of EFL students in Turkey. Demiray stated that the rapid spread of English around the world as an international means of communication has brought about the need to explore the current orientations in English Language Teaching. The departure point for her study is the belief that the teaching of writing of a global language should be different from that of any other second language. The growing need for good written communication skills in English has created a huge demand for English teaching around the world. Motivated by their desire to write in meaningful ways about meaningful topics, learners set themselves demanding goals: they want to be able to master written English to a high level. Demiray suggested that new classroom techniques and activities are needed to help learners meet these goals; the result will be new roles for teachers and learners in the classroom. Instead of making use of activities that demand accurate repetition and memorisation of sentences and grammatical patterns, Demiray recommended activities that require learners to negotiate meaning and to interact meaningfully. One of the goals of language learning is to develop writing in language use. In this light, as Lochhead and Clement (1979: 1) explain, 'We should be teaching students how to think. Instead, we are teaching them what to think'. Demiray concluded that teachers can do an excellent job by teaching our students 'how to think' through writing instead of 'what to think'.

To conclude, all symposium speakers agreed that, although it is difficult to give a clear definition of critical thinking, it can generally be seen as reasonable, reflective, responsible and skilful—thinking that is focused on deciding what to believe. Critical thinking is a learned ability that must be explicitly taught to students in formal educational contexts.

Email: gulerekincier@yahoo.com
mei.lin@newcastle.ac.uk
Danny.Norrington-Davies@ihlondon.com
demirayfatma@yahoo.com

References

Lochhead, J. and J. Clement (eds.). 1979. *Cognitive Process Instruction:Reseach on Teaching Thinking Skills*. Philadelphia, Pa.: The Franklin Institute Press.

DfEE. 1999. *National Curriculum for Modern Foreign Languages Key Stages 3–4*. London: DfEE and QCA.

Ministry of Education. 2006. *English Language Teaching Curriculum for Primary Education*. 2006.

6.4 Dialoguing with text: an exercise in critical thinking

Jenny de Sonneville and **Sara Herd** *Medical Center, Leiden University, The Netherlands*

Critical thinking is essential for students to become proficient in presenting spoken and written arguments. Students need to not only read but also engage in a constructive dialogue with the text. They should learn to ask critical questions and enter into a discussion with the author and the text. In this workshop, firstly we discussed why it is important for university students to think critically, and secondly we shared ideas on what critical thinking is. Then, we encouraged participants to engage literally with a text by writing an imaginary letter to the author.

Why is it important for students to think critically?

There is a tendency for students to accept unquestioningly the arguments and conclusions of published research; critical thinking enables students to question what they read, present their own arguments and therefore create their own meanings. Comments from participants in the workshop indicated that, in thinking critically during their studies, students are not only 'able to fulfil course requirements' but are also 'provided with life-skills'.

What is critical thinking?

Definitions of critical thinking are numerous in the literature and exchanges with the audience reflected this. Broadly, workshop participants suggested that critical thinking involves metacognitive strategies and that these strategies may be different, depending on the subject area and depth of knowledge. However, basic principles are: determining the central purpose and arguments; assessing how these arguments are developed; uncovering assumptions; examining the evidence and how it is interpreted; and constructing an alternative argument.

The task

These principles were reflected in the task for the participants. They were given a text from Robert A. Day's How to Write and Publish a Scientific Paper (1998: 209–10); this excerpt advocates the use of the active voice in scientific writing. After reading the text, participants were given the following instructions:

Compose a letter to the author of this text.
- Write an introductory greeting.
- Summarise the author's purpose and his argument.
- Consider what his assumptions are, and on what evidence these are based.
- Present an alternative argument and support your reasoning.
- Finish with a concluding sentence.

The final section of the workshop was designed to obtain feedback on the task from the participants. We used these questions:
- How was it for you to do this exercise?
- Could you use it with your students? How would you adapt it?

The discussion was lively and fruitful. One participant commented that it was more convincing to do the writing exercise herself rather than simply talk about it. Many felt resistance to having to write themselves, but agreed that it was an enlightening experience. Comments included the following:
- 'I was forced to ask myself: would I be prepared to do the task which I set my students?'
- 'It started off being difficult, but it was interesting and I then would have liked more time.'
- 'It was difficult to decide the appropriate register: how should I address the author?'
- 'The scaffolding of the text—the structure which you gave—is useful, as we could then grapple with the intellectual content.'
- 'However, the structure can be a constraint to free writing.'
- 'I enjoyed the fantasy—I could be quite indignant in my response!'

Some commented that it was a very useful exercise and they could imagine using it with students, especially for the teaching of persuasive writing. One suggestion was to ask students to read opinion columns from newspapers, to choose one letter, to examine the evidence and write a response.

The nature of the text chosen for the exercise is important. It should be a text that is related to the students' area of interest and it should give students the opportunity to be discerning. For example, in the text which we chose, the author made assumptions based on a lack of substantive evidence; it was a controversial topic and provided the opportunity to present an alternative argument.

Conclusion

On the basis of the responses of the workshop participants, we would suggest that this task enables students to engage at a deeper level with a text, questioning the assumptions of the writer, articulating their own questions and presenting their arguments, thereby developing their proficiency in critical thinking.

Acknowledgement

With thanks to Martha Boeglin (http://www.scriptoria.org) for the idea for this exercise

Email: jdesonneville@lumc.nl; S.L.Herd@lumc.nl

Reference

Day, R. A. 1998. *How to Write and Publish a Scientific Paper.* Phoenix: Oryx Press.

6.5 You think before you ask your students to think

Hiroki Uchida *Akita International University, Akita, Japan*

Introduction

A new English language programme for high schools in Japan clearly states that it is desirable for teachers to use/speak English in their classes. While this may sound very reasonable to the ears of teachers in other countries, much of Japan's long history of English education has been based on the Grammar Translation method. Japanese students have traditionally had few chances to use English in their daily life, and English has been taught as 'knowledge' rather than as a 'skill'.

Now, more teachers are interested in adopting thinking activities in their classes, though often with limited success. Many teachers believe that 'easier' topics are better for learners to think, write and talk about. This actually may not be true. In this report, I will argue against the myth that Japanese learners can talk or write about only 'easy' topics. I will show actual attempts made in Japanese high schools to improve materials and activate students' thinking skills. I will show that familiar topics do not necessarily mean students feel comfortable when they discuss them; on the other hand, less-familiar but more specific topics could work more efficiently with learners.

Topics for thinking lessons

In most cases, teachers pick topics for their students to think about from the reading materials they are using for their courses. Among topics commonly seen in EFL classrooms in Japan are 'smoking', 'recycling', 'voluntary services', and 'global warming'. Many teachers discover their students can't work with these topics; they give up, saying, 'My students can't think. They can't even brainstorm'. But when you picture a situation in which the students are asked to discuss smoking, you realise there is actually not much to say about it. No one would suggest that more people should smoke. When asked to talk about global warming, you realise this is also difficult because the topic given is too broad; you may not know how to start this discussion.

Breaking down the topic

Rather than presenting a broad topic, it is advisable to break the topic down into pieces that your students can talk about. Take 'organ donation', for example. Your students may find it easier to express their opinions in response to the following questions:

- Are you in favour of organ donation?
- Would you be willing to be a donor if you were brain-dead?
- Do you support the use of organs from people who are brain-dead?
- Imagine your mother is brain-dead. You are asked to switch off the machine that is currently keeping her heart beating. Do you think you can do it?
- When a person is brain-dead, he/she will never be conscious again. But his/her heart is beating. Do you think he/she is dead?

Results from free writing

I asked 115 high school students to write freely about two different topics:

- Global warming
- We should carry our chopsticks (instead of using disposable ones) to slow down global warming

As expected, the students had more difficulties when they were asked to write about the broader topic—see Table 6.5.1:

Topic: Global warming	
Number of words written	Percentage of students
150 words or more	3%
100–149 words	4%
50–99 words	16%
0–49 words	77%

Table 6.5.1: Free writing on 'Global warming'

On the other hand, when the same students were asked to write about the more specific topic, the number of words they managed to write showed a significant increase—see Table 6.5.2:

Topic: We should carry our chopsticks ...	
Number of words written	Percentage of students
150 words or more	11%
100–149 words	27%
50–99 words	39%
0–49 words	23%

Table 6.5.2: Free writing on 'We should carry our chopsticks ...'

Conclusion

In order to ease difficulties that your students feel in expressing their opinions, three steps are advisable: (1) choose a topic, for example, 'global warming'; (2) come up with a specific statement, for example, 'We should carry our chopsticks to slow down global warming'; (3) ask your students to find out what they should know to address this specific statement.

Email: uchida1659@aiu.ac.jp

6.6 Is CILLL the new CLIL? Critical thinking and extensive reading

Philip Prowse *Cambridge English Readers, Cambridge, UK*

CILLL is an invented acronym for Content in Language Learner Literature, chosen to highlight the recent revival of interest in content-based language teaching and its relevance to extensive reading. 'Language learner literature' is the term coined by the Extensive Reading Foundation to describe original or adapted writing intended for language learners. The aim of the session was to show that original fiction dealing with controversial or sensitive contemporary issues can stimulate a genuine response to text, rather than using it as a pretext for language practice.

Discussion of the proven language learning success of extensive reading has focused on quantity, not quality. The emphasis has been on reading as many books as possible, rather than reading to react to, and reflect on, the text; see, for example, Krashen and Ujiie (2005). While pleasure is the key to free voluntary reading, it can be argued that we could give priority to what we read and how we respond to it, not just to how much we read.

In Context or Pretext? Pulverness (1999) suggests that the cultural content of coursebooks is commonly used only to promote language learning in the narrowest sense, rather than for cultural learning. This view can also be applied to language learner literature in the case of books which masquerade as readers, but which are so full of exercises that they are in effect language practice books with an emphasis on intensive, not extensive, reading. Such books practise incomprehension, not comprehension.

Reading can be seen as a theatre of the mind, somewhere for individual private learning, as opposed to group public teaching. This argues for texts which ask their own questions, not texts which have questions added to them—in other words, reading to think.

How does this relate to critical thinking? As with CLIL, critical thinking means many different things to different people. However, most would agree that at its heart there is the skilled and active interpretation and evaluation of text. Critical thinking can be applied to extensive reading in two senses: firstly, as an aid to learning the skills of critical thinking (thinking better), and secondly, thinking about the issues raised by reading (thinking for yourself). From a useful introduction to the area (Fisher 2001), the following critical thinking skills can be identified as applicable to extensive reading, others being more appropriate to intensive reading: clarifying and interpreting expressions and ideas, drawing inferences and producing arguments.

The session then moved into a practical phase where participants listened to, or read, extracts from a number of graded readers which treated themes such as HIV/AIDS, deafness, child soldiers, asylum seekers and arms sales. Participants were invited to respond to the texts, not with the whole group, but with another participant. A range of responses were invited based on the following prompts:

- What questions does this story raise in your mind? In other words, what issues are there here?
- Choose one of the two extracts you have read and say why you have chosen it, and what it makes you think about. This is a way into students (and the teacher) giving short book talks to the class. These are not book reports but endorsements of the chosen book, hinting at content, and motivating other students to read it.
- Choose a passage which has meaning for you, rehearse it silently or on your own, then read it aloud to your partner and say why you chose it. This is natural, prepared, reading aloud to one other person with a reason for it.

In summary, the session argued for choice (individual reading, not a class reader); content (books with issues to stimulate critical thinking); allocation of class time (ideally for reading, but, if not, for completion of another task such as writing, while the teacher circulates and discusses individuals' reading); book talks where a book is recommended; prepared reading aloud of a significant passage to one other student; and, above all, for a personal response to the story. It argued against comprehension questions, exercises and book reviews/reports, while recommending the keeping of a personal reading diary and a 'want to read' list of books.

Participants were encouraged to explore ways in which a response to a story can engage their learners, so that they learn not only language, but also to reflect on life, a genuinely educational experience.

Email: philip.prowse@ntlworld.com

References

Fisher, A. 2001. *Critical Thinking: An Introduction.* Cambridge. Cambridge University Press.

Krashen, S. and J. Ujiee. 2005. 'Junk food is bad for you, but junk reading is good for you'. *International Journal of Foreign Language Teaching* 1/3. (Retrieved 11 February 2010 from www.tprstories.com/ijflt/IJFLTSummer95.pdf.)

Pulverness, A. 1999. 'Context or pretext?' *Folio* 5/2: 6.

6.7 Text interpretation: why is yours so different from mine?

Lindsay Ellwood *Expression English Language Courses, The Hague, The Netherlands*

This workshop was based on a piece of qualitative research: an investigation into the influence of cultural background on our interpretations of text.

The session began with the question: 'What do we mean by text?' The participants supplied various suggestions, and these were consolidated by a quotation from Halliday (1994: 311): 'Text is something that happens, in the form of talking or writing, listening or reading. When we analyse it, we analyse the product of this process ...'.

We then turned our attention to the question: what do we understand by culture? There were several suggestions from the participants, mostly along the lines of the following quotation: 'Culture is ... the attitudes, values and beliefs (discourses) shared by the social group one belongs to and the way members' language reflects these deeper discourses.' (Kramsch 2004: 107).

I went on to explain the reasons behind my research, which were as follows:

- I had noticed a range of interpretations of texts both inside and outside the language classroom;
- In a writer's group, with members from a variety of cultural backgrounds, and a mixture of L1 and L2 speakers, the interpretations of fiction were very diverse, both within L1 and L2 groups, and between them;
- I decided that it would be interesting to compare text interpretations of L1 and L2 speakers from different cultural backgrounds.

Therefore, as a response to these observations, an investigation was initiated to explore the influences of cultural background on the inferences drawn when reading a short story.

An explanation of how the research was set up followed. The informants were a native speaker group comprising three colleagues (English, Northern Irish and Scottish) and a non-native speaker group comprising another three colleagues (L1 speakers of Dutch, French and Spanish). The informants were asked to read a short story and then talk about their interpretations using think-aloud protocol. Think-aloud protocol asks informants to give their immediate responses to the text, without reacting to the situation around them. The verbalisation of thinking (thinking aloud) can be made without reactive effects. In order to study covert thinking, a non-reactive setting is needed in order to reproduce this type of thinking under controlled conditions. In this study, an interview was set up for each informant. Each informant read sections of the short story and then talked about his/her interpretations of each section of the text; these impressions were recorded.

After the interviews, informants were sent a questionnaire in which they were asked for background information about themselves; they were also asked to identify any points in the story where their personal experience might have influenced their interpretations.

Following this was a brief explanation of Fairclough's (2001) theory of expectations and assumptions. When we come across a situation, we draw on our schemata to find information that fits the situation, and this enables us to have expectations or make assumptions based on our previous experience. Fairclough uses three terms that identify a highly complex network of mental representations; there are close connections between them, and so there can be some overlap. Using the example of a wedding, these are as follows:

1　Schemata are mental frameworks or patterns. We match what we experience with some mentally stored information, and in this way we make sense of our environment. They represent modes of social behaviour, for example, at a wedding.

2　Frames can represent types of people or animals, or inanimate objects such as an office, or abstract concepts such as revenge, for example, a wedding venue.

3　Scripts represent the subjects who are involved in activities, and their relationships, for example, the bride, the groom and their guests, and the way they interact with each other.

In the interactive phase of the workshop, participants were given two texts, which they were asked to read; they then wrote down their immediate responses. They were asked to work in small groups and discuss their responses, focusing on the similarities and differences of interpretations in their groups. These were discussed in plenary, when some interesting interpretations were put forward, initiating a lively discussion of the wide range of participants' interpretations.

The last phase of the workshop returned to the emergent patterns in the research, which were identified as influences on informants' interpretations: motherhood, expatriate life/travel and individual experience.

In the conclusion all the points were discussed, acknowledging the diversity of interpretations that learners from a variety of cultural backgrounds are likely to produce.

Email: info@expression-english.net

References

Halliday, M. A. K. 1994. *An Introduction to Functional Grammar.* London: Edward Arnold.

Fairclough, N. 2001 *Language and Power.* Harlow: Pearson Education Limited.

Kramsch, C. 2004. *Language and Culture.* Oxford: Oxford University Press.

7 The productive skills: speaking and writing

7.1 Symposium on increasing communicative competence

Convenors: Blanka Frydrychova Klimova *University of Hradec Kralove, Czech Republic and* **Catherine Matsuo** *Fukuoka University, Japan* with
Guozhi Cai *Open University, UK* and
Elizabeth M. Anthony *University Tun Hussein Onn, Malaysia*

This symposium examined the evolving concept of communicative competence and its influence on communicative teaching approaches. Specifically, we focused on how teachers in various EFL/EIL contexts around the world (China, the Czech Republic, Japan and Malaysia) interpret and prioritise the various dimensions of competence to teach syllabi that aim to both meet the complex demands of local contexts and maximise gains in student improvement and confidence. All the presenters kept actual classroom experience front and centre, and all gave detailed demonstrations of teaching activities. This generated a lot of lively and informative audience participation, which the presenters enjoyed and appreciated. Some audience members noted that standardised tests need to better reward communicative competence in terms of ability in-the-moment to get a message across—competence in Hymes's (1972) sense—and not just give marks for correct grammar—Chomsky's original (1965) formulation of competence.

Guozhi Cai began by drawing our attention to China's increasing presence on the world stage and the breathtaking numbers of people now learning English as a result; there are perhaps as many as 50 million Chinese learning English in formal settings. To meet the demands for increased proficiency, the Chinese government issued a new national curriculum in 2000. The curriculum advocates communicative teaching approaches, including TBLT (task-based language teaching), as the way to increase proficiency. To see how this curriculum is actually being implemented, Guozhi followed three Chinese teachers of English at a Chinese university, observing and audio-recording over 80 lessons, and conducting interviews with both teachers and students. In her talk, Guozhi focused on one lesson taught by one of the teachers in her study. She showed us the textbook, which has been a recommended text for nearly twenty years (i.e. published *before* the new curriculum) and the teacher's own PowerPoint slides from the lesson, and she used audio recorded excerpts of the lesson to take us 'inside' the Chinese university classroom. Her demonstration and data findings showed that despite the fact that the teacher in question had studied for an MA in the West, and despite the national curriculum recommendations, there was a real discrepancy between the curriculum and the teacher's practice, the latter of which exemplified a transmission model (Jin and Cortazzi 1998). So, although the curriculum states explicitly that teacher-centredness should be replaced by student-centredness, in actual classroom practice, the teacher imparting knowledge and the students giving choral repetition are the dominant activities. Guozhi's preliminary data analysis suggests that the roots of this discrepancy lie in the conflicts between Western methodology and Chinese ideology.

Catherine Matsuo demonstrated the sequences of activities she uses to increase her Japanese first-year university students' speaking competence. Catherine's students have considerable grammar knowledge, but it is passive—not ready for use. Furthermore, their experience of 'spoken' English has largely been the inauthentic, decontextualised 'conversations' in text-books—in sum, sentences and semantics rather than utterances and pragmatics. Another difficulty is Japanese cultural norms, which may make students uncomfortable speaking out. Catherine's answer to these problems has been to not use textbooks at this early stage of speaking, and to 'dialogise' linguistic perspectives by combining them with Western and Japanese communication theories. Using both Western and Japanese communication models raises *both* teacher and student intercultural awareness. Explicit, propositional teacher discourse explaining communication principles such as reciprocity, co-construction, empathy and fairness makes the forms of 'natural language' in pragmatic use more noticeable to *both* teacher and students. Learning about communication rules builds students' metacognitive knowledge about speaking, allowing them to exert 'executive control' over what they are doing (saying). Thinking about communication rules takes students' attention away from feeling self-conscious about speaking, while the sense of control empowers them and makes them more intent on communicating their own messages. Because she teaches in an EFL environment where students may not come across L2 structures outside the classroom, Catherine is careful to create a syllabus that builds a semantic network. She makes meanings persist through review, but she also uses subsequent lessons to develop and expand the meaning potential of the words: returning to topics using different media and different genres shows other possible meanings of words, puts them in relationships with new/different words and brings out different syntactical relationships (Cook 2009). Most important, through the syllabus, Catherine and her students create an English world within which everyone engages his/her imagination.

Blanka Frydrychova Klimova addressed the productive skill of writing with reference to Bachman's (1990) communicative competence model. She noted how ICT is blurring boundaries between written and spoken language. Furthermore, written texts are becoming more dynamic, more hybrid in terms of genre, and more multimodal, often combining images, music and colour along with the written word. Students encounter these multimodal texts in their real lives, and may be required to create them in their working lives—making web-pages, say, in careers in tourism. However, the university course requires that the students learn formal writing, and students are expected to be able to produce an academic paper and perhaps later their thesis in English. Blanka must also contend with the fact that Czech culture is oral—students answer exams orally, and so have negligible experience in writing, even in their native language. In response to her situation, Blanka has developed a blended course in academic writing where the final aim is to write an academic paper, but where the course makes use of students' IT skills and their life experience as 'digital natives'. Thus, her course includes teaching differences between English and Czech academic writing such as citations, compiling a bibliography, and using appropriate register, but she also has students exploit their digital competence skills, for example by writing an article for Wikipedia. Because the students are creating an authentic article for Wikipedia from scratch, they are not only motivated to write but begin to recognise the usefulness and necessity of the formal writing aspects of their course, for example the importance of attending to errors and checking facts when writing for publication.

The final speaker was **Elizabeth M. Anthony**, who talked about implementing problem-based learning (PBL) as a university innovation in Malaysia and gave an in-depth presentation of students' reactions to that innovation. PBL is an alternative pedagogical model that differs considerably from the traditional 'chalk and talk' didactic approach. In the PBL learning process, ESP students learn English and content knowledge via the process of problem-solving which is then further consolidated by independent self-directed learning and team-working. Triggers in the form of ill-structured problems and FILA (Facts, Ideas, Learning Issues and Action Plan) tables used to analyse the triggers are the key elements of PBL that stimulate and facilitate the learning process. The findings reveal that the PBL approach is well received by both the ESP lecturers and the students because it provides ample and varied learning opportunities. It also offers advantages in terms of student motivation, attitude, confidence, engagement (MACE); and develops independent self-directed learning and team-working (IT) skills. Elizabeth used the MACE–IT model to help conceptualise the potential of PBL as an educational initiative for change in classroom culture. This change in the classroom culture is itself an important factor in promoting language learning. Students exhibited affirmative affect, expanded their efforts, and became goal directed, persistent, attentive, and actively involved in the learning process. All these attributes characterise students who have a desire to learn. Improved student attitude changed the classroom culture for the better, in turn creating more opportunity for language use and language development. Elizabeth's ethnographic approach case study on PBL in an ESP course extends understanding of PBL in general and in the context of second language learning in particular. Her study is relevant to researchers, lecturers and policy makers currently concerned with the effectiveness of English language learning in university classrooms in Malaysia and beyond.

Email: blanka.klimova@uhk.cz
cath@fukuoka-u.ac.jp
scai@open.ac.uk
eliz@uthm.edu.my

References

Bachman, L. F. 1990. *Fundamental Considerations in Language Testing.* Oxford: Oxford University Press.

Chomsky, N. 1965. *Aspects of the Theory of Syntax.* Cambridge, Mass.: MIT Press.

Cook, V. J. 2009. 'Developing links between second language acquisition research and language teaching' in K. Knapp and B. Seidlhofer (eds.). *Handbooks of Applied Linguistics: Vol. 6. Handbook of Foreign Language Communication and Learning.* Berlin: Mouton de Gruyter.

Hymes, D. 1972. 'On communicative competence' in J. Pride and J. Holmes (eds.). *Sociolinguistics.* Harmondsworth, UK: Penguin.

Jin, L. and M. Cortazzi. 1998. 'The culture the learner brings: a bridge or a barrier?' in M. Byram and M. Fleming (eds.). *Language Learning in Intercultural Perspective: Approaches through Drama and Ethnography*. Cambridge: Cambridge University Press.

7.2 Pronunciation matters?

Margareth Perucci and **Ian White** *Izmir University of Economics, Turkey*

Introduction

The aim of this workshop was to report on the findings of an ongoing research project concerning the integration of pronunciation in EFL preparatory classes in the School of Foreign Languages at the Izmir University of Economics. Our study investigated the reasons why the teachers in our institution, following a similar tendency of teachers elsewhere in the world, do not give pronunciation the deserved importance it should be given (Celce-Murcia *et al.* 1996; Baptista 2000).

The Pronunciation Project

The presenters had been aware for some time of the fact that students in the preparatory school had been producing an 'unnatural' pronunciation: pronunciation in which features are delivered in an artificial way either putting a strain on the listener or preventing understanding. Adding to the fact that little or no attention was being given to pronunciation during observations, it was felt that there was an urgent need to design a study to determine the reasons why pronunciation work was not being conducted in the classroom. Thus, this study investigated the matter by doing the following:

- having one of the researchers (Ian) going into the class and teaching a lesson where pronunciation was integrated when the need arose;
- having the teachers whose lesson was taught, the teacher–observers (TOs), attend an individual feedback session with the other researcher (Margareth) to report on their perceptions of the lesson;
- having the researcher–teacher who taught the lesson come for feedback and report on the pronunciation work integrated into the lesson;
- having the learners whose lesson was taught by the researcher–teacher give feedback on their perceptions of the lesson.

By the time of the conference workshop, 17 TOs had been involved in the project, four of them native speakers of English and 13 of them non-native speakers of English. At the workshop we wanted to register the work done on the teaching of pronunciation itself, which was mostly of an unplugged nature (Meddings and Thornbury 2009), and we also wanted to share the impact and reactions it had on the teachers (NS and NNS teachers alike).

The study

Ian, the researcher–teacher (RT), taught 17 lessons (50 minutes each) in place of other teachers, some of which were videoed. The RT carried on with the normal syllabus of the course and used the material that had been prescribed for that level and that teaching hour. No special pronunciation book was used. This way, it was made clear to the teachers whose lesson was taught that there would be *pronunciation within a lesson* and not a *lesson on pronunciation*. Most of the work done in the lesson came from the most 'authentic' source of material—the learners. The teachers' roles as observers focused on the integration of pronunciation carried out in the lesson. This was planned by the researchers in order to encourage the teachers to work on pronunciation in short sharp bursts, as often as was needed. As a follow-up, the TOs attended an individual feedback session and reported on their perceptions of the lesson. Based on their invaluable feedback, we were able to design an action plan to meet their needs, as presented below:

- **SIG**. A group of teachers gets together weekly for a lesson focusing on different aspects of pronunciation (Ian).
- **Visits**. Ian later makes visits to see how the teachers are integrating pronunciation into the lesson.
- **Workshops**. Ian continues workshops on aspects of pronunciation. Margareth continues workshops on pronunciation within listening.
- **A floating pronunciation teacher**. Ian will be teaching other teachers' students to collect data for a pronunciation syllabus. Teachers observe the lesson with a task.
- **A syllabus**. A syllabus tailored towards pronunciation is to be designed (Margareth and Ian).

Conclusion

The study indicated that a closer cooperation between instructors experienced in the teaching of pronunciation and those with less experience was needed. It also signalled that pronunciation might gain more importance when teachers were empowered with know-how and confidence, and when their awareness was raised.

Contributions from IATEFL participants

The video-clips shown in the workshop aroused interest among the participants. Comments such as 'creating a safe environment for the learner without the fear of being corrected', 'learner enjoyment of the lesson', and 'seeing effective pronunciation in action' made us feel more confident. A participative audience in the final session of the day further motivated us to continue the work for the 45th Conference.

Email: margareth.perucci@ieu.edu.tr

idwhite@yahoo.co.uk

References

Baptista, B. O. 2000. 'The learning and teaching of pronunciation in Brazil: linking research and practice'. *Speak Out! Newsletter of the IATEFL Pronunciation Special Interest Group* 25: 12–19.

Celce-Murcia, M., D. M. Brinton and J. M. Goodwin. 1996. *Teaching Pronunciation: A Reference for Teachers of English to Speakers of Other Languages*. Cambridge: Cambridge University Press.

Meddings, L. and S. Thornbury. 2009. *Teaching Unplugged: Dogme in English Language Teaching*. Delta Teacher Development Series.

7.3 Does English change your gestures when you present?

Robert Wilkinson *Maastricht University, The Netherlands*

When you speak in a foreign language, you probably use more gestures than when you speak in your mother tongue. This sounds like a common-sense expectation. However, does it hold true for a speaker who delivers a presentation? This paper reports a small-scale study into the use of gesture in a group of multinational advanced-level students.

Gestures are conventionally defined as the movement of hands and arms, which was the subject of this study. Other aspects of body language, such as head movements, were not taken into account. Previous research has assumed a cultural gesture transfer from L1 to L2. Bilinguals, for example, use more gestures in speaking their L2 than in L1 (for example, Pika *et al.* 2006). Researchers view gesture as a speaker phenomenon (Nicoladis 2007), helping the speaker to package information (Alibali *et al.* 2000). Thus we might expect presenters to use more gestures when presenting in their L2 than in their L1.

The purpose of this study was to investigate whether presenters' gestures differed in their L1 in contrast to the L2 (English). Two hypotheses were generated: (1) Gestures would be relatively stable in the individual, whatever the L1; (2) Individuals would use more gesture when speaking in English (L2).

Context, participants and method

The context of this study was a presentations training course in English. The participants were 11 speakers from India, Indonesia, Brazil, Mozambique and Tanzania, who had a variety of L1s: Hindi, Bahasa Indonesia, Achinese, North Moluccan, Papuan, Brazilian Portuguese, Mozambican Portuguese and Swahili. The participants were all following an intensive pre-master's programme, of which the presentations course formed a part.

The participants first gave a presentation of up to five minutes in their L1 in which they described a 'typical event' in their own culture, such as a marriage ceremony. Three weeks later they gave a similar presentation in English (L2), but on the cultural benefits of their forthcoming master's studies. Presentations were recorded on DVD. The participants were not told what the purpose of the investigation was.

Each gesture was counted according to its function (not reported here) and whether both hands or only one hand was performing it. Movements were counted as one gesture from the start of a movement until the hand or arm stopped moving.

Findings of L1/L2 gestures

Participants varied considerably in the frequency with which they made gestures, ranging from three per minute in L1 (Bahasa Indonesia speaker) to over 40 per minute in both languages (Achinese speaker). Forty per minute is almost continuous gesturing. Six speakers increased gesture frequency when presenting in English, three remained more or less stable, and two declined in frequency. (See Figure 7.3.1.)

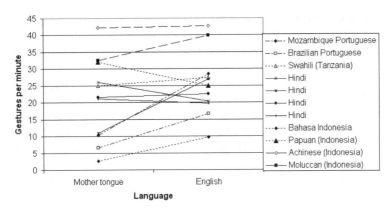

Figure 7.3.1: Gestures per minute (mother tongue, English)

A comparison was made between the percentage of gestures using both hands. Results show considerable variation: five speakers used both hands less when speaking English, three of them far less; three used both hand more frequently, and three scarcely changed. (See Figure 7.3.2.)

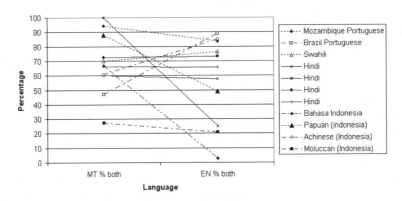

Figure 7.3.2: Gestures using both hands

Discussion

As expected, most speakers used more gestures when speaking in English. However, there was considerable individual variation in the nature of the gestures used. Variation could be a topic effect, in view of the different topics in L1 and L2.

The study has some limitations. The tasks were different, which could explain some of the difference between L1 and L2. Coding gesture is not easy, notably the difficulty of defining the start and end of a gesture. This may have led to inaccuracy in frequency. A second analyst was not used. Frequency was gesture per minute; this does not account for the individual speaking speed. Counting gesture per word would have been better.

To conclude, gesture is clearly a communicative device, but it seems to be more important for the speaker than for the audience. In English-medium training situations, one should be wary of giving comments on speakers' gestures if one does not take the individual's cultural and L1 context into account.

Email: b.wilkinson@maastrichtuniversity.nl

References

Alibali, M. W., S. Kita, and A. J. Young. 2000. 'Gesture and the process of speech production: We think, therefore we gesture'. *Language and Cognitive Processes* 15/6: 593–613.

Nicoladis, E. 2007. 'The effect of bilingualism on the use of manual gestures'. *Applied Psycholinguistics* 28/3: 441–54.

Pika, S., E. Nicoladis, and P. F. Marentette. 2006. 'A cross-cultural study on the use of gestures: Evidence for cross-linguistic transfer?' *Bilingualism: Language and Cognition* 9/3: 319–27.

7.4 Symposium on teaching academic writing

Convenor: Benjamin Haymond *Otto Friederich University, Bamberg, Germany* with

Tatyana Gudkina and **Larina Feschenko** *Amur State University, Blagoveschensk, Russia* and

Janie Rees-Miller *Marietta College, Marietta, Ohio, USA*

This symposium brought together three sets of speakers from across the globe. Beginning with Benjamin Haymond (Germany), followed by Tatyana Gudkina and Larina Feschenko (Russia), and finishing with Janie Rees-Miller (USA), the symposium dealt with an array of topics from developing a type of writing for large groups, to instructional practices for summary writing, to the assessment of an EAP Writing course.

In the first presentation, **Benjamin Haymond** addressed the question of how a university department specialising in Business English addresses the writing needs of a large student body. The presentation described the departmental dilemma, introduced their answer to this dilemma in the form of a 'Comment', and addressed student and instructor issues with this type of writing. The Business English department at the University of Bamberg has four instructors and serves more than 700 undergraduate students. Based on requirements set by the university's administration, the department must fulfil specific criteria for the testing of the students, such as a written exam in the first two semesters of a four-semester undergraduate program. The dilemma that arises is how to manage the large number of exams with limited time and staff. The solution used to solve this dilemma is the Comment. The Comment is a statement of a position of no more than 350 words. Students are required to follow standard writing rules, such as not writing in the first or second person, and not beginning sentences with coordinating conjunctions.

With this type of writing, a number of issues arise. Firstly, there is the issue of instructor training. It normally takes one to two semesters to properly train an instructor in this style of writing. Problems that typically develop are misunderstandings between a 'comment' and an 'essay', and differences in individual writing styles based on a diversity of instructor backgrounds. There is also the issue of interpretation and consistency. During exam time, with more than 400 exams, instructors need to keep their grading schemas consistent. This involves much time devoted to team work and to team evaluation of departmental exams. Regarding student issues, students have to be brought up to speed on methods of English writing style. One typical problem is the students are not always aware of how to write a comment. Based on their experiences in high school, mostly in Germany, the students are often unfamiliar with rules of directness and with organisational style, as well as having translation issues between the L1 and the L2. An additional issue is the difference in levels between students. Because English is required for most students, levels of English competence vary greatly. The Comment provides a solution to this dilemma.

In their presentation, **Tatyana Gudkina** and **Larina Feschenko** reported on the theoretical considerations behind summary-writing instructional practices and gave several examples they use in the classroom, which are designed to help students to write successful summaries. Many students find writing difficult, and summary writing is often particularly challenging. Students might fail to write successful summaries because they have poor reading comprehension skills, they lack writing skills, or they are given insufficient instructions. Traditional summary-writing instruction is product-based, which might result in a poorly developed written product. Instead, instruction should be process-based because writing summaries is not a product but a twofold process: reading (with processing and analysing the information in the text) and the writing itself.

The need to analyse text structure calls for creating specific instructional practices based on an 'information-transfer' approach first introduced by Widdowson in 1973. According to Widdowson, as cited in Swales and Feak (1997) 'Transferring information from a verbal to a non-verbal is an exercise in comprehension. Transferring information from a non-verbal to a verbal is an exercise in composition' (1997: 65). The emphasis is placed on teaching summary writing through graphic representations of various structures, such as diagrams, charts and tables.

Different types of exercises can be used to train students' skills in summary writing; specifically, they can be asked to do the following tasks: complete a table or a diagram with some parts filled and other parts left blank; decide on the functions that underlie the text information and what kind of graphic representation to use to fit the text organisation; and complete a table from which some elements of problem–solution outline are missing.

When students are asked to summarise a text, the text is taken away from them and they use their diagrams or tables to provide the information. Students are taught to use different summarising strategies depending on the text structure. At the same time, such practice in reading comprehension and summary writing can assist students in transferring their strategies for writing summaries of the one text to other texts of the same format. Another benefit of completed tables and diagrams is that they can be used to practice function words: students improve their skills in terms of relating ideas in the text using function words, which enables them to enhance their summary-writing skills. Translated into real terms, instruction based on graphic representations serves as a springboard to writing successful summaries.

Finally, **Janie Rees-Miller** discussed the results of a study on the effectiveness of EAP writing programmes at a college in the USA. The EAP writing course at a small college was assessed both quantitatively and qualitatively to determine its effectiveness in preparing international students for the required freshman composition course taken by all students at the college (Writing 101). Quantitative assessment compared the grade distribution curves in EAP in the five-year period of Fall 2004–Spring 2009 (n = 208 international students) and in Writing 101 in Spring 2009 (n = 182 students). While the grade distributions were similar, a greater percentage of students received an A in Writing 101 (33 per cent) than in EAP (16.8 per cent), indicating relatively rigorous grading standards in EAP.

For the group of 97 students who completed both EAP and Writing 101 between 2004 and 2009, the grades in both courses were roughly comparable in their distribution. However, 36.1 per cent of international students earned an A in Writing 101 compared with 19.6 per cent of the same group earning an A in EAP. As a group, international students compared favorably with American students: 72 per cent of both groups earned A or B grades in Writing 101, but a higher percentage of international students (36.1 per cent) than US students (30.6 per cent) earned an A in Writing 101. A comparison of individual international students' grades in EAP and Writing 101 revealed that 84.5 per cent of students earned grades differing by no more than one letter grade in both courses. In fact, 83.5 per cent earned an equal or higher grade in Writing 101 than in EAP. These quantitative results indicate that the EAP grade is a good predictor of the Writing 101 grade, and that EAP prepares international students both individually and as a group to compete effectively with US students in Writing 101.

The qualitative assessment found very similar course objectives dealing with essay organisation and use of sources in both EAP and Writing 101. In interviews, teachers of Writing 101 agreed that international students were well prepared in essay organisation and in finding sources, taking notes and summarising. However, they noted the wide range of proficiency in grammar and vocabulary among international students as problematic.

These quantitative and qualitative assessment results have suggested changes that can be instituted not only in the EAP course but also in ESL course offerings and in admissions and placement standards. The quantitative and qualitative means of assessment described here are practical and time-efficient, and the results can be easily understood by both students and administrators. Thus, these techniques can be easily adapted to a variety of settings.

Email:bjhaymond@gmail.com

ta-gudkina@yandex.ru

reesmilj@marietta.edu

Reference

Swales, J. M. and C. B. Feak. 1997. 'From information transfer to data commentary' in T. Miller (ed.). *Functional Approaches to Written Text: Classroom Applications*. Washington D.C.: ELP, USIA.

7.5 Two 'howevers' and 'moreovers' do not a cohesive text make

Edward de Chazal *Language Centre, University College London, UK*

Overview

I argued in this workshop for a broader and deeper understanding of cohesion than that exemplified by superficial 'bling' items like 'however' and 'moreover'—which some students overuse, coursebooks over-promote and teachers over-assess. Like coherence, cohesion is meaning-driven and complex. It is expressed through language: grammar, vocabulary and, as Halliday and Hasan (1976) argue, phonology. These language systems relate material in texts, thereby achieving 'integration ... between different parts of a text by various types of semantic and referential linkages' (Biber *et al.* 1999: 42). I proposed seven distinct cohesive phenomena, illustrated by a closely analysed text on evolution (Charlesworth and Charlesworth 2003: 4–5).

Lexis

The first system involves words. The text yielded the lexical referential sequence: 'the simplest organism capable of independent existence, a bacterial cell ... a machine of great complexity ... two daughter cells ... a single cell ... cell divisions ... the resulting cells'. The writers achieve cohesion using word-based techniques: synonyms, repetition, substitution, rephrasing and expansion. What changes is less the key technical word 'cell' than the language around it.

Cohesive noun phrases

I introduced the term 'cohesive noun phrase' to describe carefully created language to coherently link text by encoding (summarising, labelling, evaluating) a previous stretch of discourse, and moving the text forward. Cohesive noun phrases serve to connect text by referring backwards, anaphorically, and forwards, cataphorically. Participants identified the exact stretch of text that given examples ('this effort', 'our understanding') referred to—potentially challenging as this can involve several lines—then mirrored the writing process by substituting other 'label' nouns to indicate other stances: 'achievement', 'problem', 'process', 'uncertainty', 'controversy'.

Pronouns and determiners

To avoid repeating recurring nouns, and to indicate chains of reference, writers mechanically rather than creatively choose the correct grammatical device, for example, the relative pronoun 'that' adjacent to its referent; pronoun 'these'; or determiner 'its'. These are familiar and a staple of examinations. Most are anaphoric.

Contextualisers

I crystalised the concept of cohesion by including adverbials: optional contextualising structures which add circumstantial information ('during ...', 'rapidly'), linking material ('then', 'however'), plus freestanding stance and perspective elements ('of course'). The italicised adverbials in the following extract contextualise the underlying sentence.

Although there are still many unsolved problems, biologists are convinced that *even* the most complicated features of living creatures, *such as human consciousness*, reflect the operation of chemical and physical processes that are accessible to scientific analysis.

An initial concession ('Although ...') frames the argument; the maximiser 'even' reinforces the writer's stance; while the third adverbial offers an example. Reading aloud the underlying sentence without the adverbials demonstrates its 'standalone-ability', but it is denuded of cohesive contextual meaning.

Focusers

By employing grammatical transformations from default patterns such as Subject–Verb–Object, writers organise their text and lead audience focus. The transformations include fronts, clefts, inversion, ellipsis, plus certain passive and 'it'/'there' structures. For example, instead of the original 'It is therefore worthwhile to X', the writer could write the single clause 'X is worthwhile'. Similarly, the stance adverbial 'clearly' could be in its default position before the lexical verb rather than initially: 'Clearly the demand for trained scientists and engineers is increasing worldwide'. The fronted 'Worse still ...' in another sentence emphasised the writer's stance. Participants discussed and evaluated the various effects achieved in five examples, contrasting them with unfocussed default patterns.

Interactors

Visibly situating the text within the writer/audience context, what I term 'interactors' involve and interact with the audience, sharing experience and offering directives including outside text reference (exophoric). Writers do this through imperatives and inclusive language: 'we', 'see Chapter 3', respectively including and directing the audience.

Macro-text organisers

The above micro-level techniques are not sufficient for cohesion. Macro-text organisers embed non-linguistic, navigational and over-arching devices such as titles, headings, numbering, legends, iconic statements and visual means: 'the "how" question of biology' which tied in with the later iconic statement, 'the "why" question of biology'. Also falling into this category are thesis statements in essays.

I concluded by outlining activities aimed at 'knowing and noticing' cohesion: identifying and evaluating cohesive language, rewriting/reinserting text (participants did this), matching semantically similar items, constructing/improving chains of reference, and collaboratively enhancing existing cohesive material. For example, after establishing that 'moreover' signals addition, other items can substitute: 'also', 'even', or more creatively 'One further point/risk/drawback ...'. Participants saw that sophisticated writers use many techniques. My example student text contained 20 linking adverbials such as 'however' in 30 sentences; the expert text contained just one in two pages.

The participants agreed with my over-arching messages: recognising the complexity of cohesion; integrating its teaching; and when assessing student work going beyond the 'howevers' and 'moreovers'.

Email: e.dechazal@ucl.ac.uk

References

Biber, D., S. Johansson, G. Leech, S. Conrad, and E. Finegan. 1999. *Longman Grammar of Spoken and Written English*. Harlow: Longman.

Charlesworth, B. and D. Charlesworth. 2003. *Evolution: A Very Short Introduction*. Oxford: Oxford University Press.

Halliday, M. A. K. and R. Hasan. 1976. *Cohesion in English*. Harlow: Longman.

7.6 Advanced writing: what C1 and C2 writers can do

Siân Morgan *University of Modena and Reggio Emilia, Italy*

Increasing use is being made of the CEFR to benchmark assessment at local levels and this is surely a welcome development in creating a meaningful testing culture. However, although teachers are working comfortably with lower and intermediate levels, there is less familiarity with higher-level performance, possibly because there is so little of it about. What constitutes advanced production is still relatively uncharted territory, and experts are currently developing detailed descriptions of higher levels.

In this session I described a small study where I carried out a close manual analysis of argumentative writing rated as C1 and C2 at the University of Modena and Reggio Emilia. I identified grammatical, lexical and discourse features found at these levels and drew up an overview of typical performance. This profile describes the student population in question and is intended to provide a point of departure for more detailed analysis in the future.

First, we looked at previous findings on this subject (Jarvis *et al.* 2003) which suggest that highly rated writing displays clusters of different features and that multiple profiles of advanced writing may exist. I then presented the overviews of typical C1 and C2 writing performance in my institution. Finally, I commented on excerpts from essays illustrating the features at each level.

Overview of C1 writing

C1 writing is characterised by the following features:

- good control of grammatical resources;
- broad general vocabulary; specific vocabulary related to general topics for example, education;
- good collocational competence;
- audience awareness, including some genre awareness of common text types;
- good register awareness with only occasional breakdown;
- good fluency with the emergence of some natural-sounding discourse.

Comment

In general, the C1 writers in this study have good control and range of grammatical resources, although surface errors may occur when they attempt ambitious structures. Similarly, alongside good control of collocation and multi-word items, some fossilised lexical errors occasionally persist. Students at this level tend to rely on 'taught' linkers ('however'/'moreover') to structure their essays and use these mostly at sentence-initial position. We also see greater awareness of the reader–writer relationship and increasing register control. As with linkers, students use 'taught' opinion markers ('In my opinion'/'I strongly believe that'), and tend to amplify rather than mitigate their assertions ('I am firmly convinced that they are extremely useful'). Where hedging does occur, central modals are preferred. Overall, C1 writing is clear, well-organised, and grammatically accurate. We finished the first part of the session by looking more closely at excerpts from C1 essays.

Overview of C2 writing

A similar manual analysis of C2 texts formed the basis for the following profile of C2 writing:

- confident use of a wide range of grammatical resources;
- wide range of cohesive devices;
- wide range of lexis, including specific and technical vocabulary;
- use of metaphor to enhance meaning;
- natural use of collocation and multi-word units;
- high degree of sensitivity to contextual factors influencing language choice;
- fewer 'taught' rhetorical devices and a wider range of more natural items, probably acquired through extensive exposure to language and incidental learning.

Comment

C2 writing is much more fluent and sophisticated. The students working at this level have very confident control of a wide range of structures and use these appropriately for different functions, for example, to develop the argument or highlight information. Again, there may be occasional non-impeding errors as writers juggle complexity and accuracy (Foster and Skehan 1996). Students have moved on from single-word linkers and are now drawing on a wider range of devices to create cohesion over larger stretches of text. Such items include demonstratives ('In this way we …'), cleft clauses ('What is certain, though, is …'), text-organising words ('issue'/'problem'/'situation'), along with synonyms or near-synonyms ('drawbacks'/'disadvantages'/'negative aspects'). We also see a wide spectrum of lexical items used to perform interpersonal functions such as expressing opinion ('I personally feel that …'/'Indeed it is clear that …') or to express appropriate strength of claim by mitigating ('what we might call X'/'at least partially') and boosting statements ('What is certain, though, is …'). Skilful use of lexical resources such as metaphor, collocation and multi-word units make C2 writing very natural and fluent. Once more, we looked at excerpts from student writing with examples of the above features.

Conclusions

The overriding difference distinguishing C2 from C1 written performance seems to be a wider range of structures and lexis used with ease and sensitivity to contextual factors. This results in greater fluency, naturalness and more 'native-like' control of the language.

Email: sianmorgan@katamail.com

References

Foster, P. and P. Skehan. 1996. 'The influence of planning and task type on second language performance'. *Studies in Second Language Acquisition* 18: 299–323.

Jarvis, S., L. Grant, D. Bikowski and D. Ferris. 2003. 'Exploring multiple profiles of highly rated learner compositions'. *Journal of Second Language Writing* 12: 377–403.

7.7 Using I-Search papers to encourage deep reflection on writing

Sonja Tack Erten *Sabancı University School of Languages, Istanbul, Turkey*

Overview

The I-Search paper is a multi-purpose tool in the second language writing classroom: it encourages students to reflect deeply on the processes of their own writing, and at the same time it provides valuable feedback to practitioners on the quality of their course design, instruction and support. Johns defines an I-Search paper as one which 'requires extensive reflection after the completion of a demanding research writing task' (2006: 163). Although the concept of the I-Search paper has existed for nearly 30 years, there are very few attested applications of it in the literature on second language learning.

This talk related my experience of assigning an I-Search paper to 74 freshman English students as the endpoint of a research project in the spring 2009 semester at a private English-medium university in Turkey.

The project was carefully scaffolded to support learning. A number of possible resources and a detailed timetable were provided in an eight-page research guide, and core readings were discussed in class. In addition, students were taught how to search academic databases, evaluate sources and write an annotated bibliography. They also kept a reflective research diary to refer back to when preparing the I-Search paper. The first draft of the research paper received detailed peer and instructor feedback, and optional tutorials were offered.

The I-Search paper data reveals that the students were very much novice researchers: 67 per cent of respondents had never formally evaluated sources, and 79 per cent had never written an annotated bibliography. And although 68 per cent reported having written a research paper before, they described their previous attempts as less 'academic', 'accurate', 'serious', 'formal', 'detailed', 'complex' and 'sophisticated'.

What worked?

Selected student comments will illustrate recurring themes in the data.

Scaffolded approach

- The step-by-step format of the research project was very useful in making me get used to how to write a research paper ... the material provided for us and the deadlines ready for each part from the beginning of the [semester] were some of the points that were very useful throughout the writing process.

Research guide

- [In future], if the instructor would give us clear guidance about what he or she wants and a wonderful 'where to start research guide' with many starting sources in it ... I won't believe that I would need to ask many questions to my instructor.

Feedback

- My instructor gives me a very elaborate feedback that is different and more helpful than the dozens of feedback that I have received until today.
- ... drafting and feedback is a wonderful method because I can see my inadequate part, because of receiving feedback, I take great care to my paper. If my teacher didn't give to me feedback, I would not write again because I did not know it has mistake or not.

Annotated bibliography

- .. it gave me a chance to research my subject deeply and to know my sources before writing my draft. Due to the fact that I was aware of my sources from the beginning of the research project, I could write my [paper] more easily.
- ... useful for pushing us to evaluate the sources we will use and also for pushing some students to start researching and find something relevant and useful to show to your teacher.

What needed improving?

In response to comments made in the I-Search papers, the following changes were implemented for the spring 2010 semester:

- Detailed individual feedback rather than whole-class feedback is now being given on the annotated bibliographies so that students know the strengths and weaknesses of their initial research and their use of the APA format. Although this increases the marking workload, it is indispensable for providing an early confirmation or a warning to students in order to keep them on track for the first draft.
- Peer feedback was deemed unhelpful in the absence of a sufficient timeframe within which to develop adequate editing skills in students; some students complained of superficial feedback comments being made on their drafts just for the sake of fulfilling the task.

Further applications

I subsequently applied the concept of a deep reflective paper to a blogging project in the autumn 2009 semester and asked my students to write an I-Blog paper. A very good example is posted on my student's blog—see Olgaç (2010). Please feel free to contact me for a copy of my I-Search paper questions.

Email: srtack@gmail.com

References

Johns, A. 2006. 'Students and research: reflective feedback for I-Search papers' in K. Hyland and F. Hyland (eds.). *Feedback in Second Language Writing: Contexts and Issues.* New York: Cambridge University Press.

Olgaç, O. 2010. 'My I-Blog paper'. *Onur's Freshman English Blog,* January. (Retrieved 24 April 2010 from http://onursfreshmanengblog.blogspot.com/2010/01/18-my-i-blog-paper.html.)

7.8 Dos and don'ts of using writing portfolios in the EFL classroom

Natalya Eydelman *University of Leeds, UK; Novosibirsk State University, Russia*
Hornby Trust Scholar

My presentation was devoted to a discussion of how to introduce and use writing portfolios in academic writing courses. Even though the writing of portfolios has been used in writing instruction for more than 20 years (Hamp-Lyons and Condon 2000), in my teaching context they have been used for about five years. I have chosen to use them as a tool for instruction and assessment because they help both the students and the teacher to reflect on their progress and future needs. Also, they help to develop students' self-assessment skills and make them more autonomous learners (Little 2009).

My students are English majors at a large university in Russia; their language proficiency ranges from A2 (intermediate) to B2 (advanced) according to the CEFR. Generally, they have a good command of English but their writing skills require improvement for academic achievement and effective communication. The course is taught in face-to-face mode and electronically through the course blog.

Creating a portfolio is a challenging task for the students, particularly because it is their first experience in doing it. Thus, throughout the semester they are offered different activities to help them master their writing skills and build their knowledge and understanding of the purposes and process of creating a portfolio and benefiting from it. At the beginning of the semester I introduce the students to the concept of the writing portfolio, show sample portfolios and help them understand the procedures and activities leading to the creation of a portfolio. Throughout the semester, students post their essay drafts and journal entries on the blog for peer feedback; write summaries of articles they have read (usually taken from English-language newspapers); and write reflective notes about their own essays. Having reflected on my students' portfolio writing experience, I have formulated a number of points that can contribute to the success or failure of incorporating portfolio work in English instruction.

Dos

The main components of successful portfolio creation are as follows:

- Students should be provided with models of different components of the portfolio for discussion and reflection; this can be done in the classroom and/or electronically depending on the teaching context.
- Students should be given plenty of opportunities for writing in meaningful contexts.
- Instruction in the writing process is necessary, since this helps students to understand better how to approach writing, how to make use of their strengths as writers and how to work on their weaknesses.
- Students should be given a lot of practice in peer-editing, which is a natural component of the process approach to writing. This can be done online through a blog. This allows them to practise writing and critiquing each others' reflective pieces they need to write for the portfolio.

Don'ts

What factors can make incorporating writing portfolios problematic? This was the question I addressed last in my presentation; my thoughts are as follows:

- Consider your students' needs, interests and strengths. Creating a portfolio may be too much for them in their particular circumstances.
- Do not start alone but team up with your colleagues and get support from them. Without such support you may encounter some problems that can result in you abandoning the whole idea of using portfolios in the instruction.
- It is a good idea too to pilot portfolio writing with a small group of students first to see how it works. In my case I introduced portfolio writing in the instruction in one group of 15 students and only a year later started using it with the other groups I teach.
- Consider your class size too. Maybe it is just too big to make portfolio writing part of the instruction.
- If you are going to work online, have a close look at the technology available in your teaching context. Is it reliable?

Is portfolio writing worth trying? My experience has shown that it is because it helps to develop students writing skills more completely and makes the process of learning more meaningful and purposeful.

Email: eydelman.natalia@gmail.com

References

Hamp-Lyons, L., and W. Condon. 2000. *Assessing Portfolio: Principles for Practice, Theory, and Research.* Cresskill, N.J.: Hampton.

Little, D. 2009. 'The European Language Portfolio: Where pedagogy and assessment meet'. 8th International Seminar on the European Language Portfolio. Graz, 29 September–1 October 2009.

7.9 The feasibility of using blogs to teach writing in English

Kuang-yun Ting *St John's University, Taiwan*

Introduction

English writing exercises are often seen as difficult tasks for many students. However, if given sufficient feedback, students might be willing to participate more in writing tasks. One characteristic of a blog is that it provides writers with a forum for their thoughts and communications with others (Stock 2009). This paper will discuss a research project on the use of blogs in writing courses.

The research project

This research project explores learners' perspectives of writing using both a class blog designed by the teacher and a BBC student blog. The participants were students from different university departments and programmes (for example, bachelor's, master's and doctoral degrees). They followed a course called 'Basic Writing' twice a week for two hours over a period of two months in 2009.

Writing tasks were divided into three stages: writing on paper, writing on the class blog and writing on the BBC student blog. In the first four weeks, students brainstormed ideas; organised topic, supporting and concluding sentences; and then presented their work to the whole class.

From the fifth week onwards, students posted their work on the class blog, the topics being taken from the themes in the coursebook—for example, the signs of the zodiac were introduced in short sentences in one unit. In addition, students were requested to write a short paragraph about an animal. In order to increase the challenge of the task, each student had to choose a different animal and they had to post their work as soon as possible. If they saw the animal they wanted to describe was already posted on the blog, they had to choose another one.

In the seventh week, students posted their comments on the BBC student blog on the BBC *Learning English* website which contains many topics raised by learners from different countries. Students chose a topic of interest to them and commented on it.

Findings and discussion

According to student opinion, as revealed in a questionnaire and follow-up interviews, most of the students liked the way their writing work was posted on the class blog—see Table 10.4.1.

Writing on paper	Writing on our class blog	Writing on BBC student blog
7%	80%	13%

Table 10.4.1: Students' favourite writing task

80 per cent of the students liked to post writing exercises on the class blog. The main reason was that they could read other classmates' articles. If they were not clear about the homework, they could also find the information on the class blog; this shows that the blog was an interactive platform for learners.

All the students agreed that blogging was a very useful way to practise English: 87 per cent of the students felt that the writing task was interesting and challenging because they knew that someone would read their work. Participants' comments were, in fact, similar to Rollinson's (2005) views on writing for a real audience.

Conclusion

Some suggestions and reflections about teaching writing through blogs are proposed. First, in a writing class, students should be encouraged to experiment with writing tasks without fear of being criticised. Instead of giving more formative instructions, teachers should provide students with real audiences which include themselves and also people unknown to them. In this way, students are motivated to assume greater responsibility for the quality of their writing. Second, teachers should propose meaningful writing tasks to restore students' lack of interest and motivation for writing even though they may consider writing as a difficult task. Third, blogs can be used as a medium on writing courses. When students publish their work on a class blog, writing assignments become meaningful. Students can, in this way address real audiences, of which they themselves form a part.

When students publish their work on a popular blog, they tend to be motivated to take their writing more seriously. At the same time, students often acquire a sense of achievement when their writing work is posted on a blog.

Email: k.y.ting@gmail.com

References

Rollinson, P. 2005. 'Using peer feedback in the ESL writing class'. *ELT Journal*, 59/1: 23–30.

Stock, M. 2009. *The School Administrator's Guide to Blogging*. New York: Rowman and Littlefield Education.

8 Preparing learners for specific situations

8.1 Online discussion: can it help international students ease into British university life?

Barbara Skinner *University of Ulster, Coleraine, Northern Ireland*

Introduction

International students arriving at UK higher education institutions often find the first stage of the period of transition from home to British university difficult. Research has shown that the difficulties relate to finding themselves in a new culture and being hesitant to discuss problems of a personal nature face-to-face (Pederson 1991; Parker *et al.* 2001). This presentation looked at a project at the University of Ulster in Northern Ireland which encouraged students to explore their feelings by participating in a series of online WebCT discussion tasks to help mitigate any disabling effects of arriving in a new country.

Methodology

The participants in the project were 55 students (42 Chinese, four Japanese, three Taiwanese, three Polish and three Italian) aged 18–35, studying on a six-week pre-sessional English language programme. They were divided into six groups, that is, three groups on each of the two university campuses where the pre-sessional takes place, with about nine members in each group. They took part in a 45-minute WebCT discussion each week for five weeks. The WebCT discussion topics were formulated based on problems which may occur during the initial stages of cultural adjustment. These tasks acted as a springboard for students to express their thoughts and feelings.

Week 1: The 'Arrival and first impressions' task elicited memories of their journey to Northern Ireland and their first thoughts of being in the country.

Week 2: The 'Who am I (culturally speaking)?' task asked participants to consider how cultural differences affected their image of themselves.

Week 3: The 'Expectations versus reality' task asked them to compare their expectations of the university and Northern Ireland with the reality of being in the new country.

Week 4: The 'Culture bumps' task asked students to study examples of 'cultural clashes' and then to present awkward cultural situations they had experienced and to explain how they had dealt with them.

Week 5: The 'How others see us' task asked students to examine how their own cultural mores may be seen through the eyes of the host country.

Six 'critical issues' (loneliness, health, accommodation, lack of competent English, finance and independence) were identified. An illustration of 'loneliness' follows; in this case, a student misses family life and, three weeks into his stay, still uses Chinese time to know what his family at home are doing:

- I have been in Northern Ireland for almost four weeks and it's quite different from what I thought before I came here. I live in a single room, it's not as if we live together for four people as in our country. The people here who cook in the kitchen do not let me do my preparation so I eat very late. I can't stand potato and I will never eat them at home. I still lead a Chinese lifestyle, even use the Chinese time on my clock to know what my family are doing. There are no more opportunities to ask mum or dad for anything now. There have been some surprises and some bad things for me. I can only say 'bad luck'. I hope it will be a bit better from now on.

Various forms of advice were offered:

- You seem to be sad. You must hold on to your family but do not obsess with them. Why not ring them once every two days? You can use international phone card which is cheap.
- I feel the same and always convert the time to Japanese time so I can understand if my parents are at work or not. It is OK to think about them if you want to.
- I advise you to be with your Chinese friends more and to tell them about your family. Try not to worry about at home and enjoy this time. Don't stay in your room too much. Normally there are people cooking in the kitchen you must talk to them and watch the TV. You have to be strong to not feel unhappy. Do you have a best friend to talk?

This student shows symptoms of second stage culture shock (Gullahorn and Gullahorn 1963): hostility towards the host culture for not letting him cook at a time he wants and intrusion of cultural differences, the 'bad' food. This feeling grows out of a real difficulty in adjusting to the new surroundings.

This project showed that an online discussion facility as an alternative way to express international students' emotions during this period of transition may help toward supporting them through this exciting but difficult time.

Email: B.Skinner@ulster.ac.uk

References

Gullahorn, J. T. and J. E. Gullahorn. 1963. 'An extension of the U-curve hypothesis'. *Journal of Social Issues* 19/3: 33–47.

Parker, G., G. Gladstone and K. T. Chee. 2001. 'Depression in the planet's largest ethnic group: the Chinese'. *American Journal of Psychiatry* 158/6: 857–64.

Pederson, P. 1991. 'Counseling international students'. *The Counseling Psychologist* 19/1: 10–58.

8.2 English-medium instruction and ESP: a collaborative approach

Claudia Kunschak *Shantou University, China*

Introduction

With the increasing proficiency of English learners reaching university, the professionalisation of language teaching at the tertiary level (Wen and Hu 2007), and a trend towards English-medium instruction across Asia, English for Specific Purposes (ESP) or Content-Based Instruction (CBI) is rapidly becoming the preferred mode of instruction. The process of instituting such modules is clearly not without challenges as it typically involves more than one department, requiring institutional support as well as teachers ready to assume the task of collaborative planning and team-teaching (Du 2009). However, given students' need for support in English-medium classes as well as the demand for English-proficient professionals on the globalised market, universities and colleges will need to follow suit. This paper reports on the development and implementation of an ESP programme in business, journalism and law at a medium-sized public university in Southern China and hopes to contribute to the discussion of challenges and successes of such programmes in tertiary institutions across the globe.

Background

English-medium instruction in the colleges of business, journalism and law was introduced together with the English Enhancement Program (EEP) established in 2002; this led to an influx of international teachers, the provision of a wide range of co-curricular activities for students and an expectation that those students would be successful participants in this globalised society upon graduation. From a series of semi-structured interviews with students, graduates, teachers and professionals conducted by the researcher, it quickly became apparent that while HR directors were pleased by the English level of graduates from this university, teachers and students voiced concerns about the demands of English-medium instruction and the lack of appropriate support classes. With these data in mind, the English Language Center (ELC) of the university decided to launch tailor-made ESP support programmes for the relevant colleges.

A step-by-step approach

Based on the results of the initial qualitative research conducted in 2007–2008, a step-by-step approach to developing, implementing and evaluating the ESP initiative was drafted. The first step consisted of gaining institutional support, which was obtained by referring to the initial data and appealing to the university's mission of internationalisation and professionalisation. Next, potential teachers within the ELC and collaborators in the respective colleges had to be identified and invited to participate in the project, which was also submitted as a funded research proposal to the university authorities. The entire team then drafted, revised and implemented a needs analysis that was administered to students in all three colleges across grade levels (30 per college and year; 120 total per college) in the spring of 2009. In the autumn, teams of ELC teachers, one international and one Chinese teacher each, started to develop pilot programmes by meeting with their content collaborators, observing their classes, and studying their syllabi and teaching materials. New course proposals were then submitted to the university's Teaching Affairs Office and the new ESP modules went live in the spring semester, 2010. Currently, evaluation of the pilot is being carried out through classroom observation, initial, mid-term and exit surveys, as well as through interviews with teachers and students involved. Data will be analysed over the summer months and will wash back into the next stage of course consolidation in the autumn semester of 2010.

Challenges and solutions

Common obstacles in the development of such courses that were also encountered to some extent in this project include the following: insecurity on the content level among English teachers, mirrored by insecurity on the English level for content-course faculty; departmental turf wars; lack of support from the institution; unclear or exaggerated expectations; and lack of release time or extra credit for teachers, as well as lack of time or open credit on the part of students. In order to overcome such obstacles, the team advanced arguments such as: the character of the course as a language class, not a content class; the facilitation of teaching and grading for content teachers; the clear message of the data from the quantitative needs analysis; the emphasis on the voluntary nature of the project for teachers and students; the requirements of the global workplace; and the relevance of language training that students would receive to their degree subjects.

Conclusion

English for Specific Purposes is a natural extension of English for General Purposes at any tertiary institution, even more so in English-medium instruction. Though its initial implementation may be arduous and fraught with obstacles and doubts, student needs, market demands and teaching considerations call for it. By following some general guidelines including needs analysis, team building, institutional support, professional conduct, flexibility and persistence, as well as detailed documentation, some solid foundations for future success can be laid.

Email: claudiakunschak@yahoo.de

References

Du, J. H. 2009. 'Content and language integration in tertiary education in China: a case study in Wuhan Law College'. *The Asian ESP Journal* 5/1: 4. (Retrieved 18 June 2010 from http://www.asian-esp-journal.com/May_2009_jdh.php.)

Wen, Q. F. and W. Z. Hu. 2007. 'History and policy of English education in Mainland China' in Y. H. Choi and B. Spolsky (eds.). *English Education in Asia: History and Policies.* Seoul: eduKLC.

8.3 Investigation of a multiple intelligences profile for engineering students

Adrian Millward-Sadler, Annette Casey and Dietmar Tatzl

FH JOANNEUM, University of Applied Sciences, Graz, Austria

Background

Teachers of English for Specific Purposes (ESP) frequently comment on the challenges of teaching language to non-language students. Many practitioners experience these challenges first-hand when they take their painstakingly prepared materials into class, only to find that their choice of language learning activity or planned approach for transferring content is simply not accessible to the target group in question.

The following describes a study inspired by Howard Gardner's theory of Multiple Intelligences (MI). It aims to ascertain tertiary students' multiple intelligences profiles and to suggest ways to adapt teaching materials in an ESP classroom, with a view to not only making the materials more accessible to the students, but ultimately to improving their motivation for language learning in engineering degree programmes specifically.

With this in mind, students in the department of Vehicle Technology at the University of Applied Sciences in Graz, Austria were surveyed using a questionnaire to evaluate their strengths and weaknesses according to Gardner's theory. This survey was then extended to include the department of Aviation at the same university. As a comparison, a group of translation students from the nearby Karl-Franzens University was surveyed using the same questionnaire.

Theory of multiple intelligences

In 1983, Gardner presented his theory of MI, proposing that rather than measuring intelligence according to the traditional IQ system, we should view human ability to solve problems using a set of intelligences (or skills or aptitudes), which are essentially 'procedures' for learning. The seven, and later eight, intelligences he defined are as follows:

- *Linguistic*: the ability to communicate and use language in a variety of ways; sensitivity to meaning, word order, sounds, patterns in language; the ability to acquire foreign languages with relative ease.
- *Visual-Spatial*: the ability to understand and create visual images using charts, diagrams, drawings; the ability to read maps.
- *Musical*: the ability to recognise and create sound patterns; sensitivity to rhythm, pitch, tone quality.
- *Kinaesthetic*: the potential to use one's body to create something or solve a problem; good coordination and refined motor skills.
- *Interpersonal*: awareness and sensitivity to others; the ability to interact with ease and confidence; good collaboration skills.
- *Intrapersonal*: awareness and understanding of one's own strengths and weaknesses; awareness of one's own emotional states and those of others.
- *Logical*: the ability to analyse problems logically, do calculations in your head, make logical arguments based on facts and figures.
- *Naturalist*: awareness of the world around you; interest in and understanding of the classification of species.

Gardner suggests that each individual has a 'blend' of these intelligences, in other words a mixture of procedures which are employed when learning, and that some of these are more prevalent than others—see, for example, Gardner 1995. Identifying these prevalent intelligences and tailoring activities towards them can help instructors create pathways for their students into subject material, in this case ESP.

Data collection

Data for this survey was collected by means of a learning questionnaire (adapted from Berman 1998) between 2006 and 2009. Three test groups from the departments of

Vehicle Technology (n = 167), Aviation (n = 52) and the Institute of Theoretical and Applied Translation (n = 46) participated in the study, with a total of 265 students investigated. The survey contained eight sets of six statements, each set relating to a separate intelligence. Students rated each statement, making it possible to create individual intelligences profiles displaying the respondent's learning preferences.

Results

Table 8.3.1 shows the striking match of prevalent intelligences among engineering students, whereas the control group from the Institute of Theoretical and Applied Translation (ITAT) deviates considerably from Vehicle Technology and Aviation students.

	Vehicle Technology	Aviation	ITAT
1	Interpersonal	Interpersonal	Interpersonal
2	Kinaesthetic	Kinaesthetic	Linguistic
3	Logical	Logical	Intrapersonal
4	Spatial	Spatial	Spatial
5	Linguistic	Linguistic	Musical
6	Intrapersonal	Intrapersonal	Logical
7	Musical	Musical	Kinaesthetic
8	Naturalist	Naturalist	Naturalist

Table 8.3.1: Comparative ranking of dominant intelligences

A more detailed analysis of selected year group data from the department of Vehicle Technology and the Institute of Theoretical and Applied Translation can be found in Millward-Sadler *et al.* (2010).

Conclusions

The results of this survey suggest that one approach at optimising learning conditions for engineering students consists in an application of the theory of Multiple Intelligences. The multiple intelligences profile for engineering students discovered in this study provides a backdrop for adapting current materials, and may pave the way to increased learner motivation and success if learners' strong intelligences can be employed to improve their English language skills.

Email: adrian.millward-sadler@fh-joanneum.at
annette.casey@fh-joanneum.at
dietmar.tatzl@fh-joanneum.at

References

Berman, M. 1998. *A Multiple Intelligences Road to an ELT Classroom.* Carmarthen, Wales: Crown House.

Gardner, H. 1999. *Intelligence Reframed: Multiple Intelligences for the 21st Century.* New York, N.Y.: Basic Books.

Millward-Sadler, A. J., A. Casey and F. Newman. 2010. 'Facilitating engineering students in the language classroom: multiple intelligences profiles to improve foreign language competence'. *Proceedings of the 2010 American Society for Engineering Education Annual Conference & Exposition*, Louisville, Ky., 20–23 June 2010.

8.4 The globalisation of English: implications for the Business English classroom

Robin Walker *Freelance, Lieres, Spain*

Implication 1: Different roles mean different goals

The globalisation of English is now an undisputed fact. One of the major effects of this is that English has taken on the role of lingua franca in many contexts. The Toyota–Peugeot factory in the Czech Republic, for example, uses English as a lingua franca among the staff who work there, as do the Nokia factories in Finland. English is also the working language for major international trade associations such as the G7, BRIC or ASEAN. That is to say, the globalisation of English has added a new role to the existing ones of English as a native language, as a second language, and as a foreign language. This new role, that of English as a lingua franca (ELF), requires us to rethink our goals for the Business English classroom. It is no longer appropriate to assume that what native speakers do in business is automatically relevant to what happens between non-native speaker (NNS) interlocutors.

Implication 2: Language users determine correct language use

One critical outcome of English becoming a lingua franca is that it will be modified through use. The principal mechanism through which this will happen is contact with the speakers' first languages, a mechanism has already given rise, for example, to Indian or Nigerian Englishes. One apparent danger of language contact is that the changes it generates might go in different directions depending on the L1s in play. This could lead to the development of mutually unintelligible variations. Graddol (2006) contests this outcome, and even suggests that it is frequently the absence of native speakers in ELF interactions that results in communication being successful. In addition, Widdowson (1994) has argued that non-native speakers have the right to make such changes since ownership of the language belongs as much to them as to its native speakers.

Implication 3: Learners need training in exploiting meaning(s)

Research has been going on for some time as to the nature of ELF. In terms of grammar, certain features of ELF, such as the 's' of the third person singular of the verb, are regularly seen to differ from standard native speaker (NS) English without impacting negatively on communication. ELF is also characterised by lexical variation. In some cases, such variation is the result of poor English or of performance mistakes, and is not automatically effective. Thus, 'May I forguest Please reftain no check good' (seen on the door of a public toilet) is neither good ELF nor good EFL—nor good anything. The English used completely fails to convey any intended message. In contrast, 'Please do not plug out!' (found by a telephone jack-point in a Prague hotel), is entirely effective. Even though 'plug out' does not conform to the NS norm, which only permits 'plug in', the ELF coinage not only displays a full understanding of the meanings of 'plug' and 'out', but also reveals competence in the functioning of English phrasal verbs. The NNS author of the sign has merely 'played' with the potential for meaning of the language. Legitimate, effective creativity of this sort characterises ELF vocabulary, and learners need training in such creativity if they are to make the most of their own language resources.

Implication 4: Accents are normal and are not the same as intelligibility

The area of ELF most people are familiar with is pronunciation. Analysis of empirical data from NNS–NNS spoken interactions gave rise to the Lingua Franca Core (LFC) (Jenkins 2000). Jenkins suggested that mutual intelligibility would be retained when speakers are competent in the main areas of the LFC, namely:

- the consonants of English (except voiced and voiceless 'th'),
- the correct treatment of word-initial consonant clusters,
- variation in vowel length (as opposed to vowel quality),
- tonic stress placement.

In addition to facilitating ELF intelligibility, the LFC offers teachers and learners significant benefits: it provides them with a lighter workload, and it is broadly achievable through classroom teaching. Lastly, the LFC allows speakers to retain their L1 identities through their L2 accents. Until now, 'accent' has been judged in terms of distance from a standard NS phonological norm, generally RP or GA, with 'foreign' accents being equated to poor intelligibility.

Email: robin@englishglobalcom.com

References

Graddol, D. 2006. *English Next.* London: British Council.

Jenkins, J. 2000. *The Phonology of English as a Lingua Franca.* Oxford: Oxford University Press.

Widdowson. H. G. 1994. 'The ownership of English'. *TESOL Quarterly* 28/2 377–89.

8.5 English for the public sector in Europe

Rhoda McGraw *Ecole Nationale des Ponts et Chaussées, Paris, France*

Global interactions increasingly require civil servants in Europe to communicate in English, even when they are working locally. Indeed, the effective use of English may be a factor in the survival of public services today. In this presentation I discussed using content-based instruction to meet the rapidly changing needs of European government employees.

I work for a French ministry which is currently in charge of sustainable development. In an engineering school run by the ministry, I teach English to public administrators at all stages of their careers, from pre-service to preparation for retirement. The talk focused on my experience of designing and running mixed-level, content-based courses for people whose present or future government jobs require the use of English both within and outside Europe. The courses explore areas such as urban planning, transport and utility networks, public finance and sustainable consumption. Classes are structured around collaborative tasks involving the integrated use of all four skills. Although learners' ideas and questions arising from their work are a major source of material for the courses, other sources include research centres, national and international government agencies, non-governmental organisations and the popular press. The presentation used course descriptions, sample activities and student writing to illustrate how two of the courses have operated and how the learners have contributed and responded.

After emphasising the importance of adapting instruction to local contexts and to specific fields of public endeavor, I suggested some general ways in which the needs of civil servants might differ from those of private-sector employees. Many of the learners in my courses report that they believe they are working for the public good. Some of them also say that they have the luxury of being able to take the time necessary for an intellectual approach to political issues, trying to find the best outcomes for the greatest number of people. Yet they know they must finally be pragmatic and seek consensus. In my experience, materials designed for teaching Business English do not often fit with their values and perspectives.

Since the official language in our ministry is French and many big companies now use English in their offices in France, my students have fewer opportunities than private-sector employees to use English with each other in the workplace. The resulting lack of practice means that they can feel at a disadvantage when working internationally, especially in public–private partnerships. Nevertheless, they still see their use of English as an advantage in international negotiations because it helps them seem neutral.

When session participants were invited to share their own experiences and impressions, a lively exchange ensued. Almost all of the audience members were themselves teaching English to government workers, mainly in Europe. Many had been using materials designed for the private sector and had noticed learners complaining that their courses were not specific enough. One person reported such difficulties even though she herself has a degree in public administration. Although everyone had observed a lack of materials and guidance for teachers of civil servants, participants did not agree on whether or not we can define English for the public sector across fields and national boundaries. A need for further exploration of the topic is apparent.

If the public sector is to retain any voice at all in the contemporary political climate, in Europe and elsewhere, government as well as business workers must be equipped to communicate effectively in English. I hope that those who attended the session left with a notion of one way to approach their teaching as well as a renewed sense of its political and social significance.

Email: rhoda.mcgraw@mail.enpc.fr

8.6 Developing workplace English programmes in Botswana

Modupe M. Alimi *University of Botswana, Gaborone, Botswana*

Why workplace English in Botswana?

This paper discusses the need for suitable workplace English programmes in the emerging multicultural work environment of Botswana, a country with a land area the size of France and a population of 1.6 million. Because of its political stability and economic growth (it is the world's largest exporter of diamonds and houses one of the world's unique ecosystems), Botswana has attracted workers from different linguistic and cultural backgrounds.

At independence, Botswana retained English as its official language and adopted Setswana as its national language. Thus, unlike many countries in West Africa where English completely dominates the indigenous languages, in Botswana English competes with Setswana in a number of domains. As a result, the linguistic landscape of the workplace seems to be divided into two overlapping types: workplaces where English is predominantly the tool of oral and written communication (EEWP) including the mining industry, and workplaces where both English and Setswana are used for oral communication with English dominating the written mode (ESWP) such as the commercial arm of the aviation department. The increasing linguistic and cultural diversity of its workplaces is a key reason for the need to develop workplace English programmes in Botswana.

Workplace English needs

This paper focuses on four major industries in Botswana: mining, tourism, aviation and health. The establishment of the Diamond Trading Company of Botswana, a joint venture with De Beers, is expected to yield massive 'transfers of skills and commercial activity to Africa' (BBC News). This development, which is evidence of the increased globalisation of Botswana's workforce, will probably sustain the dominance of English as the language of official functions in the mining industry while Setswana will remain the language of interaction for establishing and maintaining social relationships.

Tourism has also expanded significantly as it currently accounts for about 10 per cent of total employment (World Travel and Tourism Council 2007). Many private and public institutions now run certificate courses in travel and tourism. Also, travel and tour companies have multiplied, resulting in two cadres of workers in the industry: the highly specialised group and the more general group. This implies that both specialised and informal English skills will be in demand.

The work environment in the commercial arm of the aviation department has leaned more towards ESWP because of the powerful prevailing forces of national identity and cultural consciousness. Announcements of flight schedules and boarding are relayed first in Setswana and second in English. However, the Civil Aviation Authority of Botswana (CAAB), established recently, is expected to hire many professionals such as mechanical and electrical engineers from outside the country. This development will probably alter language use in the industry in favour of English, especially because the industry will need to conform to the complex set of language competency standards prescribed by the International Civil Aviation Organisation (ICAO).

The health sector attracts many NGOs and donor organisations and is expected to grow further with the planned recruitment of Cuban medical doctors and the opening of Bokamoso private hospital, which intends to offer many specialities that are currently not available in the country; this situation will likely promote the dominance of English.

Response to these needs

It is obvious that the general proficiency English programmes based solely on ELT practitioners' perception of learners needs, offered by most departments of English in Africa, will not suffice for these growing sectors because such programmes are not aimed at specific needs. Though the specificity of learners' needs has been criticised, the importance of defining 'learners' specific needs and their actual language difficulties in their professional lives' (Johns and Dudley- Evans 1991: 303) cannot be underestimated as these are crucial for successful workplace interaction. The process of identifying the workplace English needs for the mining, aviation, health and tourism industries in Botswana requires the development of a comprehensive needs analysis specific to each of these workplaces. It will also entail the full participation of employers and employees of the workplaces and the relevant language departments.

The above is the challenge to which the department of English at the University of Botswana must respond by being proactive in marketing its expertise to these industries and by offering to develop appropriate workplace English courses for them. Responding in this manner will position the department strategically to create and engage in strong partnerships with these workplaces, and promote capacity building. Ultimately the department will broaden its programmes to make them more relevant to the globalised workplace.

Email: alimimm@mopipi.ub.bw

References

BBC News http://news.bbc.co.uk/1/hi/world/africa/country_profiles/1068674.stm.

Johns, A. and T. Dudley-Evans. 1991. 'English for Specific Purposes: international in scope, specific in purpose. *TESOL Quarterly* 30/2: 297–314. (Retrieved 26 March 2010 from http://www.jstor.org/stable/3587465.)

World Travel and Tourism Council. 2007. 'Botswana: the impact of travel and tourism on jobs and the economy'. (Retrieved 25 February 2009 from http://www.botswanatourism.co.bw/news_events/.)

8.7 ELT Community Policing

Enid Jorsling *Halton Multicultural Council, Oakville, Ontario, Canada*

For many international professionals immigrating to Canada, the opportunity to work in their former profession seems an impossible dream. This is particularly true for police and other law enforcement professionals as their occupation requires a high level of professional English fluency. As one of the most challenging professions in terms of language communication, policing demands a language competency that is often seen as beyond the reach of adult ESL learners.

This poster presentation gave an overview of an innovative, high-level English language training programme, ELT Community Policing, created to meet the needs of adult learners who aspire to joining the police service in Canada. All applicants complete an English language assessment and must meet a minimum language requirement of Level 7 on the Canadian Language Benchmarks (CLB), the official Canadian standard for measuring the language proficiency of adult immigrants. The programme utilises a specialised curriculum and is continuously adapted to address gaps in specific language areas. Delivered part-time, evenings and weekends over an intense, four-month learning period, the programme aims to give participants the English language skills required to accomplish specific goals, the primary goal being passing the police entrance examination.

Any ELT programme that attempts to address this complex language barrier must embody a unique and comprehensive approach that uses authentic materials to teach those aspects of language learning that are specific to this occupation. The delivery of the programme illustrates how realistic forms of spoken and written communication in this very demanding profession are employed in the classroom. In order to prepare for the examination and move into the constable selection process, learners work at developing competencies, public speaking, report writing and problem analysis, and they practise the complex communications required for handling situations that arise daily in the working life of a police constable.

Participants begin developing specific language skills by analysing work tasks vital to the profession. Exercises provide opportunities for intensive practice of language structures related to specific work situations. For example, for work tasks that utilise skills in interviewing, analysing and acquiring specific information, participants use extensive practice writing, forming, as well as asking questions, reading, analysing and solving mystery stories. Grammar is reviewed as needed, and is based on the errors learners consistently make. A full review of verb tenses of regular and irregular verbs is completed, giving participants opportunities to rehearse and refine the appropriate use of tenses through extensive practice. These exercises help to focus on proper usage, expand their understanding of the tenses, and make the relating and writing about events in the past a smoother process—a very important detail in the work of the police officer. Other practice exercises include describing people (faces, features, build), places and events.

In order to develop writing competence, activities focus on producing specific documents police officers complete daily. One key approach is the posing and treatment of open-ended questions. This model of short-paragraph, written responses fits the standard of police report writing: expressing facts concisely. Practice also includes preparing accident reports after viewing events online, and writing numerous summaries and factual reports of past events.

While the main goal of the programme is language skills development, participants are also educated about the constable selection process, local police services and community policing procedures. The style of policing in this region is community based; in order to be effective, police officers maintain a connection with their communities and this is reflected in local policing procedures. The programme relies heavily on an ongoing partnership with Halton Police Service, which provides technical expertise and internship/mentorship opportunities. Supporting agencies help to bring the realities of police work into the classroom through presentations that highlight their service to the community; they also provide opportunities for volunteer work, an integral part of the programme. Among them, the Ontario Justice Education Network (OJEN), an organisation that promotes justice education in the province, provides participants with an introduction to the Canadian legal system.

Throughout their training learners receive motivation and encouragement from a variety of sources. Guest speakers who have completed the selection process and now work as police officers using English, their L2, return to provide firsthand accounts of their challenges and successes.

Email: ejorsling@halton-multicultural.org

9 Teaching young learners: cognition, curriculum and culture

9.1 Plenary: Students' minds and imaginations

Kieran Egan *Simon Fraser University, Burnaby, British Columbia, Canada*

Introduction

In this paper I will outline a somewhat new way of thinking about the process of students' education. It focuses on the kinds of 'cognitive tools' or learning 'toolkits' students develop as they grow up in a society like ours. In schools and in most currently dominant psychological theories of development, short shrift is given to some of the most powerful learning tools students have available to make sense of their world and experience, and of the languages that surround them. We tend also to think of the imagination as something of an educational frill—something to try to engage after the hard work of learning had occurred. I will try to show that focusing on central features of students' learning 'toolkits' makes it clear that the imagination is one of the great workhorses of learning, and that we ignore it at the cost of making learning more ineffective than it should be and much schooling more tedious than it need be. In particular, the imagination can make learning other languages more engaging and meaningful than it commonly is.

I will begin by sketching the main ideas that have accumulated historically into our current conception of education, in order to indicate what is distinctive about the approach I will be recommending. The first and oldest educational idea is that we should shape children to the norms, values, and beliefs of the adult society around them. In the jargon of textbooks, we call this socialisation. We recognise this idea of education when items in the curriculum are justified on the basis of their future social utility. So reading, writing, computing, sex education, consumer economics, basic common knowledge, other languages, and so on, are all justified in terms of their importance for someone who wishes to get on and be a good citizen today.

The second educational idea was largely Plato's. As he chatted with the best and brightest of Athens, he concluded that well-socialised citizens were more or less contemptible. Their ready acceptance of the conventional norms and values of the society they grew into seemed to him appalling, as such beliefs, he showed, were typically a collection of confusions, illusions, stereotypes, prejudices, and dogmas that didn't bear much scrutiny. Plato conceived of education as the process of seeking the truth about reality. For Plato, the mind is made up very largely of the knowledge that it accumulates, and accumulating a lot of the right kind of disciplined knowledge can turn the mind from its easy acceptance of whatever conventional rubbish happens to be fashionable to an austere and disciplined search for what is true, good and beautiful.

The third idea is largely derived from Jean-Jacques Rousseau. He shared Plato's view that early socialisation generally taught children a load of nonsense that was immensely difficult to dislodge once learned. But he thought Plato was wrong in his view that children's minds were shaped very largely by the knowledge that they accumulate. He argued that the mind has an internal, spontaneous, natural developmental process through which it grows, and proper education is the process of furthering its fullest development. So education became for Rousseau a matter of facilitating the fullest development of a natural psychological process, and thereby fulfilling as far as possible the potential of each individual student. This has become the anchoring idea of 'progressivism'.

Pretty well all modern conceptions of education, from the most radical to the most conservative, are compounded from these three ideas. No one holds one of them to the exclusion of the other two, of course; it's a matter of the proportions in which they are mixed. So the more radical conceptions tend to combine a large amount of Rousseau with a small dose of socialising and go very sparingly with the Plato. The conservative tends to stir in a good measure of Plato, a healthy dose of socialising, and go light on the Rousseau. The average politician throws in a very large dose of socialising, is very sparing of Rousseau, and sprinkles in just a little bit of Plato.

How else can we think about education? We can think of it as learning to use as well as possible the cognitive tools developed in our evolution and cultural history. I think we can re-conceive education as the process whereby we acquire as fully as possible the major symbolic tools invented or discovered in human cultures. Each major set of tools generates for us somewhat distinctive kinds of understanding. I will briefly sketch these main sets of tools and describe the kinds of understanding to which they give rise.

But what does a 'cognitive tool' look like? Imagine you are on the plains of Africa 75,000 years ago. It is mid-day and very hot. Ahead of you is a large lean-to built around a thorn tree. You can wander inside the shelter, and you can see and hear the small tribe working and talking. At the back of the lean-to, on the most comfortable skins, a corpulent gentleman lies snoring. He is clearly held in high regard by the tribe. You discover that he is held in high regard because a dozen years earlier he invented the past tense.

Everyone is using the past tense now, including neighboring tribes, through whom it is passing like wildfire, and your tribe is receiving much praise for its invention. The past tense adds to people's ability to articulate features of our experience with greater clarity and scope. But, you learn, the corpulent gentleman at the back of the tent has twin daughters, and it was actually the daughters who invented the past tense, and their father has since taken the credit. The daughters are now young adults and, more sensitive to intellectual property rights, plan a launch of the subjunctive in the following week.

Well, someone invented the past tense and the subjunctive. They didn't just happen. The invention and elaboration of these features of our language adds to our ability to make sense of our experience and to articulate it to others. When we learn a language, we pick up endless tools of this kind, which become for us tools for thinking and learning. In the 75,000 years since our scenario on the African plains, human beings have invented a huge array of cognitive tools that can enhance our ability to think, to learn and to understand our world and our human condition. The simplistic scenario is designed to illuminate a little Lev Vygotsky's (1962, 1997) conception of development as picking up sets of cognitive tools as we grow up in a society. So I want to explore a conception of education that sees the process as *maximising for us the array of cognitive tools we pick up as we interact with the cultural world around us.*

The body's toolkit

The first tool we have available for understanding the world is our body. If you have a body—you might want to check this now—you will have a set of sense-making and learning tools available to you; these are tools that remain with you for the rest of your life, though they change somewhat over time.

Senses

The inescapable elements of our body's toolkit are our senses—our sight, hearing, touch, taste and smell, which we value more or less in that order. These senses are stimulated in our earliest years, and babies take a particular delight in games that combine a number of them: plops, clicks and squeaks that create, then follow, patterns that involve sight, touch and taste. Our senses are necessary for our initial understanding of the world and allow us to perceive and deal with a certain range and scale of the phenomena of our environments.

Emotions

A central feature of our bodies' meaning-making toolkit is its emotional nature. These emotions will persist and develop as the most basic orientors and organisers of our cognition throughout our lives. The way in which we respond to the physical and social world around us depends, importantly, on our emotions: from an early age we experience profound emotional patterns such as expectation and frustration, or satisfaction, of the expectation.

Indeed the way we interpret events, including our later ability to analyse them critically, will always be shot through with emotions. Delight, distress, elation, horror, satisfaction, anger, compassion or fear constitute elements of the underlying matrix that shape our responses, and thus even rationality itself. If we recognise the foundational development of our bodies' emotional core, we will be less likely to see cognition, and cognitive tools, as somehow separate from our emotional lives; however sophisticated our thinking becomes it will always be oriented and shaped by the emotions of the body within which it occurs.

Pattern and musicality

Stephen Mithen's *The Singing Neanderthals* (2005) has helped to show how profoundly we are musical animals. Our musicality seems a central feature of our body's toolkit, perhaps, as Mithen suggests, from early in our evolution as modern humans. We look for meaning in patterns from our earliest years, even when what we see, hear or touch may be quite random. We begin to construct that uniquely human kind of meaning on the back of these patterned regularities our senses deliver to us. There is, of course, a huge amount of recent research showing the importance of pattern recognition in infants' learning, in language learning and visual recognition of their world. (See, for example, Kirchhoff and Schimmel, 2005; and the multitude of studies from the Stanford University center for Infant studies: http://www-psych.stanford.edu/~babylab/index.html.)

Humour

Another prominent component of our bodies' toolkit is humour. While educators have typically neglected humour, or treated it as some relatively casual frill, the presence of humour in our earliest interactions suggests that its stimulation and development might be profoundly important to us, and consequently should be considered as a constituent of any adequate programme of education. It is useful to remember that humour, in many of its forms, is based on incongruity. Ability to deal easily and pleasurably with incongruity contributes to flexibility of mind, which is an important component of an educated person. Humour is important for many things, not least the delight it can give to experience, but it has a distinctive educational importance in its contribution to flexible, imaginative and creative thinking.

Our bodily sense of humour becomes evident in such early activities as the mutual sticking out of tongues, tickling, the hiding and revealing of peek-a-boo, and other forms of pretend that so delight babies and elicit laughter. All our behaviours seem accessible to a sense of humour, both to enrich the experience itself and to recognise it as parts of contexts that we can also transcend.

There is a range of research now available showing a number of dimensions of learning that are aided by humour. (For a good summary of this material, and further support, see Garner 2005; see also Garner 2006.)

Many other learning tools of the body could be explored (Egan 1997). But these few will suffice to suggest how we might see the body as providing a set of important 'tools' whose development can properly be seen as appropriate for an educational programme. Their value to all learning—perhaps especially learning languages—is, I hope, evident.

The toolkit of language

When we become fluent users of an oral language, we acquire a further toolkit for sense-making. All people who can use an oral language, or some other form of language, such as signing, will have the following tools available in varying degrees.

Story form

One implication of being an oral language-user is a responsiveness to stories. All oral cultures that we know of have developed and used stories. Shaped by logical and psychological constraint, the invention of language seems to imply the inevitable development of stories.

But what are stories? How are they distinguishable from other narratives? If I say, 'He shot Tom', you will likely have no particular or precise response (unless, perhaps, your name is Tom). If I elaborate this narrative and add that 'he' is a handsome, well-groomed young man who loves his grandmother, and that Tom is generally scruffy, bearded, picks his nose in public and uses foul language in front of children, you may begin to feel glad that he shot Tom—given the conventions of fiction today. But if the narrative is extended further, telling you that 'he' and the grandmother are leaders of a drug-pushing operation who specialise in selling to kids outside schools, and also that Tom, despite his unprepossessing exterior, has a heart of gold and is taking terrible risks to stop the grandmother's and her grandson's nefarious operations ... well, you will properly begin to feel sorry that he shot Tom. When we know securely how to feel about 'He shot Tom', we know we have reached the end of the story.

Stories, then, are narratives that fix our emotional orientation to the elements that make them up. No other narrative form can do this. We ascribe affective meaning to events, and to people, and to our own lives, by plotting them into provisional or partial stories. The reason we might reasonably consider the story as the most important social invention is that they orient the emotions of their hearers to their contents. We can, of course, make sense of our experience in a number of other modalities, but to whatever degree our emotional orientation is involved, then the plotting of events into partial or provisional or over-arching stories will be involved. We are creatures who understand an important dimension of our experience and our world in story shapes.

Binary opposites

Forming and mediating between binary opposites also seems to be another development of the kinds of sense-making we employ prior to language development. Fairy tales such as *Cinderella, Hansel and Gretel* or *Jack the Giant Killer* are all built on top of powerful, abstract, binary oppositions such as security and anxiety, pleasure and pain, expectation and satisfaction, happiness and sadness, and so on. Bettelheim analyses the 'manner in which [children] can bring some order into [their] world by dividing everything into opposites' (1976: 74; see also Propp 1985; Zipes 1991).

Jokes

In much the same way as physical rhythm transforms into our language, so too do our earliest bodily games and humour give birth to jokes; the physical fun of peek-a-boo becomes the fun of the concocted language of riddles, puns and other forms of jokes. Maybe you know when cooks are mean? 'When they beat eggs and whip cream.' Jokes such as these, which typically delight young children, rely greatly on incongruity. They also make visible features of language that might otherwise be taken merely as behaviours. That is, the child has to recognise that while whipping and beating are often expressions of meanness, they are not so in the case of cooks in their kitchens. The humour comes from recognising the different meanings of the same words in special contexts. So we learn to see language as an object, not merely as a behaviour. This develops 'meta-cognition' which is crucial to the development of flexible and creative language use (Herriman 1986).

Images

Like humour, the array of images available to our minds, while somewhat limited in our early years, is suddenly enriched immensely by the acquisition of language. We seem unable to not form images as we hear events described in words, and a range of the effects of stories depends, to a great extent, upon listeners' ability to form images in their minds. These can be so intense initially that most people seem able to recall with surprising clarity the images they formed when listening to stories in their early years (Cowan 1998). The ability to call up precise and rich images is a unique feature of our minds and is clearly connected with the development of the imagination.

The toolkit of literacy

Once children become fluently literate they can pick up a whole new toolkit. Literacy in general can deliver to the developing mind a new kind of conception of reality (Bruner 1986). The impact of coming to terms with this new intellectual world generates a new set of cognitive tools, which we can deploy in teaching, because we can be sure all children who are literate will also have these tools, in addition to the ones explored above.

The extremes of reality

The initial literacy-driven exploration of reality is of its extremes, of the strange, the bizarre, the wonderful. It is not just coincidental that one of the world's most popular books with newly literate children is the *Guinness Book of Records*, nor that the best-selling texts are such papers as the *National Inquirer*. A rather odd part of the folklore of teaching is that students' exploration of the world will be more enthusiastic if we begin with what is immediate and relevant to their everyday experience. But we can readily observe that their interest is most commonly and energetically engaged by the exotic, the strange, the wonderful, by the limits of reality and the extremes of experience—with who had the longest finger nails ever, rather than the structure of their local neighborhood.

Associating with the heroic

While the exploration of this newly problematic reality can be exciting, it can also be threatening. The threats can be significantly relieved by associating with someone or something that seems best able to overcome them. So associations are formed with embodiments of those human qualities that transcend the everyday constraining and threatening world; whether it is an association with the outrageousness of a pop-singing Lady Gaga (and her freedom from having to behave conventionally, and her money and power) or with the skill and strength of a sports star (and his/her skill, money and power).

Accumulation of details

Nearly all young people begin a hobby or a collection at about age seven. The activity reaches a peak of intensity at about age eleven, and usually dies out at about age fifteen. What is going on? Why do nearly all students engage in this kind of activity? Why do we see this powerful spontaneous intellectual engagement in nearly all children? An adequate explanation is beyond what I can manage here, or anywhere, but we can see it as a response to young people's orientation to reality. Santa Claus and the tooth fairy have been left behind, and the real world is worryingly extensive. One way we can achieve some security is to gain exhaustive intellectual control over some part of it. Commercial interests, of course, are very alert to this engagement, and so they produce sets of collectible objects that have the twin requirements of being moderately extensive but also limited and exhaustible. We can draw on this cognitive tool when teaching almost anything. All topics have within them some area of knowledge that is both moderately extensive and also exhaustible.

Human knowledge

I sometimes suggest to my students that there is no knowledge in the library or on the internet. What they find in these places are only codes, which we can reconstruct into knowledge if we become familiar with the tools of literacy. But no one derives the same knowledge from any particular set of codes, and the only source of knowledge is in living human tissue, in our brains. This leads to a simple principle: that all knowledge is human knowledge; that it is derived from human hopes, fears and passions; and that if we want students to understand the knowledge—reconstruct it from the codes in their minds—they need to see it in the context of the human hopes, fears and passions that generated it in the first place or within which it finds a living meaning today.

Well, I could go on characterising additional cognitive tools in each category above, and also I could extend this description to further sets of toolkits. Given the shortage of space, let me instead recommend finding further details in Egan 1997, or, for a more practically oriented book, Egan 2005. The implications for how these kinds of observations lead directly to methods of teaching can be found on the website of the Imaginative Education Research group (www.ierg.net).

Conclusion

What I want to suggest is that we can re-conceive education as an enterprise aimed at ensuring for each child as full as possible an acquisition of each of these toolkits. Each set of cognitive tools yields a somewhat distinctive kind of understanding, and we can describe the educational process as a series of kinds of understanding (Egan 1997). Acquiring them ensures that the sensible aims of education embodied in the old ideas will be achieved incidentally; a person who gains in significant degree the use of the toolkits briefly described above will necessarily have to acquire a lot of knowledge, will have to attain significant psychological maturity, and will become socially competent. What will not happen is traditional socialisation to conformity, nor the acquisition of particular 'élite' knowledge that privileges one against others, nor the pursuit of some supposedly proper developmental process; and we will leave behind us the enervating battles among these incompatible aims.

These are not stages we pass through; they are kinds of understanding we accumulate and that coalesce to some degree. This scheme does not describe a psychological process through which we spontaneously develop as we grow older; rather, it characterises forms of thinking evoked in individuals today, as they were evoked in our cultural history, by the development of particular symbolic tools. If these tools are not supported by appropriate educational activities, they will not be acquired in any adequate way, and the forms of understanding they stimulate will not develop.

Education as the acquisition of intellectual tools is not some straightforward progressive scheme, but rather is a process of gains and losses. That is, each kind of understanding, while ideally coalescing in significant degree with previously acquired kinds, also suppresses something of the previous kinds. So, for example, the elaborated literacy that produces Romantic understanding suppresses some elements of Mythic understanding—we sense that there hath passed away a glory from the earth, as Wordsworth put it, when the anaesthetising power of literacy and theoretic thinking remove us a little from that early vivid participation in the natural world.

Each of the set of cognitive tools mentioned above also gives us clues to how we can teach more effectively, engaging students' imaginations in learning.

Email: egan@sfu.ca

References

Bettelheim, B. 1976. *The Uses of Enchantment*. New York: Knopf.

Bruner, J. 1986. *Actual Minds, Possible Worlds*. Cambridge, Mass.: Harvard University Press.

Cowan, N. (ed.). 1998. *The Development of Memory in Childhood*. New York: Psychology Press.

Egan, K. 1997. *The Educated Mind: How Cognitive Tools Shape our Understanding*. Chicago: University of Chicago Press.

Egan, K. 2005. *An Imaginative Approach to Teaching*. San Francisco: Jossey-Bass.

Garner, R. 2005. 'Humor, analogy and metaphor: H.A.M. it up in teaching'. *Radical Pedagogy* 6: 2.

Garner, R. 2006. 'Humor in pedagogy: How ha-ha can lead to aha!' *College Teaching* 54/1: 177–80.

Herriman, M. 1986. 'Metalinguistic awareness and the growth of literacy' in S. de Castell, A. Luke and K. Egan (eds.). *Literacy, Society, and Schooling*. New York: Cambridge University Press.

Kirchhoff, K. and S. Schimmel. 2005. 'Statistical properties of infant-directed versus adult-directed speech: insights from speech recognition'. *The Journal of the Acoustical Society of America* 117/4: 2238–46.

Mithen, S. 2005. *The Singing Neanderthals: The Origins of Music, Language, Mind and Body*. London: Weidenfeld and Nicolson.

Propp, V. 1985. *Theory and History of Folklore* (A. Liberman, ed.). Minnesota: University of Minnesota Press. (First published Moscow 1927.)

Vygotsky, L. 1962. *Thought and Language* (E. Haufmann and G. Vakar, trans.). Cambridge, Mass.: MIT Press.

Vygotsky, L. 1997. *The Collected Works of L. S. Vygotsky* (R.W. Rieber and J. Wollock, eds.). New York: Plenum.

Zipes, J. 1991. *Spells of Enchantment*. New York: Viking.

9.2 *ELT Journal*/IATEFL Debate: **Content and Language—an ILlusion?**

Amos Paran *Institute of Education, University of London, UK* and
Sheelagh Deller *Pilgrims Teacher Training, Canterbury, UK*

Amos Paran

Although in some contexts the successes of CLIL are well documented, overall it remains an illusion, for two main reasons: firstly, because these contexts are limited; and secondly, because the research evidence for CLIL is scant.

The limits of CLIL success are obvious: it works in countries and contexts where literacy is high and education is socially valued. Unsurprisingly, the country most associated with CLIL success is Finland, which has always come out first or second in the

Programme for International Student Assessment (PISA) tables. It is noted for a high literacy level, with major emphasis on learning the mother tongues at a very high level. Teachers in Finland are educated to degree level and have high social standing.

Another factor is the status of foreign languages in general. CLIL works in countries where foreign languages are perceived as a necessity (because the local language has a small number of speakers) and where there is easy and plentiful access to English in the community; for example, films are subtitled rather than dubbed. It works where teachers are trained to teach two subjects (for example, Germany, Austria and Switzerland); in places where secondary schools are selective (for example, Switzerland); and where there is additional selection of who enters the CLIL classroom, or where students choose whether they wish to enter a CLIL or bilingual programme.

In countries where these requirements are not met, the implementation of CLIL or of bilingual teaching has failed. The implementation of bilingual teaching in Malaysia has just been rescinded, with the educational qualification of teachers seen as a major factor. In some countries the teachers' level of English is not high enough. In other countries—for example, Italy—where schools have been forced to incorporate CLIL into their curriculum, there are myriad stories of confusion and, indeed, failure.

My second point concerns the grounds for deciding to implement CLIL. In many contexts, this decision is politically motivated, with politicians aiming at easy solutions for raising English language achievements, focusing on visible policies. These moves ignore evidence from educational research that highlights the problems of wholesale implementation of language policies in inappropriate contexts and inappropriate ways. Importantly, although research into CLIL is steadily growing, most of it looks at classroom factors and case studies. There is almost no research into the learning outcomes, and whatever research there is focuses on language achievement, rather than investigating achievement in the content area, comparing CLIL classes and L1 classes. The dangers are obvious: relying on CLIL can result in learners who may know English, but whose understanding of carrier content is shaky. Indeed, research from Hong Kong suggests that there are significant differences in achievement in History and Geography between children who were taught these subjects in their L1, and those taught in English.

CLIL is therefore an illusion, because the benefits claimed for it cannot easily—let alone automatically—be transferred to other contexts. It is an illusion, because it can only succeed where there is massive investment in teacher training. We would not buy a drug that had not been properly tested; why are we willing to initiate wide-ranging educational reform without the necessary evidence in appropriate contexts?

Sheelagh Deller

CLIL is a reality—but a work-in-progress reality. Like all work in progress, it may run into problems from time to time, but my premise is that CLIL is not an illusion if it is done well. And that depends on when, where and how we do it. I think there are five things that need to happen to make CLIL a reality and not an illusion:

- In many cases it seems to work best if it is not used 100 per cent, so that some lessons of the same subject are taught in the mother tongue and some in the foreign language: 'soft' CLIL as opposed to 'hard' CLIL. In this way there is no danger of students not being able to speak about and understand the subject in their own languages.

- There should still be pure language lessons. In a language lesson we focus on the language. In a CLIL lesson we need to infiltrate the language the students will need in order to understand, speak or write about the subject. We do not spend a lot of time teaching and practising it—but we do need to give frameworks and examples and sometimes translations.
- There needs to be adequate training before implementation—and perhaps the time has come for there to be a CLIL module in pre-service training.
- Not all students and teachers will benefit from or be able to cope with CLIL, so both the teachers and the students need to be selected appropriately.
- New CLIL teachers need to be given more time for preparation and collaboration.

When CLIL is done well, it can result in two specific positive outcomes. Firstly, using the target language for a real purpose, rather than teaching about it, is likely to produce better results in terms of language use. In CLIL, language items are introduced when the subject demands it. The language content is subject led; the language is the vehicle. Secondly, when used properly in the right environment with the appropriate people, CLIL can motivate students and prepare them for further education abroad, and for the global workplace. They will become more employable.

Nothing we do can be effective and work for everyone all of the time. But if something works for some people most of the time, it is worth pursuing. And I find it hard to believe that students who have been put through the CLIL process come out of it with nothing.

I am as much pro-CLIL as many methodologies. Just because it doesn't always work doesn't mean we should never do it. There is a lack of hard evidence for or against it, but it does work in the right place with the right people, if it is done well. Most approaches, CLIL included, have great things to offer, but as we know we need to pick the bits that suit the situation.

CLIL is definitely not an illusion. It is a reality. But it is a baby. And babies take time to develop and find their feet. CLIL is in the process of doing that and I hope that it is given the right environment, support and time to help many students and to provide a positive challenge for many teachers.

Points from the floor

- Is there a difference between 'CLIL' and 'content-based instruction'?
- Is there evidence that students really understand the language they are using in a CLIL lesson?
- How many primary teachers around the world really speak English well enough to be able to teach other curriculum areas through it?
- What will happen to 'smaller' languages around the world if English becomes a widespread medium of instruction, even at school level?
- CLIL often works better on a local level than as part of a major national project.
- CLIL is a rebellion against the transmission model in terms of content teaching, and against a grammar-based approach in terms of language teaching.

Illusion or not, CLIL attracted a large audience to the event and generated some lively discussion. Nothing was settled, but there was general agreement that this had been one of the best *ELT Journal*/IATEFL debates so far.

9.3 Evaluating an LEA-wide CLIL programme (primary and lower-secondary education)

Sandra Lucietto *Free University of Bolzano, Italy*

Introduction

CLIL (Content and Language Integrated Learning) emerged in 1994 as a pragmatic response to the EU political goal of enabling EU citizens to communicate effectively in three EU languages (L1 + 2) (Maljers and Marsh 1999). After spreading in mainstream education through grass-rooting, CLIL has recently acquired higher status in academic research, becoming one of the Research Networks of the Association Internationale de Linguistique Appliquée (AILA) in 2006, and has won governmental support in many contexts. Yet, few studies have been carried out so far to evaluate CLIL programmes, this being a research area still needing further development (European Commission 2007).

The study

The PhD evaluative study I presented at the conference aimed to explore and understand the effectiveness of a CLIL programme (30 per cent of the primary curriculum taught in English or German) launched and supported by the Autonomous Province of Trento (Italy) LEA in 2005–2006. The study was carried out within the interpretive paradigm, with strong elements of Complexity Theory emerging during the field-research phase, which focused mainly on macro- and micro-management, school support, teacher development and teaching practice. The presentation raised interest, and was followed by a question-and-answer session.

Methodology

The main research questions were:

- What are the programme's management structures (macro/micro-level)?
- What are its success factors/critical features?
- Are stakeholders satisfied?

To answer these questions, I collected and triangulated data from all CLIL teachers, teacher trainers, head teachers, LEA managers and politicians, the academic supervisor, and a sample of children/parents. The research design included classroom observation and feedback (61 classes), teachers' questionnaires (n = 114), and semi-structured individual and group interviews (n = 41). The results of the study can be used by policy makers and educators to identify strengths and weaknesses when starting a similar programme, and by academics to compare/contrast the programme and the research methodology with others elsewhere.

Selected findings

Teaching practice

Classroom observation showed teaching practice was distant from recommended CLIL methodology guidelines (for example, Mehisto *et al.* 2008): classroom activities mainly consisted of listening to the teacher, following instructions and doing low-thinking-skill individual work (drawing, copying, etc.). Only three teachers (3/31) engaged pupils in task-based, group/cooperative learning activities.

Teacher support

Teachers' feedback sessions/questionnaires highlighted that the LEA-organised CLIL training did not address teachers' needs to be guided through this new learning environment. The interview with the academic supervisor in charge of the programme's scientific reliability (an expatriate British national) revealed that his methodological guidelines to teachers had been to 'do what you've always done, only change the language'.

Management

Lack of continuity characterised management at the micro-/macro-levels. Thirteen schools were in the programme in 2008–2009: in eight of them, the head teacher had changed once since 2004–2005 (lead-in year); in four, the heads had changed twice; only in one school had the head teacher remained the same. Of the 28 head teachers involved in total, nine were newly appointed heads in their probationary year.

As to the LEA management support structure (*Comitato tecnico-scientifico*), the turn-over in five years included three Chairs of Education, three Project Coordinators (one year the position remained vacant) and three Organisational Coordinators. The academic supervisor himself was only appointed in 2006–2007. Other members in the management support team also changed, or left without being replaced.

Success and success factors

Surprisingly enough, at least 50 per cent of pupils in each class showed satisfactory *comprehension* of the EFL; language *production*, however, varied greatly between German and English classes and from pupil to pupil. As to *content*, teachers declared they were generally satisfied with pupils' results.

When asked about the programme's success factors, teachers almost invariably ticked themselves in first, followed by their team-teachers. It was their own care for the children and commitment to the programme that had 'rescued the results', as they put it, in spite of little guidance from the LEA and no recognition from their head teachers. Head teachers also considered the teaching teams to be the main success factor, and whilst less explicit, they also ranked the LEA support to schools and teachers as very low.

Conclusion

The study highlighted many drawbacks in management and support, and teachers' disappointment with their working terms and conditions. Head teachers were generally more positive, yet appeared to simply take for granted that CLIL teachers should work longer hours than non-CLIL teachers, despite being on the same salary. Children and parents were generally satisfied: pupils said CLIL was 'more difficult than normal school', but they did not want to stop it. Parents were grateful for the opportunity given to their children and proud of their results: they reported great motivation and some spontaneous use of the FL at home, and insisted that the programme should continue into lower-secondary education.

Email: sandra.lucietto@vodafone.it

References

Maljers, A. and D. Marsh. 1999. 'From vision to pragmatism: Content and Language Integrated Learning as a key factor in achieving plurilingualism in Europe'. Report presented at the Strategies for the Promotion of Linguistic Diversity in Europe Conference, Noordwijkerhout, 1999. (Retrieved 11 November 2008 from http://www.upf.edu/dtf/alpme/links.htm.)

European Commission. 2007. *Final Report, High Level Group on Multilingualism.* Luxembourg: Office for Official Publications of the European Communities.

Mehisto, P., D. Marsh and M. J. Frigols. 2008. *Uncovering CLIL. Content and Language Integrated Learning in Bilingual and Multilingual Education.* Oxford: Macmillan

9.4 From language learner autonomy to the promotion of a plurilingual competence

Marcella Menegale *Ca' Foscari University of Venice, Italy*

Background to the study

Much of the existing research into effective language learning has elected CLIL (Content and Language Integrated Learning) as one of the most valuable pathways towards plurilingualism. However, after carrying out various projects in this area, I concluded that something more was needed for students in order to develop plurilingual competence. Language learner autonomy (LLA) appeared to be the solution. Finding that LLA had not been thoroughly investigated with specific connection to plurilingualism, and that most of the research pertained to tertiary education (for a comprehensive survey, see Benson 2001), I decided to focus my PhD investigation on young students, considering how LLA could support their plurilingual competence.

Aims of the study

I investigated learners' and teachers' perceptions of the following:

1 LLA, comparing students' awareness of their learning process and teachers' actions directed towards its promotion;
2 in-class and out-of-class learning, comparing students' attitudes and teachers' efforts.

The findings have helped me to extrapolate some teaching implications fundamental to the development of plurilingual competence.

Method

Students (n = 473) and teachers (n = 44) in Italian middle and secondary schools took part in the project by answering two anonymous online questionnaires. Data were then analysed as follows:

- students' answers were related to three main domains underpinning LLA: affective, cognitive/metacognitive and communicative dimensions (Jiménez Raya *et al.* 2007);
- teachers' answers were analysed according to their view of LLA, their knowledge of their students' beliefs and their perception of in-class and out-of-class learning.

Results

Data showed that students had different beliefs about their roles as language learners, depending on their personal learning biographies and experiences. Consequently, they revealed different degrees of willingness to engage in learning: a great majority of the participants (77 per cent) expressed the *desire* to take charge of their learning, fixing objectives, deciding materials, taking part in evaluation, and so on; however, a considerable number (49.8 per cent) declared a *current incapacity* for doing it, expecting teachers to decide everything and refusing to become more responsible for the process of their learning. It was evident that, despite teachers' affirmations that they did provide regular training in learning strategies, most of the students did not know what to do in difficult situations, revealing a lack of strategic competence.

As language learners must primarily be considered language *users* (Little 2007) not only within the classroom but also outside, it was crucial to understand the participants' use of the target language(s), how they exercised the knowledge acquired at school in their private life and how they brought their outside learning into the classroom. Most of the students (86 per cent) thought that the kind of language learned/used at school and that learned/used outside school were notably different, claiming that what they generally processed in their private life was not the language usually found in coursebooks. Additionally, some answers suggested that they were not completely aware of the opportunities available to them to use foreign languages: only 45 per cent reported using a foreign language frequently in their free time, but then 99 per cent admitted dealing with it every day, when using computers or listening to music. An analysis of teachers' answers revealed that even teachers were not well informed about their students' language habits and had some misconceptions about their pupils' use of foreign languages.

Conclusion

These findings call for a twofold intervention:

1 Students should be helped to develop a greater awareness as language learners and language users.
2 They should be provided with more opportunities to apply prior knowledge and out-of-class experiences in classroom learning, and vice versa.

Learning must be intellectually challenging and needs to be connected to students' daily reality where formal study and homework mix with songs, web chats, computer games and contacts with the surrounding multilingual and multicultural community. Today, more and more students are plurilingual before they come to school; this demands the implementation of a plurilingual curriculum, intended to valorise each student's repertoire, including his/her mother tongue as a point of reference for the building of a wider language system.

The other requirement regards synergy in knowledge: improving mutual cooperation not only among the language teachers but also among the entire teaching team will allow students to work on inter- and trans-disciplinary projects that facilitate connections among the different subjects learnt at school and between in-class and out-of-class learning.

Email: menegale@unive.it

References

Benson, P. 2001. *Teaching and Researching Autonomy in Language Learning*. Harlow: Longman/Pearson Education.

Jiménez Raya, M., T. Lamb and F. Vieira. 2007. *Pedagogy for Autonomy in Language Education in Europe—Towards a Framework for Learner and Teacher Development*. Dublin: Authentik.

Little, D. 2007. 'Language learner autonomy: some fundamental considerations revisited'. *Innovation in Language Learning and Teaching*, 1/1: 14–29.

9.5 Vision to village

Clare O'Donahue *British Council, Chennai, India*

Introduction

In a relatively short time significant changes have taken place in government primary schools in Tamil Nadu, South India. This paper describes how three organisations worked together to build on one man's vision in order to respond to the current demands for English by parents, teachers and children across the state.

From 2002 to 2007 a 'silent revolution' took place when MP Vijayakumar, Director of Sarva Shiksha Abhiyan (SSA), the Government of India's flagship programme for the Universalisation of Elementary Education, implemented activity-based learning (ABL) for children aged 5–9 years. ABL within Tamil Nadu is described as:

> selected practices of Montessori pedagogy for multi-grade and multi-level classrooms that has now been extended to 37,500 government and government-aided schools in the state. (Schoolscape 2009: 2)

The resulting change in primary school experience for children has been remarkable but such is the demand for English that many parents are making uninformed choices to remove their children from vernacular-medium government provision and send them instead to the growing number of private English-medium schools.

It was against this background that UNICEF, the SSA and the British Council's *Project English* set about developing English language teaching for children in government schools as they progressed through and beyond the ABL system. A large-scale cascade programme was realised, which would directly train 900 Master Trainers and 120,000 teachers, with the partners working together to identify critical success factors.

Success factors

Shared expectations

A needs analysis initiated stakeholder involvement and engagement. Everyone, from the State Director through to local teachers, children and administrators, was consulted, with their ideas being taken forward to ensure that needs were met. The three organisations agreed and clearly communicated that the overall aim would be to boost teachers' confidence in speaking English and introduce active-learning techniques, thereby increasing the children's opportunities for speaking English. This would be achieved in the local context and within the existing recently implemented English curriculum.

Engagement and ownership

A challenging aspect of educational change programmes is how to ensure teacher 'buy in', without which there is little hope of changing existing practice. A certain amount of adaptation needs to take place when existing beliefs and practice are being challenged. The teachers in Tamil Nadu had recently been through a 'sea change' with the introduction of ABL and, as those targeted for the English programme had already seen and heard their colleagues working in different ways with younger learners, they were eager to try out different methodologies themselves. During a monitoring visit to a remote school, one teacher enthused about the English training programme, describing in detail how the new ideas were being implemented in the classroom. When asked which cascade training he had attended, he replied, 'Unfortunately, I did not attend the training; I have learnt all this from my friends and colleagues who did!' Affirmation from peers within their own local community can only encourage ownership and acceptance.

Defined roles and responsibilities

During the initiation phase, roles were defined which took account of and recognised the knowledge and expertise of each partner. The SSA shared their project-planning strategies; similarly UNICEF shared their extensive knowledge of the participants and local education systems and advised accordingly. The British Council was able to provide top-quality, experienced trainers to start the cascade process and, through its reputation, was key in motivating participants and generating enthusiasm. Crucially, an atmosphere of reciprocal learning was established.

Ongoing monitoring and evaluation

State-wide monitoring and evaluation was conducted throughout the programme by all partners at all levels. Key findings were shared and consulted on with subsequent action agreed and, wherever possible, implemented immediately. Partners were responsive to local needs, being appropriately flexible in their approach.

Maintaining quality

Specific logistical arrangements were implemented to maintain quality and minimise risk. Relatively small batches of 40 participants were trained, and only one layer to the cascade reduced the risk of transmission loss. The Master Trainer programme was residential with venues undergoing a rigorous check. The participant selection process was transparent and fair and during delivery teachers and trainers were encouraged to work together to share knowledge and skills.

Conclusion

Initial monitoring has indicated that impact from the programme is already being seen and that consultation, communication and careful planning have been the key to success. The three partners have already begun working in another state and will continue the roll out to 25,000 teachers in Tamil Nadu.

Email: clareodonahue@in.britishcouncil.org

Reference

SchoolScape. 2009. *Activity Based Learning. Effectiveness of ABL under SSA. A report of the baseline and year end surveys.* (Retrieved 22 November 2010 from http://www.education forallindia.com/evaluation-of-activity-based-learning-of-tmail-nadu.pdf.)

9.6 Children with EAL: comparing withdrawal sessions with teachers and teaching assistants

Clare Wardman *York St John University, York, UK*

Introduction

Schools in the UK are now highly diverse in the terms of the nature of bilingual learners. In the UK, 'mainstreaming' has been the government education strategy for linguistic minority children since the Swann Report of 1985 and the Commission for Racial Equality in 1986 found that separate provision led to social division and was therefore considered to be tantamount to racial discrimination (Leung 2003). However, most primary school-aged children with English as an Additional Language (EAL) receive additional funded support in their education. This support is often offered through withdrawal from the mainstream classroom and is taught by either specialist EAL teachers funded by Ethnic Minority Achievement Grants or by teaching assistants.

The studies

The research design comprises two case studies set within this very diverse context of mainstream provision for English language learners (ELLs). Both studies use a variety of methods to collect data, including classroom observation and semi-structured interviews, and both adopt a qualitative approach to data analysis. The first seeks to uncover beliefs of teaching staff about 'ideal' practice in terms of classroom and small-group interaction, and the second compares the interactional opportunities for ELLs provided by specialist EAL teachers and teaching assistants during withdrawal sessions.

The findings

The participants were all confident that they would continue to offer the same approach to classroom interaction if they were able to live in the 'ideal' world; they all expressed the opinion that a balance between withdrawal sessions and whole-class interaction offered the best for the child and commented on the importance of developing cognitive ability alongside linguistic skills.

The National Association for Language Development in the Curriculum (NALDIC) has said that more EAL specialist teachers are required. Most of the individual support for ELLs seen during the studies came from TAs and, although their achievements are often remarkable, we can see from data in both studies, especially regarding questioning strategies, that teacher training does seem to lead to a more considered teaching approach. One class teacher expressed her concern about unqualified TA support, especially when they are involved in some level of bilingual work, and it is likely that her views are similar to those of other teachers in the schools.

This leads to the second study, which considered precisely those differences between teachers and teaching assistants where interaction with ELLs is concerned. It was found that in terms of session macro-structure, the specialist teachers built in sections to their sessions for personalisation and general conversation that were missing in the TAs' lessons. Initiation Response Feedback/Evaluation (Mehan 1979) scripts were more often incomplete in TAs' interactions and contained more extension of the feedback stage in teachers' classes. Additionally the nature of the questions asked in those IRF/E structures differed significantly, with the TAs asking significantly more closed display questions than the specialist language teachers, who were more likely to pose closed referential questions. It was also interesting to note that, whilst the TAs used no open referential questions at all in their sessions, the specialist teachers asked between 10 and 20 per cent of their questions in this way. The personalisation of learning that the teachers adopt is considered likely to increase engagement and achievement.

Implications and conclusion

It is heartening to see teaching staff feel that they have, to an extent, found the right balance of support for ELLs, in terms of the classroom/withdrawal split. This remains an area for further investigation, however, as some researchers have expressed concern over the teaching community embracing withdrawal as a standard provision without strong evidence (Franson 1999).

It is suggested, on the basis of this study, that local authorities and schools should reconsider any decision to save money by cutting the number of EAL specialist teachers working with ELLs and should provide more training opportunities for TAs and teachers.

The studies are limited in scope due to the sample size as well as the narrow focus. However, this paper offers a picture of the current EAL situation in some relatively typical schools, which may be of interest to practitioners and other researchers. Further areas for research include, but are not limited to, the impact of differentiation for ELLs in the context of success in a classroom where it is not practiced, the nature and success of bilingual support in the UK and the provision of training for EAL teaching staff.

Email: clarewardman@gmail.com

References

Franson, C. 1999. 'Mainstreaming learners of English as an Additional Language: the class teacher's perspective'. *Language, Culture and Curriculum* 12/1: 59–71.

Leung, C. 2003. 'Integrating school-aged ESL learners into the mainstream curriculum.' *Working Papers in Urban Language and Literacies, Paper 21.* London: King's College London.

Mehan, H. 1979. ' "What time is it, Denise?": asking known information questions in classroom discourse'. *Theory into Practice* 18/4: 285–94.

9.7 Promoting and assessing reading skills: the QAR method

Sanja Wagner *The English Academy Circle, Darmstadt, Germany*

In language classes a variety of texts are used as 'rich language input' from the very beginning. Every teacher relies upon the fact that once the pupils have learnt the alphabet and they know the vocabulary and grammar, then they can read and understand what they have read. However, reading for understanding is a much more complex process, involving different strategies which enable the reader to construct the meaning encoded in the text. These strategies include the following: activating prior knowledge; anticipating meaning; activating inferences and patterns; creating/referring to mental models; recognising difficulties; choosing a strategy according to the difficulty; and self-monitoring/checking comprehension.

In order to improve the learner's readings skills it is most important to make these invisible thinking processes visible. If we want our pupils to use strategies while reading, we must explicitly show them first what strategies there are and how to use them—in all subjects. One of the very effective and transparent ways of instruction in how to get the meaning out of the text is the Question-Answer-Relationship (QAR) method, developed by Taffy Raphael *et al.*

Teachers use questioning strategies to guide and monitor comprehension and to promote higher-level thinking in their students. However, many students often avoid answering questions, relying on the better ones who will do that for them. How to find the answer in the jungle of words, some of which they don't even understand? Through visualisation and modelling, the QAR strategy helps students locate information, analyse text for information, and determine when inference is required. It encourages learners to be more efficient and strategic readers.

Depending on where the reader finds the information he/she needs, the questions are divided into two primary-source QARs: 'In the book/text' or 'In my head/my knowledge'. These are again each divided into two core QARs: 'Right There' and 'Think and Search' or 'Author/Text and Me' and 'On My Own'. This is demonstrated in Figure 9.7.1.

RIGHT THERE I can find the answer in the text. I can point to it and write it down.	**THINK AND SEARCH** The answer is in the text but not in one place. I must look at different text parts / elements and combine the information. I must use my own words. 
AUTHOR/TEXT AND ME The answer is not given in the text. Part of the answer is in the text/graphic, but I must add to it what I already know about the topic. 	**ON MY OWN** I can find the answer from my own knowledge and experience. 

Figure 9.7.1: The QAR method

Using my own material, I showed how to introduce this strategy in a five-step instructional model, as shown in Figure 9.7.2:

Question·Answer·Relationship·¶

¶
Read each question very carefully and think about how to find the answer. You can find the information directly in the text, in one sentence or in different passages/parts of the text; or do you need your HEAD, that means your knowledge and experience to find the answer.¶
1.→Look at the KEY WORDS in the questions, look for them in the text and you will find the answer. If not use your HEAD.¶
2.→Underline the words or passages which give you the information for the answer. ¶
3.→Write the answer next to the question in the grid. In the last column you explain how you've found the answer. ¶
¶

Question·category¤	Question¤	Answer¤	How did I find the answer (possible answers)¤	¤
Right·there You can find the answer in one sentence in the text (one word or short phrase). Look for words used in the question. You can use the same words. ¢	¤	¤	¤	¤
Think·and·search¶ The answer is in the text, but not in one place. You must put together different pieces of information from the text. You must use your own words in the answer.¤	¤	¤	¤	¤
Text·and·you¶ The answer is not in the text. You must use your knowledge and combine it with the information from the text.¤	¤	¤	¤	¤
On·my·own¶ The answer is not in the text. You must use your own experiences and/or background knowledge. You must give your opinion or judgement.¤	¤	¤	¤	¢

¶

Figure 9.7.2: Materials for practice

- explicit explanation of the method; take a picture instead of a text;
- demonstration through *think aloud* how you look for and find the answer in a given text (modelling);
- guided practice (questions on the text with the help of cards and grids for self-reflection); pupils work in pairs;
- coaching, giving advice; pupils present their answers and the way they found them;
- independent application; pupils work on their own self-assessment and goal setting.

This strategy promotes different reading styles (skimming, scanning, close reading) and strategies and by meta-cognitive discourse ('How did I find the answer?') encourages higher-level thinking. It makes visible the invisible processes that occur while reading. Above all, it helps the teacher as well as the learner to monitor and to assess reading skills and strategies in a transparent way.

QAR is an effective strategy for improving reading comprehension at all levels. It proved very useful in mixed ability classes (age 14–16) at a state comprehensive school with a high percentage of migrant children. Using visuals and grids for self-reflection, a teacher guides and monitors the learners in a very simple and transparent way. It helps both the struggling learners and the advanced ones. Besides promoting higher-level thinking this strategy also encourages students to be active, strategic readers of texts.

Email: sanja-wagner@web.de

Reference

Raphael, T. E., K. Highfield and K. H. Au. 2006. *QAR Now. Question Answer Relationships (Theory and Practice)*. New York: Scholastic.

9.8 Key factors in learning and teaching English for young learners

Samuel Lefever *University of Iceland, Reykjavík, Iceland*

Introduction

This presentation looked at the reading and oral skills in English of Icelandic children. Children (aged 8–9) who had received no formal English instruction were tested for reading comprehension and oral production. The participants were Grade 3 pupils from five schools (n = 182). In the first part of the study the children were asked to complete a set of four reading comprehension tasks. These were based on an international test of English for young learners and intended for use after 100 hours of English instruction. The average percentage of correct answers was 49 per cent, and there was no significant gender difference. The results show that many eight-year-old children are beginning to build up some early literacy skills in English, such as an understanding of basic vocabulary and common phrases.

In the second part of the study a random sample of the participants (n = 51) took part in a test of oral production. The children were individually shown pictures of familiar scenes and were asked to describe them and answer questions in English. They were also asked to talk about their hobbies, families or other topics of interest. The test began with simple questions that could be answered non-verbally (by pointing) and progressed to more demanding, less structured tasks requiring more understanding and oral production. Their responses were recorded and then categorised into three levels of competence. Group 1 was the group with the least oral competence. At this level the children could understand simple instructions and questions in English but had difficulties in answering in English due to a lack of basic vocabulary. They tended to answer in Icelandic or non-verbally. About half of the participants (49 per cent) were categorised at this level.

A little more than one fourth of the participants (27 per cent) fell into the second level of competence. In group 2 the children could take part in a simple conversation with occasional prompting. They understood instructions and could answer questions in single words and short phrases. They had basic vocabulary in English but occasionally used Icelandic words. Language mistakes did not impede comprehension or communication.

The remaining quarter of the participants were categorised in group 3 (24 per cent). Here the children showed a surprising level of communicative competence. They could respond without hesitation and appropriately and did not code-switch. They had a better understanding of syntax and grammar and a wider vocabulary. Some of the children were eager to express themselves in English and could share stories about themselves.

A clear gender difference was exhibited in the oral production part of the study. The boys were equally distributed between the three levels of competence whereas 75 per cent of the girls were categorised in the group with the lowest competence—see Figure 9.8.1. More research is needed about possible reasons for this difference.

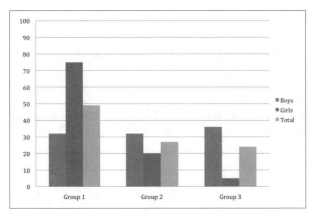

Figure 9.8.1: Percentage of students in each group

Discussion

The findings of the study show that many children in Iceland are not true beginners when they start learning English at school. Many of the children showed competence levels of A1–A2 on the Common European Framework grid. The results lend support to interactionist theories of language acquisition which view the communicative give-and-take of natural conversations with other speakers as being crucial for language learning (Long and Porter 1985, in Peregoy and Boyle 2008). Other important factors of language learning seen in the study were self-confidence and motivation to learn and use the language. Children's desire to use English for communication and their willingness to try to express themselves—negotiate meaning—are key ingredients in their English learning. Another key factor is ample access to English, both in and out of the classroom. Access provides children with opportunities to use English for their own purposes and expand their learning.

Implications

Several implications for teaching English to young learners can be drawn from the study. Teachers need to focus on communicative language teaching and provide rich opportunities for comprehensible input: lots of exposure to English by using it in instruction, reading or telling stories in English, using songs and games, etc. Children also need ample opportunity to produce English in the classroom. They learn English by using it, by participating in songs, games and trying to make themselves understood in communicative activities. It is important that classroom tasks are meaningful and encourage social interaction through pair and group work. In addition, it is important to keep children's motivation to learn English alive by building on what they already know.

Email: samuel@hi.is

Reference

Peregoy, S. and O. Boyle. 2008. *Reading, Writing and Learning in ESL* (5th edition). Boston: Pearson Education, Inc.

9.9 Jewish and Arab children communicate across linguistic borders

Maureen Rajuan *Achva Academic College of Education, Israel*
International House John Haycraft Classroom Exploration Scholarship Winner

Introduction

The research project was carried out by Jewish student teachers in an elementary Bedouin school under the supervision of their pedagogical advisor in the English Department of an Israeli teacher training college. The purpose of the project was as follows:

1 to promote intercultural understanding between Arab and Jewish children;
2 to change attitudes and stereotypes;
3 to teach and use English as a neutral language to bridge cultural differences; and
4 to involve student teachers in the research process.

The Israeli educational system is divided into two main sectors, the Jewish sector and the Arab sector; the medium of instruction is according to the native language, with Hebrew used in the Jewish schools and Arabic in the Arab and Bedouin schools. Both Jewish and Arab children are required to learn English according to the same curriculum of the Ministry of Education.

The emphasis on English as a neutral language common to both Bedouin and Jewish children, as well as the medium of instruction for the educational intervention by the Jewish student teachers, served to neutralise the issue of language as a cultural barrier (Abu Raas 2000; Doye 1999). English became the medium of communication between the Bedouin children and their Jewish student teachers, as well as a potential means of communication with Jewish children.

The psychological theory underlying the educational intervention of this project was based on the principles of Raviv *et al.* (1999):

1 Developmental factors form the basis for concept formation and it is, therefore, important that the concepts presented to young children be on a concrete level. Friendship, as the main theme of the educational intervention, was chosen as an age-appropriate concept for young learners.
2 External sources of information serve to enrich and change existing information and stereotypes. The educational intervention was based on presentation of materials designed to compare and contrast the Arab and Jewish cultures. Some examples include holidays, religious artefacts, traditional clothes, foods and customs, folk tales and legends representing both cultures.

Method

Procedure

Jewish student teachers designed a 'friendship unit' that was taught once per week in English only in two Bedouin sixth-grade classes. The research tools were administered in Arabic by the Bedouin English subject cooperating teacher; she also translated the children's responses into English.

Research tools

Two research tools, designed by the student teachers, were administered before and after the educational intervention:

1 A questionnaire relating to attitudes towards knowing about and being friends with Jewish people.
2 An open-ended free-association task asking the pupils to complete the sentences 'Arabs are ...' and 'Jews are ...' in order to investigate the children's attitudes and stereotypes towards the other.

Results

Stereotypes were shown to decrease to a significant degree on the free-association task. Cultural differences were frequent in the pre-test. Categories that were elicited from the data showed stereotypes, such as 'different religion', 'different language', animals ('dog', 'donkey' and 'pig'), 'immodest clothing' and others. These cultural differences decreased significantly and were replaced by neutral and positive statements in the post-test. Examples of these include 'friends', 'want to meet people' and 'want peace'. Results are summarised in Table 9.9.1.

	Before	After
1 Questionnaire	Bedouin children know very little about Jewish people and have met very few Jewish people, but are highly motivated to know more and meet more.	Bedouin children report that they know a lot more about Jewish people and feel that they know more Jewish people.
2 Free-association task	Stereotypes: negative – 57.0% neutral – 20.7% positive – 22.3%	Stereotypes: negative – 25.5% neutral – 17.5% positive – 57.0%

Table 9.9.1: Research findings

Discussion

Our research findings point to three major conclusions. The first is that stereotypes are variable and given to change, according to the newer social view, through educational interventions of a limited and focused nature. We have found that one effective strategy for the changing of stereotypes among young children is the strengthening of their own self-image. Another is the comparison of one's ethnic group with other 'out groups' of differing characteristics.

The second conclusion is that age-specific interventions are effective at the early stage of concrete concept formation. Children can relate to the concept of friendship in the context of their own lives when confronted by information and encounters with other ethnic groups.

The third conclusion is that learning English as a neutral language can bridge barriers related to cultural, religious and ethnic connotations of the native language. English, when taught as a language of communication, is perceived by children as a tool for connecting to the similarities they share with other children.

Email: msrajuan@mscc.huji.ac.il

References

Abu Raas, R. 2000. 'Learning strategies and second language learning'. *English Teacher's Journal.* English Inspectorate, Israel Ministry of Education 53: 68–74.

Doye, P. 1999. *The Intercultural Dimension: Foreign Language Education in the Primary School.* Berlin: Cornelsen Verlag.

Raviv, A., L. Oppenheimer and D. Bar-Tal (eds.). 1999. *How Children Understand War and Peace.* San Francisco: Jossey-Bass Publishers.

10 Teaching with technology

10.1 Teaching the mobile generation

Nicky Hockly *The Consultants-E, Barcelona, Spain*

Learners are coming to class increasingly wired up: iPods, mp3 players, mobile phones, digital cameras—many of our learners already use these devices in their daily lives. How can we get learners to use these devices to help them learn English? Can teachers easily start to integrate mobile learning into their teaching practice? If so, how? These are some the questions we set out to answer in the workshop.

But let's take a step back. What exactly is mobile or m-learning? Let's start with what it's *not*. Don't equate the words 'mobile learning' with 'mobile phone'. There is sometimes a misconception that mobile learning means SMS or text messaging. It doesn't. Simply put, mobile learning is learning that takes place via portable, WiFi enabled, handheld devices. This includes smartphones (like the iPhone), e-readers (like the Kindle or Sony e-reader), small laptop computers (also called 'netbooks'), the iTouch, and even gaming consoles such as the Nintendo! If it's small enough to put into your pocket or handbag, it can be classified as a handheld device and therefore suitable for mobile learning.

It's up to us, as teachers, to let our students know about the options and apps which are increasingly available to them—many of them for free—and which they can download and use for their own out-of-class, on-the-move learning. The use of handheld devices as a research tool can be integrated into the curriculum inside the classroom as well.

Teachers need to be aware of the wider issues involved in implementing mobile learning before they start. There are a number of questions that you as a teacher need to ask yourself from the outset, to ensure (1) that you know *why* you are implementing mobile learning and *what* you want to achieve, and (2) that you are clear about the choices you have to make. I imagine these issues as a series of clines or continuums. Each cline lends itself to a series of questions.

- **in the classroom ───────────────────────── on the move**
  Are you going to get your learners to use handheld devices regularly *in the classroom* (for example, to access dictionaries, to research on the web, to take polls …)? Or are you going to encourage your learners to use their own handheld devices *outside* the classroom for independent study (for example, to play games, to listen to podcasts, to learn vocabulary …)? Or both?
- **class sets ──────────────────────────── own devices**
  What handheld devices will your students use? And *whose* devices will they use? Will your institution invest in class sets (for example, of iTouches or netbooks), or will your learners need to use their own devices? Or both? What if only some learners have handheld devices, or if everyone has a different make of phone? What

kind of classroom-based work can you do if everyone has a different device and operating system?

- **rich content** ──────────────────────── **discrete content**
What about the content that will be used on the mobile devices? Is it going to be *rich* content that includes multi-media (images, audio, video), the chance to interact with others via social networking, and access to web resources? Or are you going to focus your learners on *discrete* content such as quizzes, polls, SMS, simple games, and apps? Or both?

- **push content** ──────────────────────── **pull content**
How is this mobile content going to reach learners? Are you going to 'push' content out to your learners? In other words, are you going to be responsible for sending mobile-friendly content to learners? Or are learners to 'pull' in content themselves? In other words, are they going to search for mobile-friendly content on their own, depending on their own interests and needs? Or both? And how does this fit into the clines above? Will you focus mainly on pushed content for learners' out of class work, and mainly on pulled content in the classroom? Or the other way round? Or a mixture of both, in both contexts?

- **strategic use** ──────────────────────── **discrete use**
Related to the previous cline, is your use of mobile learning overall going to be *strategic*, that is, learners use handheld devices as a resource and tool covering a wide range of functions, in every class? Or is your use of mobile learning going to be *discrete*, that is, learners use handheld devices every now and again, for 'one-off' activities? Or both? How about strategic use of class sets of handheld devices in the classroom, and discrete use as optional for out of class self-study work, for example?

Providing answers to these questions can, I hope, help teachers towards a more principled and structured implementation of m-learning with their learners. Starting with a discrete use of apps is one of the easiest ways of introducing m-learning to your learners, for example. See http://www.emoderationskills.com for more EFL-related m-learning advice and ideas.

Email: nicky.hockly@theconsultants-e.com

10.2 Breathing life into eLearning

Sharon Hartle *University of Verona, Italy*

Overview of the presentation

This presentation evolved into a snapshot of my experience with online teaching over the past decade at the University of Verona, Italy. It was included in the Interactive Language Fair, and as a result was not a traditional workshop, but was an interactive blended presentation, structured in three parts to reflect the type of work being presented. The blended presentation comprised the following components:

1 A 30-minute video

This was shown twice and is now available on YouTube in four parts (http://www.youtube.com/watch?v=L_O7x8G5YH0). It shows some of the ways that technology has been used in the form of separate blogs, wikis and forums in the past, and how these have now been brought together in a more systematic approach under the umbrella of the eLearning site on the University of Verona homepage. The final part of the videos takes a more in-depth look at some of the ways in which sites and materials on the VLE are actually used with learners.

An important point which is also made, however, is that VLEs are being under-exploited in some cases because some tutors use them as a materials deposit or a digital notice-board. Whilst this is a valid way of organising materials and notices, and while simply making materials available online for learners is useful, it has the unfortunate effect of encouraging these learners to think that this is the main aim of a VLE; this is rather like saying that the main aim of a laptop is to do word processing. VLEs can be used to do so much more.

2 A face-to-face session

In this part of the presentation, delegates were given a guided discovery questionnaire; the questions were designed to help them navigate the display of examples of materi-als, which was set up on my notice-board at the fair. The display included mainly learner work taken from our eLearning site and our wiki. This was very successful in that individuals had much more opportunity than they would in a 'traditional' presentation to interact with me and to discuss their own situations and experiences, as well as being able to choose what they wanted to look at.

3 A page of my Wikispaces site

This was prepared for delegates to see some of the work being done. Unfortunately this is not possible within the university eLearning site, which is protected by a password, but I often link the work being done on the university site to the wiki too. This site is available for all those who are interested at http://hartledistancelearning. wikispaces.com. (Go to the page entitled Harrogate IATEFL 2010.)

By looking at some of the work being done online, participants gain a much better idea of what these activities mean and how useful and motivating they are for learners, who can access them at any time they wish.

Some conclusions

Over the past decade my work has been transformed by the growing presence of technology in the university and the different opportunities available. What were once used as separate tools have become blended into a whole new approach where work done in the classroom then flows over the boundaries of the classroom walls and into learners' homes and onto their Personal Learning Networks (i.e. contacts that individuals develop through such forums as Twitter and use to share their work or insights with each other). The online space provides an area which becomes a real online social network for some learners, so that they use English as a means to com-municate much more naturally.

It is true that this type of approach involves labour-intensive dedication from the tutor, but the reward lies in seeing the way learners are motivated to spend hours on their English, too. Their level of English improves as they are encouraged to do more and more in a much more autonomous way. In the end they bring their own worlds, knowledge, likes and dislikes not only into the classroom but into the VLE as well, so that we are approaching an experience which is truly learner centred.

Email: sharon.hartle@univr.it

10.3 Setting up self-access through eLearning

Richard Pinner *engnet-education.com, London, UK*

Many large multinational language schools and universities have Virtual Learning Environments (VLEs) for their learners. Amongst the benefits of VLEs are increased access to course materials and information, as well as additional ways to communicate with tutors and peers. Many smaller institutions, which do not have the same resources as larger ones, may also wish to set up their own VLEs for students, but they may not know where to start.

The session was designed as a hands-on and practical workshop for teachers who wished to know exactly what was involved in setting up a self-access VLE. It discussed the cost involved, a comparison between commercial and open-source VLEs, the steps and procedures one might take in setting the site up, and a few golden rules, learned from experience, about what needs to be in place from the outset in order to save time in the long run.

Moodle was used as the main example because it is free and by far the easiest and most accessible option (Machado and Tao, 2007).

Getting started

Figure 10.3.1 shows the basic steps needed to set up a fully functioning Moodle VLE.

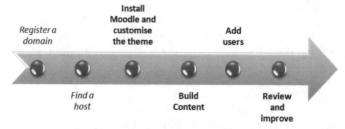

Figure 10.3.1: Setting up a Moodle VLE

The first two steps are in italics because if your institution already has a website, Moodle can be installed directly onto that. There are also companies that are Moodle Partners and that can offer hosting and design packages. The installation and theme (appearance) customisation require some specialist technical knowledge, but the other parts require only a limited proficiency with computers.

Time and money

A great deal of discussion about eLearning focuses on ideas and possibilities, but this talk was mainly aimed at practicalities. As such, time and money were big considerations. Commercial VLEs can cost tens of thousands of pounds; likewise, purchasing content packages can be too expensive for smaller independent institutions. A Moodle installation can be done for less than £50 if you do it yourself, but there are hosting packages and other costs that need to be considered. In terms of time, it takes about half a day to install a Moodle on an existing website, provided it has an SQL database and other features readily in place. Building the content, implementing and analysing it, however, takes a lot longer and will require teacher training and learner training; it is to be considered more of an ongoing process.

Creating content

The best way to get content is to give the teachers and their classes their own course within the Moodle and allow them to create their own content and upload documents and links which are related directly to what is going on in class. While grammar and vocabulary drills are often popular, more interactive content such as WebQuests, tasks and forums are more likely to promote authentic and lively discussion in my experience. (See Godwin-Jones 2004 for a good summary with some practical ideas.) It is also possible to use the VLE to provide links to other content such as RSS feeds. For example, the BBC's *Learning English* page has regularly updated news feeds which you can add to your site at no charge. One important thing to consider if creating content is having a naming convention and keeping everything in organised files.

Implementing

As mentioned earlier, a big part of the successful implementation of a VLE will be in training the users and creating an architecture which allows for all the users to quickly and easily navigate to their course areas. Because the expense of Moodle installations is reasonably low, it is recommended that time and money be invested in the users and the planning of the system. Try to approach it from all angles: How will the students, the teachers and the administrators experience the site? How can it be set up to be as user friendly as possible? When asking these questions, it helps to join the Moodle community (www.moodle.org) or speak to another institution that has already been through these steps. As Moodle is open-source, all this information is often readily and freely available.

Conclusion

With a little effort and time, any institution can set up a VLE for their students to use. Once in place there are many ways to expand the VLE, but giving teachers and students ownership is more likely to lead to successful organic growth through user input.

Email: richard.pinner@engnet-education.com

References

Godwin-Jones, R. 2004. 'Emerging technologies: language in action: from WebQuests to virtual realities'. *Language Learning and Technology* 8/3: 9–14. (Retrieved 24 January 2010 from http://llt.msu.edu/vol8num3/emerging/.)

Machado, M. and E. Tao. 2007. 'Blackboard vs. Moodle: comparing user experience of learning management systems'. *37th ASEE/IEEE Frontiers in Education Conference* October 10–13 2007, Milwaukee, WI. (Retrieved 28 March 2010 from http://fie-conference.org/fie2007/papers/1194.pdf.)

10.4 Using eXe Editor for developing course content for ESL learners

Kalyan Chattopadhyay *Bankim Sardar College, University of Calcutta, India*
Hornby Trust Scholar

Can teachers design and generate professional-looking learning resources in web-based courses without having proficiency in web-publishing tools like Dreamweaver or Frontpage? My answer is yes they can, with the use of eXe. eXe is an eLearning XHTML editor that allows educators to create content offline and present it to learners in a variety of formats. Pedagogical tips are provided, which help content creators to develop appropriate resources, and the programme allows for the regular updating of materials.

I demonstrated how I used eXe with teachers in my context to create a structure for a tertiary-level ESL course in India, and how I used it to develop teaching resources. I focused on how these resources were used with learners, how they were assessed, how the course content was modified and updated, and how the learners benefited from the use of such materials.

First, I outlined those institutional, tutors' and learners' requirements that prompted me to select eXe as a content-development tool. Among the major institutional concerns were the following: the need to generate content for online courses; the appeal of making that content available through various formats; the potential for reusability of the resources developed; the desire for minimum investment in staff training as well as computer hardware and software; and the provision of continuing support to content developers. From the tutors' perspective, they required a tool for content creation which had a structure and some useful and pedagogically sound devices; these needed to be interoperable with the VLE that the institution was currently using. Tutors also specified that the selected tool should be easy to use, that they wanted to develop course content in both an online and offline environment, and that they needed to be able to update the content. Finally, the learners' requirements included the ability to access the content in both online and offline modes, the availability of a variety of learning activities, and the provision of some self-assessment tools.

I demonstrated how learning resources and activities can be easily modified and updated in different formats using eXe. I also showed how teachers could collaborate to develop course content, by drawing on each other's content, publishing it as IMS- (Information Management System) or SCORM- (Sharable Content Object Reference Model) compliant content, and finally exporting it to any VLE. During the presentation, teachers realised that they did not need advanced web-publishing skills to operate eXe.

I faced a number of challenges while working with eXe, which I shared with the participants. First of all, I had to convince the institution that eXe is an effective and reliable content-authoring tool. Although administrators appreciated the low investment in hardware/software and staff-training to run eXe, they expressed concern about the lack of support available. I needed to demonstrate that that eXe does not

Figure 10.4.1: A course developed using eXe and uploaded to Moodle as a SCORM package.

require support from its creators, that its tools and interface can easily be customised to suit the institutional requirements, and that an in-house support mechanism can easily be established. The next challenge was to convince the tutors that they could handle the tool with minimum effort; I also needed to encourage them to work collaboratively on content generation. Other challenges included maintaining a schedule for content generation, making the content available to the learners in time, and ensuring that the content was always accessible. Finally, I shared some examples of materials (through screenshot and by accessing the VLE live) from a Business English course that I have produced using eXe—see Figure 10.4.1.

During the presentation teachers found the tool friendly enough to design, develop and present web-based materials or CD-ROM-based courses without prior knowledge of content-editing scripts. I believe that I was able to communicate the usefulness of eXe and to show teachers how to organise their own course content in a pedagogically and logically sound manner.

Email: profkalyan@gmail.com

10.5 Breaking down the classroom walls: web-based tasks with real outcomes

Ann Foreman *British Council, Bilbao, Spain*

How can we motivate our students to see learning English as not just another academic subject but as a communication tool that will be useful for them throughout their lives? My method for tackling the problem is to create tasks which are relevant to them and which produce tangible results.

Case study: presenting a recipe task

Here's a sample task I've used with a group of adult students. We had set up a class blog and identified pronunciation as an area they wanted to focus on—see http://tiny.cc/136in. First, the students studied a model. In pairs, they selected a recipe from Videojug (http://www.videojug.com/), a website that uses videos to give advice about how to do things and that contains hundreds of recipes. Each video includes a text version of the instructions. The students paid attention to sentence stress and intonation and made a note of any new vocabulary they felt was critical to their understanding of the recipe. We commented together on what language, intonation and word stress were used in the recipes and reviewed new vocabulary.

The students then changed partners and took turns to describe the recipe they'd looked at to their new partner, who hadn't seen it. Back in their original pairs, they decided on a recipe of their own to present.

With help from me, a volunteer from the group demonstrated how to use VoiceThread (http://voicethread.com/) to present their recipes. VoiceThread is a web resource which allows the user to create an online slideshow with a recorded commentary. I used the demonstration as an opportunity to highlight the language that students needed for the task for example, 'What about that photo?' 'No, not that one, this one', 'Scroll down a bit further' and 'It's my turn'. The students noted this language down; afterwards, they practised this process language in pairs via a little role play.

Working again in pairs, they found photos of the ingredients of their recipes on the internet, uploaded them to VoiceThread and recorded their recipes. Once completed, they embedded their VoiceThreads into post on their blog. I then spent time with each pair listening to their VoiceThreads and focusing on any problems they'd had. Finally, everybody discussed and commented on each other's recipes.

An example of the completed task can be found at http://tiny.cc/sbl9m.

Using a collaborative platform and employing scaffolding techniques

I always use a blog, or some other collaborative online platform, for task-based work. Setting one up is a combined effort between me and my students: they choose its title and layout and invite themselves to become members. This establishes from the outset their ownership of the blog and helps them to see it as a space where they can express themselves freely.

Putting tasks on the class blog takes the spotlight off me and gives me time to devote to individual students and make use of the scaffolding techniques that are so productive in language learning. I listen to or read with each student what they have produced, and by gauging where they're at, help them by hints and prompts to bridge the gap between what they have achieved and what they would like to achieve.

Task design

I try to design tasks that cover a content area that's wide enough for students to pick a particular aspect that interests them, that requires them to be creative, and that stretches them without overwhelming them. Challenging students to be inquiring and creative motivates them to think for themselves, collaborate with their classmates, reflect on what they know and need to know, structure their thoughts and, ultimately, find the language that suits the occasion.

Real results

It's really important that the platform for all this is the internet, an authentic communication channel, and that students are using their language skills to negotiate with the real world. When students publish their work on the internet, they experience real and tangible results from their efforts; by contributing to the body of information and knowledge that all of us have access to, they actively break through the confines of the classroom.

So, to come full turn to where we started with the sample task: from one who has had the opportunity to try out the recipes published by the students, the proof is in the pudding—and they are very tasty indeed!

Email: foreman@ydemas.com

10.6 Points to consider when using technology

Josefina C. Santana *Universidad Panamericana, Guadalajara, Mexico*

This paper will describe three projects that used technology in the classroom in an attempt to engage students more actively in learning English. The projects formed part of a larger study that explored how classroom interaction changes when technology is added to the mix. The three projects discussed here used wikis, podcasts, and Skype in diverse ways and with mixed results. The author concludes that it is not technology that makes a task more attractive, but rather the opportunity to interact meaningfully with others.

Introduction

English is a graduation requirement for students at many Mexican universities. Students in one university were not engaged in learning the language: they attended classes irregularly and did not participate actively. It was thought that adding a technological component to the classes would make these more interesting and engaging, and that this engagement would lead to enhanced learning. Thus, information and communication technologies (ICT) were incorporated into different classroom tasks.

ICT is an umbrella term that relates to any device that can digitally store, retrieve, transmit, receive and manipulate information; this includes mp3 players, personal computers, mobile phones, digital cameras, and such. The use of these devices is very common among young learners nowadays. The study hypothesised that adding ICT to the class would provide interest and make the class more engaging.

Context, participants and task

The study took place at a small, private university in western Mexico from June 2008 to May 2010. Participants were three groups of students and their teachers.

- Group 1 consisted of ten students who were taking a TOEIC exam preparation course in an intensive summer session. Their in-class project was to use technology to help them learn the vocabulary needed for the exam. The ten students were divided into two teams of five members each. Each team was given a list of 300 words or phrases with instructions to learn those words, to make sure their team-mates learned the words, and to make sure the other team also learned the words. Thus, at the end of the four weeks, each student would have learned 600 words. The students chose to use wikis for their projects.
- Group 2 involved 15 students at a B1 level and their course instructor. The students were divided into three teams of five students each. As a final integrating project, students were asked to select one of the topics from their course book and to develop a podcast based on that topic. They were to research the topic, write up the script for the podcast and produce it. The topics selected were a local legend, the history of an electronic device, and the history of a local product, specifically, tequila.
- Group 3 formed part of an external project. The university was approached by another university in the United States with an offer to form part of a language exchange via Skype. In this project, 15 intermediate learners of English in Mexico were matched with 15 intermediate learners of Spanish in the United States. The students would meet via Skype six times in the course of a semester to speak for 30 minutes in English and for 30 minutes in Spanish on a series of predefined topics.

All three groups were videotaped while working on their tasks in order to analyse their patterns of interaction.

Discussion

Groups 1 and 2 created well-designed wikis and podcasts, but they tended to divide the work among the individuals and to work alone. There was little interaction among them, and thus, little opportunity for language practice. There was no change in attendance patterns among participants in these groups compared to those in traditional classes, and the videotapes do not show evidence of added engagement among the participants; in fact, some students are shown napping in class.

On the other hand, videotapes of Group 3 show that students were actively engaged in speaking to peers in another country. Attendance on days that included the task was good, and students reported being interested in continuing the project into another semester.

Conclusion

Based on the analysis of student interactions and student reports, it can be concluded that adding technology for its own sake did not engage students; participants did not seem to value ICT *per se*, but rather, for the opportunities it provided for interaction with others.

Email: jsantana@up.edu.mx

10.7 Skills learning in computer-mediated intercultural collaboration: what ESP students say

Rachel Lindner *Munich University (Ludwig-Maximilians-Universität), Germany*
IATEFL Learning Technologies SIG Travel Scholarship Winner, and
Vida Zorko *Ljubljana University, Slovenia*

This article outlines the methodological rationale and design of a computer-mediated intercultural exchange between ESP students of Sociology at Munich and Ljubljana Universities. It also reports on research findings regarding students' perspectives on skills learning in this educational context.

Methodological rationale for the exchange

Today's students are expected to acquire discipline-specific and transferable competences for participation in a globalised society. In ESP, resulting changes to study needs have given rise to questions of methodology and content. E-literacies, for example, that build on 'old' study skills (for example, note-taking and text analysis) may help students navigate and assess English-language net resources. E-literacies are equally pertinent in an academic-literacies approach to ESP, which views learning as an acculturation into an academic community. Warschauer (2002), for example, suggests introducing computer-mediated communication (CMC) into the EAP classroom to help scaffold students' entry into the world of academic discourse. If we add an intercultural dimension—computer-mediated *intercultural* communication (CMIC)—we can temporally and geographically increase opportunities for the kind of interaction that students may encounter beyond the EAP/ESP classroom (Warschauer 1997). Drawing on Train (2006), communication between non-native speakers of English may more appropriately reflect English usage in academic and professional circles today, and as such should be considered in the design of computer-mediated intercultural exchange. This thinking was key to the design of the exchange described below.

Exchange design

Participants: Seven German and eleven Slovene ESP Sociology students took part in the exchange. Participants were non-native speakers of English with an approximate proficiency of B2+ and varying experience in computer-assisted language learning and CMC in academic contexts.

Tools: A wiki with integrated forum was chosen as the central online space for the exchange. Students were invited to use other web tools to support in-group collaboration, such as email or chat.

Scaffolding: The exchange process was scaffolded in phases, as shown in Table 10.7.1.

Task: Working in small, culturally diverse groups, students were asked to study, reflect on and debate a selection of audio-visual materials on the subject of society and communication in the age of Web 2.0, thus linking students' study subject with the concerns of telecollaboration. At the end of this phase, they were asked to summarise their discussions and present them in group presentation pages, using further film, visuals or text sources they had found to support their arguments.

Phases	Action
Pre-task phase	• familiarisation with the online environment • socialising • in-wiki discussion for raising awareness of CMIC issues
Task phase	• collaboration on study-relevant, scaffolded tasks in culturally diverse groups (using CMC tools of choice) • in-wiki presentation of group results
Post-task phase	• exchange reflection • peer–peer (wiki and class discussions) • teacher–group (written feedback on each group's process and product) • student–teacher (anonymous online survey) • teacher–teacher (comparison of feedback analysis)

Table 10.7.1: Phases of the exchange process

Findings

Feedback in the post-task phase fed into a qualitative focus group interview with German participants aimed at surfacing students' perceptions of skills learning in the exchange. Some key findings are summarised here.

Using the web and CMC tools in a subject-specific context

Some students had surprisingly little experience of using the web for studying; they reported gaining confidence in accessing and navigating the English pages of Sociology sites, improving study skills for navigating between online language aids and texts they were reading, viewing or writing, and the useful familiarisation with CMC tools for study contexts.

Reduced inhibitions in non-native speaker interaction

Students appreciated an English 'course' that involved developing English skills without overt language skills learning. The choice and relevance of the materials for their study field motivated students to cope with a large input of reading and audio-visual materials, to interact extensively and to work collaboratively on task output. Students said the common non-native speaker status reduced inhibitions in communicating, which in turn supported motivation and facilitated output.

Awareness of strategies for ELF communication

Students reported developing an awareness of strategies for lingua franca communication such as particular attention to their use of vocabulary and carefully checking meaning with each other to avoid misunderstandings.

Communicative competences for collaboration

Students were highly motivated to discover that they could collaborate effectively in culturally diverse online groups. Besides linguistic, computer-mediated and intercultural communicative competence, they were aware of needing and developing collaborative skills, such as organisation, negotiation and social skills for successful teamwork.

Becoming members of a community of practice

Students used the exchange for extensive comparison of their study cultures. Finding out about the sociological discourse beyond their familiar study sphere was understood to be a sociological competence, suggesting awareness of the importance of the wider academic community of which they intend to become a part.

Conclusion

The methodological rationale for the exchange was to a large extent confirmed by students' responses. This suggests a valid place for CMIC between non-native speakers in ESP for developing communicative competences that are relevant for students academically and professionally and for introducing students to a community of practice beyond the walls of the ESP classroom.

Email: rachel.lindner@onlinehome.de

vida.zorko@fdv.uni-lj.si

References

Train, R. 2006. 'A critical look at technologies and ideologies in internet-mediated intercultural foreign language education' in J. A. Belz and S. L. Thorne (eds.). *AAUSC 2005: Internet-mediated Foreign Language Education.* Boston, Mass.: Thomson Heinle and Heinle.

Warschauer, M. 1997. 'Computer-mediated collaborative learning: theory and practice'. *The Modern Language Journal* 81/4: 470–81.

Warschauer, M. 2002. 'Networking into academic discourse'. *Journal of English for Academic Purposes* 1/1: 45–58.

10.8 AVALON to Shakespeare: language learning and teaching in virtual worlds

Joe Pereira *British Council, Porto, Portugal*

Introduction

Current advances in technology and the impact of socio-constructivist learning principles in online education have made virtual worlds such as Second Life viable and accepted environments for learning. Here I will describe two projects I am involved in within Second Life, which in distinct ways provide opportunities for language learning.

Virtual worlds in education

A virtual world can be described as a 3D environment, accessed via a computer connected to the internet, where the user interacts with the environment and other users through an avatar—a 3D virtual representation of the user. Other inherent characteristics of these environments are that they are persistent (they continue to exist outside the user's direct interaction); they are scalable (they allow for hundreds of users from geographically dispersed areas to be in the same space simultaneously); and, unlike other computer-mediated communication tools, they allow for a very high level of social presence (the ability of participants in a community to project themselves socially and emotionally as 'real' people).

The use of virtual worlds for education has garnered a great deal of attention and research from many fields in the last few years. Language learning, in particular, is an area which can benefit from the affordances offered by this technology, namely from the communication tools, the socio-constructivist learning environment and the possibility of authentic communication with people from all over the world. The most popular social virtual world and the one with the largest educational community is Second Life, which is where the following two projects have taken place.

Language Learning Quests

In order to get teenage learners from around the world interested in the English-practice and community-building opportunities offered by Second Life, the British Council set upon building three islands which would contain replicas of famous British landmarks and cultural references, such as the London Eye, the Giant's Causeway and Shakespeare. These references were then integrated into digital game-based learning tasks which we called Language Learning Quests (LLQs).

These LLQs can be compared to adventure video games, such as *Myst*; they have a clear pedagogical focus but still incorporate many of the learning principles found in video games in their design. An in-depth explanation of the rationale behind their design and a case study can be found in Pereira (2009). This is an example of using Second Life for the autonomous learning of English as a by-product of engagement during play.

The AVALON project

The Access to Virtual and Action Learning ONline project is a two-year European-funded project which aims to create materials and guidelines for best practice in teaching in 3D virtual environments and to run a pilot teacher-training course in Second Life with language teachers. The materials and best practice guidelines were initially created during various language learning courses such as Business English, Italian and North-Sami, which were offered for free. The materials were then refined and improved during the teacher-training course which involved five experienced tutors and over 20 practising language teachers as students.

Lessons learned

As a way for young learners to have access to authentic language in a safe and engaging environment, the British Council's Second Life for Teens islands have been a success. Research on the Language Learning Quests has found that they are a fun and motivating way for young learners to practise their English autonomously. However, research has also found that learners expect more gaming elements to be implemented, and that the four skills need to be more evenly catered to in their design. The three islands are currently being transferred onto the Second Life main grid, and we can now expect adult users to take advantage of the LLQs for autonomous learning as well.

The AVALON project has been incredibly successful so far. A second iteration of the Business English course is being run and the teacher-training course received over

80 applicants and very positive feedback. It is expected that a future training course will be offered as a paid course and this may continue as interest grows. The project has also created an ever-growing community of educators who engage in discussion and host educational events in Second Life and other platforms. Access to the community and further information can be found at http://avalon-project.ning.com

Email: joep@theswanstation.com

Reference

Pereira, J. 2009. *Language Learning Quests in Second Life: A Framework for Blending Digital Game-based Learning and Virtual Worlds.* Unpublished Master's Dissertation, University of Manchester, Manchester, UK. (Retrieved 18 June 2010 from http://theswanstation.com.)

10.9 Before and after Twitter: Personal Learning Environments

Graham Stanley *British Council, Barcelona, Spain*

Overview

A Personal Learning Environment (PLE) is a flexible system that helps people take control of and manage their own learning. It consists of a number of different tools (blogs, wikis, social networks, etc.) that a teacher or learner chooses, around which he/she builds a group of people that can be turned to for knowledge, help, advice and support. This is the teacher's or learner's Personal Learning Network (PLN). There has been a considerable rise in the number of English language teachers using the microblogging service Twitter (www.twitter.com), which is an online social network where people express themselves through brief statements (called tweets) of no more than 140 characters. This tool has started to make it easier for teachers to manage their own learning and professional development, and to communicate with others in the process. There are fewer English learners using Twitter at the moment, but I believe teachers can help learners to help themselves through building their own PLE.

Teachers who tweet

In Malcolm Gladwell's book *The Tipping Point* (2000), the figure of 150 ('Dunbar's number') is given as representing the maximum number of individuals with whom a person can have a genuine social relationship. Gladwell says, 'putting it another way, it's the number of people you would not feel embarrassed about joining uninvited for a drink if you happened to bump into them in a bar' (page 179). Some people are now questioning whether this number is being changed by today's social media. The interesting thing about Twitter for teachers is that is brings people together who wouldn't normally ever meet online. Unlike previous specialist email groups and communities of practice, which are usually private and centre around groups of teachers with special interests or from specific countries or areas, the PLN that teachers build around the people they know on Twitter is public and more general; the monitoring of keywords (called 'hashtags' in Twitter because they are usually prefaced by #) means that through serendipity your PLN can include strangers who provide answers to questions and/or links to resources.

Appealing to teachers in my PLN before my talk, and asking them to describe changes they had experienced since Twitter, was illuminating. A wide range of responses were received; here is a selection:

- #beforetwitter I didn't know your whole life story, #aftertwitter I know where you live, what car you drive and the colour of your socks
- #beforetwitter I had a limited network, #aftertwitter I have access to my network's network
- #aftertwitter suddenly many opportunities have opened, resources are plenty
- #beforetwitter I used to go on the web, #aftertwitter the web is brought to me
- #beforetwitter my staffroom consisted of 15 teachers, #aftertwitter it has spread across the globe with 100s of colleagues
- with Twitter you get much quicker feedback, much more immediate than with blogging
- #beforetwitter cold, boring, stressful #aftertwitter warm, reassuring, engaging, energising, motivating, creative life
- #aftertwitter means having a constantly updated global resource and a motivated staffroom

What became clear from the many comments is that building a PLE with Twitter at the centre has given those teachers who have done so a very useful network of people they can turn to.

Students who tweet

Can the idea of using a PLN with Twitter at its centre be used to support language learning as well as teacher development? I decided to ask some of my young adult students if they wanted to use Twitter. Making it optional meant that only 10 per cent of them decided to do so. Since then, however, I have seen the number grow to 20 per cent. Apart from connecting to me and each other, they have found other people in their own networks who also use Twitter, and some of these are English speakers. How are they using the tool? Apart from tweeting in their own language, they are also using English. I have seen a number of them use Twitter in the following ways:

- to help each other with grammatical questions,
- to chat to each other in English in a light-hearted way,
- to chat to English-speaking friends and contacts,
- to ask me about information regarding English class and exams,
- to respond to some of the things that I have been tweeting about.

What conclusions can be drawn from this?

It's early days, but Twitter is being used for teacher development and this should continue to grow. Twitter also shows promise as a tool for informal learning with language learners.

Email: graham.stanley@britishcouncil.es

Reference

Gladwell, M. 2000. *The Tipping Point*. London: Abacus.

10.10 English as a lingua franca: creating and sharing an online introductory tutorial

Rachel Wicaksono *York St John University, York, UK*

English as a lingua franca (ELF)

English is a lingua franca when at least one person in a conversation is multilingual and the chosen language of communication is English. You are a potential ELF user if you speak English as an additional language or if you speak English (in any of its social, regional and national varieties) as your main language and you are talking to an additional language speaker.

Research into ELF has taken both a *systems* approach (comparing the grammar, vocabulary and pronunciation of ELF with other varieties of English) and a *strategies* approach (noticing how multilingual speakers monitor each other's talk and accommodate their grammar, vocabulary, pronunciation, rate of speaking, volume, gestures, eye contact and so on). You might assume that if you have grown up speaking English, ELF should be easy. In fact, monolingual 'native speakers' of English have often had less practice at monitoring and accommodating speakers of other languages than speakers who live in multilingual communities or who have put a lot of effort into learning an additional language (Smith 1983).

Many UK universities like to encourage students to work in mixed-nationality (and therefore often, though of course not always, multilingual) groups. In a previous study (Wicaksono 2008), I noticed how students cited 'communication problems' as a drawback of mixed-language groups. I started to think about how to internationalise student group talk but wanted to avoid offering advice to students about how best to communicate. The achievement of understanding is not context-free, and ways of communicating effectively depend on the task, the people talking and their situation. Instead, I decided to try to raise my students' awareness of how they actually talk to each other and the effects these ways of talking have on the group and their achievement of a task. Instead of 'ten top tips for effective communicators', I wanted my students to notice how ELF arises in specific contexts of use, sensitising them to the role played by their own communication strategies, attitudes and linguistic identities.

Creating the tutorial

I worked with four of my own students to create an awareness-raising activity, which we decided to call an 'introductory tutorial'. All four students recorded mixed-language classroom activities, transcribed short extracts from their recordings and spent many hours discussing their transcripts with each other.

Over about six months, we designed the activity which forms the basis of the tutorial. Students (we designed the activity so that it can be used with students from any discipline) do the activity in mixed-language groups, either in class, or as an independent group-study activity. The activity takes about four hours to complete and is made up of five stages: form a group; choose a recording device; make a recording of a discussion; transcribe part of the discussion; compare and discuss the transcriptions. We wanted the tutorial to be engaging, so we decided to include audio (extracts from the classroom talk) and video. We used Audacity to edit our sound files, Windows Movie Maker to edit our videos and Wimba Create to transform our materials into HTML (and create flashcards, internal and external links, etc.). We also wanted the tutorial to be accessible and so we made the further decision to publish it online.

Sharing our work

The resulting web pages, *Introducing English as a Lingua Franca: An online tutorial* are hosted by the York St John digital repository (http://www2.yorksj.ac.uk/ EnquiryCommons/elf/) and are available in three formats: online; customisable Word pages; and HTML for uploading as a learning module into a virtual learning environment. All formats are licensed under a Creative Commons license. This means that anyone may use the tutorial or any of its components in their own projects as long as they credit the source, their work is not for profit, and they share the outputs under the same license. Subsequent presentations of our work have resulted in ideas for an improved version of the tutorial, which we hope to release later this year.

Lessons learned

We hope that the tutorial contributes to the development of students as applied linguists, able to generate context-specific findings relevant to language use in their own situations. (For more on this 'bottom-up' approach to applied linguistics, see Hall, Smith and Wicaksono forthcoming.) Finally, we hope that by working through the tutorial, students will start to see the part played by language in the creation of roles, attitudes and linguistic identities, and subsequently in the ongoing internationalisation of UK universities.

Email: r.wicaksono@yorksj.ac.uk

References

Hall, C. J., P. H. Smith and R. Wicaksono. Forthcoming. *Mapping Applied Linguistics: A Guide for Students and Practitioners.* Abingdon: Routledge.

Smith, L. E. (ed.). 1983. *Readings in English as an International Language.* Oxford: Pergamon.

Wicaksono, R. 2008. 'Assessing mixed nationality and mixed ability group work' in R. Atfield and P. Kemp (eds.). *Enhancing the International Learning Experience in Business Management, Hospitality, Leisure, Sport and Tourism.* Newbury: Threshold Press.

10.11 Using audio tools, e-readers and virtual worlds in an online MA–TESOL and Applied Linguistics

Gabi Witthaus and **Alejandro Armellini** *Beyond Distance Research Alliance, University of Leicester, UK*

Introduction

This report discusses the integration of audio tools (podcasting and voice boards), Second Life and e-readers into curriculum delivery for an online MA–TESOL programme. The study is part of a two-year, JISC-funded research project called DUCKLING (www.le.ac.uk/beyonddistance/duckling/). The project was established in response to a number of challenges identified in the programme—primarily, the need for more peer interaction, greater variety in delivery approaches and technologies, and enhanced flexibility in curriculum delivery for students who tend to travel a lot.

Each of the DUCKLING technologies was piloted separately, starting in March 2009. Data from the interventions is still being gathered and analysed; preliminary findings are discussed below.

Audio tools: podcasts and voice boards

In addition to an extensive series of podcasts on phonology and phonetics, a suite of podcasts on World Englishes was produced to illustrate aspects of language variation, comprising commentaries by speakers of English representing 'inner circle', 'outer circle' and 'expanding circle' varieties (Kachru 1985), reflecting on their experience of using English. The evidence suggests that the impact of these podcasts has been extremely positive. Students encouraged the course team to consider ways of using audio more interactively, resulting in the subsequent voice board intervention.

Voice boards are similar to online discussion boards, with users also having the option to leave a recorded message. For this study, a series of 'e-tivities' was developed, following Salmon's (2002) five-stage model. Six volunteer students participated. The feedback was overwhelmingly positive, with students commenting that the audio added a human dimension to their studies and helped overcome the sense of isolation they felt as distance learners. A plan has now been put in place to roll out the e-tivities across all the modules.

Second Life (SL)

A series of e-tivities using SL, also following Salmon's (2002) model, was piloted for the optional CALL (Computer Assisted Language Learning) module. Six volunteers participated in this pilot, which ran over seven weeks. Optional SL training was provided in two short sessions at the University of Leicester's Media Zoo island in SL. Students then visited SL individually, in their own time, and observed EFL classes at an in-world language school (Languagelab.com, with whom we had an informal partnership), with the aim of considering the uses of virtual worlds for EFL teaching. The lesson observation protocol formed the basis of subsequent reflections by students via asynchronous discussion on the Blackboard discussion forum. Although students identified some drawbacks to the use of SL—mainly related to the technology demands of the platform—they highlighted a number of benefits of SL, such as the relaxed, sociable environment and the opportunities afforded for learners to speak to native speakers around the world. The CALL e-tivities are now available as an open educational resource for the use of other institutions and individuals. These e-tivities have also provided a transferable model for the use of SL as a flexible environment where no real-time meeting of the cohort is required. This model provides a significant departure from the typical approach in the literature of using SL as a synchronous meeting place for student cohorts (for example, Edwards *et al.* 2008).

E-readers

In order to make the programme delivery more suited to mobile learners, the in-house module materials for two pilot modules were delivered to students on an e-reader, the Sony PRS 505, as well as on Blackboard as usual. Unfortunately, journal articles and e-books could not be included on the readers (with the exception of one textbook from Routledge), as the major publishing houses with whom we negotiated were reluctant to consider new models for distribution. Eight students participated in the first pilot and nine in the second. Student responses to the initiative have been extremely positive. Apart from the obvious benefits of mobility, several students have described fundamental changes in their study habits resulting from the use of their e-readers, mainly because they can now access their reading materials for short periods during the day, whenever they have a little free time. Furthermore, many students indicated that they use their e-readers in conjunction with other technologies such as printed materials, netbooks and iPhones, demonstrating that multiple devices can co-exist for use in different contexts.

Conclusion

Although the pilots involved small numbers of volunteers, those who participated have remained committed and enthusiastic throughout each intervention, and the qualitative feedback gathered is indicative of the potential benefits that these technologies may have when used on a larger scale. Table 10.11.1 summarises the findings so far.

Technologies \ Challenges	Interaction with peers	Materials 'dry'	Variety in teaching approach	Mobility	Flexibility
Podcasting		■		■	■
Voice boards	■	■			■
Second Life		■		■	■
E-readers				■	

Figure 10.11.1: Learning technologies and the challenges they addressed

Email: gabi.witthaus@le.ac.uk

alejandro.armellini@le.ac.uk

References

Edwards, P., E. Dominguez and M. Rico. 2008. 'A second look at Second Life: virtual role-play as a motivational factor in higher education' in K. McFerrin *et al.* (eds.). *Proceedings of the Society for Information Technology and Teacher Education International Conference 2008.* Chesapeake, Va.: AACE.

Kachru, B. B. 1985. 'Standards, codification and sociolinguistic realism: The English language in the Outer Circle' in R. Quirk and H. G. Widdowson (eds.). *English in the World: Teaching and Learning the Language and Literatures.* Cambridge: Cambridge University Press.

Salmon, G. 2002. *E-tivities: The Key to On-Line Learning.* London and New York: Routledge.

11 Testing, feedback and evaulation

11.1 British Council Signature Event: English and development: the impact of testing on learning

Philida Schellekens *Freelance, London, UK* and
Melissa Cudmore *British Council, London, UK*

For a long time English language testing has been delivered predominantly 'top down': national governments and test designers have largely driven the testing agenda. However, there is growing awareness that teachers and test users are also key stakeholders who should have a say in how language skills are assessed. This is not least because tests often influence what is taught, the so-called washback effect, with at its most extreme end the notion that 'if it is not in the test, it is not taught'. This paper sets out some of the key considerations that affect testing, teaching and learning. You will also find reflected contributions made by the Signature Event participants, who came from countries such as Zimbabwe, Nigeria, China, France, Canada, Rwanda, Japan, Turkey, Cameroon, Congo, India, Ethiopia and the UK. And, to give a flavour of the sizes of test populations, we have also included snapshots of China and the UK.

Validity and relevance

Test design tends to focus on two major criteria: results must be valid, and the test must measure what it is supposed to measure. However, candidates, parents, universities and employers also want to know whether the test reflects what learners will need to do in real life. For example, employers prioritise speaking and listening skills as key to employability, yet these skills are still largely unassessed in many regions, for example, the African continent, China and India. The main reason often stated is that speaking is difficult to test reliably. However, another consideration is the classroom environment. As participants at the Signature Event pointed out, class sizes of over 40 students make it hard to teach and assess spoken language skills and many teachers are under-confident about their own oral skills in English and hence are hesitant to teach speaking and listening.

Equality of opportunity and fairness

Testing also needs to address the concepts of equality of opportunity and fairness in testing. In many countries we see major variation in opportunities to learn, access to resources and the quality of language teaching. This applies at national, regional and local levels. For example, a study by Rea-Dickins, Guoxing and Afitska focuses on the effect of teaching Zanzibari children in their L1 and L2, Kiswahili and English respectively. They comment on test fairness, social consequences and the effect of classroom language use on learner engagement and achievement in formal examinations: 'educational disadvantage prevails in the majority of classes conducted [in a] language that is not their mother-tongue' (2009: 206). Rubagumya questions whether English can help Africa become part of globalisation; or whether it will marginalise the majority of African people even further. He contends that 'learning English should not be at the expense of learning African languages, [...] nor of getting meaningful education' (2004: 141). The variation in access to language learning opportunities should prompt the testing and teaching community to do its utmost to achieve fairness of testing and achievement. It could be argued, for example, that locally devised tests, based on a sound understanding of local learning contexts, provide a fairer and more realistic test base than tests intended for the international market. We should include in this debate whether students learn most effectively in their own language or in an international language such as English.

Profile of China
- Population of 1.3 billion in 2008
- 27 million Chinese *university* students took English tests in 2008
- Major investment in teaching and testing English, with new initiatives monitored and improvements made over time
- Positive washback is an explicit government objective

Cheng and Curtis (2009)

Political, educational and historical context

A third consideration is that tests do not exist in a vacuum. We often find that a nation's political, educational and historical contexts underpin the role of exams in society. For example, in China tests have traditionally been seen as an instrument to select the cadre of civil servants. Students' career prospects are determined by English language exams throughout the educational system. Non-English majors need to pass the English test to get their diploma, regardless of whether they ever intend to use the language (Cheng and Curtis 2009). As one of the contributors to the Signature Event said, the role of English in China appears to be changing from a gate-keeping exam to English being used as a practical skill to communicate with the rest of the world.

Profile of the UK and its newcomers
- Population of 5m people (2001 Census)
- 3.5m residents born in countries where English is not the national language
- 924,000 Eastern Europeans registered to work in the UK (2004–2009)
- 11200 work permits awarded to people from outside the European Economic Area (2009)
- 30,000 people sought asylum in the UK, for example, from Iraq, Somalia, Afghanistan (2009)
- Of the 4m+ second language speakers in the UK, an estimated 33%–50% lack English to function in society and in work

Home Office (2009); Office for National Statistics (2001)

This change alone has implications for teaching and testing. Another example of the influence of the political and educational context is found in England and Wales where government departments categorise English language teaching for migrant and refugees as part of literacy for native English speakers. Even though their learning trajectories are very different, there is only one set of national standards for these two target groups. This has had a largely negative effect on learning and testing (Schellekens 2009). Thus a nation's educational and political history can have a marked impact on the language classroom.

Local versus global

Tests should not just suit the domestic market but, as students and employees become more mobile, national standard setting bodies may also need to anticipate the international dimension. For example, students who have learnt particular language skills, strategies and study skills which are valued in their native country may find that these are not seen as effective when they go abroad. Fox and Curtis report on this for Chinese students (Fox and Curtis 2009) but the same issue is likely to occur with transfers between other countries. This aspect could have major implications for the choice and design of tests. But should national governments and test designers adjust test content to the needs of possibly a small minority of students? And how should teachers respond when they are likely never to have experienced a different learning environment themselves?

Conclusion

The discussion at the Signature Event indicated that there is major interest in testing and its impact in the classroom. The issues raised also showed how complex testing is and how many variables potentially interact with each other. It was also interesting to see that not only developing countries struggle with the interaction between testing and teaching and learning. We see a similar situation in countries such as England and Wales.

The aspects raised in this paper indicate that testing and teaching should not stand on their own. It seems logical that the better the correlation between the needs of the learner, test design and classroom practice, the more relevant the test outcome will be. The Signature Event closed with a call for participants to contact the British Council with references to research on this topic and ideas for further research.

Email: philida@schellekens.co.uk

Melissa.Cudmore@britishcouncil.org

References

Cheng, L. and A. Curtis. 2009. 'The impact of English language assessment and the Chinese learner in China and beyond' in L. Cheng and A. Curtis (eds.). 2009. *English Language Assessment and the Chinese Learner*. New York and London: Routledge.

Fox, J. and A. Curtis. 2009. 'IELTS: International English Language Testing System' in L. Cheng and A. Curtis (eds.). *English Language Assessment and the Chinese Learner*. New York and London: Routledge.

Home Office. 2009. *Accession Monitoring Report May 2004 to March 2009*. London: Home Office UK Border Agency, DWP, HMRC, and Communities and Local Government.

Rea-Dickins, P., Y. Guoxing and O. Afitska. 2009. 'The consequences of examining through an unfamiliar language of instruction and its impact for school-age learners in sub-Saharan African school systems'. *Language Testing Matters, Studies in Language Testing* 31: 190–214.

Rubagumya, C. 2004. 'English in Africa and the emergence of Afro-Saxons: globalisation or marginalisation?' in M. Baynham, A. Deignan and G. White (eds.). *Applied Linguistics at the Interface*. London: BAAL and Equinox.

Schellekens, P. 2009. 'Cause and effect: the impact of the skills for life strategy on language assessment'. *Language Testing Matters, Studies in Language Testing* 31: 103–17.

11.2 Assessment practices and beliefs: strengthening assessment literacy in EFL teachers

Dawn Rogier *Zayed University, Abu Dhabi, United Arab Emirates*

The study

This presentation focused on research into the assessment knowledge and practices (assessment literacy) of intensive English programme (IEP) teachers. The goal of the study was to identify IEP teachers' beliefs about the importance of knowledge in various areas of assessment, their own perceived expertise in assessment, and their desire for future language assessment training.

It has been estimated that teachers spend as much as 50 per cent of their time in assessment-related activities (Stiggins 1991) and that appropriate and effective assessment is a necessary and important part of teaching. When instruction and assessment work together, student achievement increases. Given the role of assessment as an integral part of the teaching and learning process, it is surprising to find that pre-service and in-service teachers often don't have the necessary skills to properly administer effective assessment in the classroom. Past research indicates a lack of general effective assessment education and little supervision of assessment activities of teachers once they are in the classroom.

Much of the past research has looked at assessment literacy in regard to elementary- and secondary-school teachers in the USA. This presentation discussed the results of a small-scale research project looking specifically at IEP instructors in a tertiary programme in the United Arab Emirates. Participants completed an online survey designed to indicate their beliefs about their knowledge of assessment, the purpose of assessment, the use of various assessment methods and the perceived need for further training.

Results

The research indicated that these particular IEP teachers are no different from teachers studied in past research. Most (54.4 per cent) felt that their formal education had not provided the skills necessary for assessing student performance, and 70 per cent indicated that they had never received any training on test development. Teachers indicated that their professional knowledge of assessment was gained 'on the job' through trial and error and in discussion with colleagues. The majority of teachers (76 per cent) also expressed a desire for more professional development in testing and assessment. The area of statistics and measurement was ranked as the least important area for teachers to have expertise, while 100 per cent of the participants felt that expertise in the ability to use a broad variety of assessments measures to assess students was important.

Discussion

Based on comments about how English-language teachers come by their assessment knowledge, there needs to be sustained professional development to achieve assessment literacy. It is also important to help teachers to use the information from assessment to adjust teaching practices, to provide evidence of student performance and to guide the curriculum review process. Assessment in language teaching should not be thought of as just a series of tests to measure student learning. The information from assessment should not only provide feedback to students, but should be used as a means for teachers and programme administrators to review instructional practices and curricular objectives. This is an area that needs attention as more than 38 per cent of instructors in my study indicated a low ability to use assessment results to identify strengths and weaknesses in teaching. As Brookhart points out, in order for teachers to 'own the goal of high-quality assessment, they must be convinced that assessment is just as important to student learning as [...] effective classroom management or lesson design' (2001: 10).

It is equally important that programme administrators determine the role assessment plays in the classroom. Research indicates that 'teacher professional development is more effective when it is school embedded, cooperative and sustained over time [...] organized within and/or across schools and focuses on improving practice over time through the sharing of knowledge, experience and expertise' (O'Leary 2008: 112). Without the support of programme administrators it is difficult for teachers to find the time necessary to create assessments that are integrated with classroom instruction, to review and evaluate these assessments, and discuss them with their colleagues. Also, financial support and recognition of time spent on professional development is needed. If programme administrators do not see assessment as an integral part of the teaching experience, or if they think that the instructors are already proficient, assessment-related professional development will be neglected. Problems will occur when assessment is taken out of the hands of teachers—or *seen to be* taken out of the hands of teachers. Without the expectation that teachers are responsible for assessment, it will likely get pushed aside due to the teachers' many other job responsibilities. We then de-skill the teachers and do not allow them the experience necessary to develop assessment literacy.

Email: Dawn.Rogier@zu.ac.ae

References

Brookhart, S. M. 2001. 'The standards and classroom assessment research'. Paper presented at the Annual Meeting of the American Association of Colleges for Teacher Education. (Retrieved on 20 November 2010 from http://www.eric.ed.gov as document ED 451 189.)

O'Leary, M. 2008. 'Towards an agenda for professional development in assessment'. *Journal of In-service Education* 34/1: 109–14.

Stiggins, R. J. 1991. 'Relevant classroom assessment training for teachers'. *Educational Measurement: Issues and Practice* 10/1: 7–12.

11.3 Teaching and testing: bridging the gap

Melanie Shaul *Tichon Hadera, Bet-Eliezar and Oranim Academic College of Education, Israel*
Trinity College London Language Examinations Scholarship Winner

Introduction

When using summative assessment, it is vital that students' prior knowledge be taken into consideration. When students' past experiences are brought into contact with their present and future, students interact with their culturally based background knowledge (Vygotsky 1978, 1986) and academic change is facilitated. Through testing, students' earlier conceptions re-emerge as a new cognitive skill resulting from their ability to reorganise material in their own words via background knowledge. Testing should facilitate the link between prior experience and classroom learning, through intervention based on appropriate strategies.

The study

In order to examine the effects of using a Vygotsky–Sternberg assessment plan on students' achievement, research was conducted with 22 junior-high, at-risk EFL students in Israel. Tests were designed to assess reading and writing proficiency. Students were given three tests; these included both questions based on formal knowledge learned in the classroom and questions which combined classroom knowledge and the students' own background knowledge. Upon completion of the three tests, questionnaires were administered and follow-up interviews were conducted with the class.

Findings

Testing targeted what students were able to do alone while involved in inner dialogue with themselves. As testing progressed, students began to develop and comprehend tasks that were at first difficult for them; they processed questions and acted on them through their own personal thinking style so that thoughts and actions were organised, coherent, and suitable. In other words, learning advancement stemmed from informal knowledge coming from experiences outside the classroom as well as explicit formal knowledge taught in educational institutions (Sternberg, 2007).

When tested using the Vygotsky–Sternberg assessment plan, students showed a marked improvement from test 1 (69), to test 2 (85) and test 3 (92). These elevated grades on all three tests suggest that the Vygotsky–Sternberg assessment plan may have a cumulative beneficial effect on students' achievement. Furthermore, students demonstrated a dramatic step-like increase throughout the testing process, thus revealing the benefits of an assessment plan which includes both learned classroom material and students' personal knowledge. For example, students were asked to explain and give examples from the text to the following questions: 'If you were the speaker in the poem, would you marry again?' One student whose parents were divorced answered: 'Yes, I would marry again because not all the guys are like the speaker's husband from the poem. The poem talks about bad things like *'bombs'*. We, the women, need to show the bad guys that we deserve more. We deserve the good guys.' In another question, students were asked: 'Is it ever justifiable for someone to commit suicide?' A student whose best friend had recently committed suicide answered: 'Yes, because we can't stop them. The speaker in the poem '*only wanted to lie with her hands turned up and be totally empty*' like my friend.'

Students' responses to the questionnaire yielded similarly positive results. It was found that 100 per cent of the students enjoyed taking a test that employed the use of their background knowledge, 90 per cent stated that they felt as if they were thinking in a different way, and 70 per cent felt better in their testing because they could explain their answers. When asked to reflect on how they felt about the test questions based only on classroom material compared with questions which combined both classroom material and their own knowledge, most of the students stated that the combination of formal and informal knowledge caused them to think differently: 'The answer came from my brain and I had to think and not copy from the text.' Many of the students stated the questions which were based only on classroom material did not induce thinking: 'I didn't need to think because the answers were in the text.'

Conclusion

This research showed that students' exposure to a Vygotsky–Sternberg assessment plan can lead to higher academic achievement. Furthermore, the exposure to an alternative assessment plan showed students that they were thinking differently while answering test questions that were socially and culturally rooted. Further studies, with larger samples, controlled for language proficiency are needed to enable further generalisations for the results found in the current study. Nevertheless, based on the results from the tests and students' feedback on the questionnaire, it can be assumed that a specific testing method which employs background knowledge can aid in advancement of students' proficiency.

Email: ymontn@hotmail.com

References

Sternberg, R. J. 2007. 'Culture, instruction, and assessment'. *Comparative Education* 43/1: 5–22.

Vygotsky, L.S. 1978. *Mind in Society*. Cambridge, Mass.: Harvard University Press.

Vygotsky, L.S. 1986. *Thought and Language*. Cambridge, Mass.: MIT Press

11.4 Determining ELF intelligibility through authentic assessment

Maria Parker *Duke University, Durham, North Carolina, USA* and
Brenda P. Imber *University of Michigan, Ann Arbor, Michigan, USA*

This session focused on the following topics:

- understanding the complexity and challenge of determining English as a lingua franca (ELF) intelligibility; and
- addressing that challenge pragmatically by exploiting the teaching of paraphrasing.

Participants first engaged in an informal intelligibility rating task and then reviewed a task illustrating a variety of features that can be taught within paraphrasing. They ended by viewing a context-based rubric and intelligibility rating scale that serve as authentic assessment tools for a variety of discourse and pronunciation features.

We began with the most straightforward and generally agreed-on definition of ELF: the English spoken between/among speakers who do *not* share a common first language. Following our introduction, participants engaged in a task illustrating the complexity and challenges of setting intelligibility standards. They carried out the following tasks:

- watched a five-minute video conversation between three ELF speakers,
- rated the speakers on a 1–3 scale (1: easiest to understand; 3: hardest to understand),
- discussed their individual ratings in small groups,
- reported on the differences among their ratings.

The resulting lack of agreement supported our position based on Levis' (2006) perspective that assessing intelligibility is indeed an elusive target.

Having illustrated the difficulty of finding a quantifiable standard, we turned to the pressing questions confronting ELF teachers:

- how to determine course curricula and objectives,
- where to look for pedagogical guidance to help us develop materials to meet ELF course and learner goals.

Despite the importance of pronunciation (a handout of Jenkins' Lingua Franca Core featuring a reduced sound inventory was made available), time constraints required that we focus on the most productive resource for materials and instruction, namely the prominence of paraphrasing in ELF discourse. The literature on ELF reveals that speakers tend to restate more than native speakers; this is not surprising considering that ELF speakers have no common language, no shared cultural references, no shared connotations, differences in denotation, and a variety of NS models to pattern after

So, having found agreement rather than complexities, we examined the transcripts of the speakers in the intelligibility rating exercise. At one point, one of the speakers says, 'I f- I, I find that people eat up words, like they, they, they, they speak like one sentence in one word or something like that'. The speaker is indeed attempting a paraphrase of 'eat up words', allowing us to assess his proficiency level and provide optional phrases. Further exploration of his transcript revealed additional features that we could include in the task-based rubric as set out in Table 11.4.1; this provides an authentic assessment tool to measure what the student is doing in various areas, and to rate his current proficiency level in those areas.

Task-based rubrics such as this are easily adaptable authentic assessment tools that realistically reflect instructional objectives, and they provide students as well as instructors with descriptive, quantifiable, and formative perspectives on the current degree of proficiency. Prior to the conclusion, participants also viewed an example of an intelligibility rating index that could be created as an authentic assessment tool (copy available on request).

Feature	Number or level
Paraphrase attempts *'eat up'* = *'they speak like one sentence in one word'*	1
Discourse strategies 'I find that …' the 2nd *like* *'or something like that'*	3
Verbal stratagems/formulaic expressions *'I find that …'* *'something like that'*	2
False starts 'I f- I, I find …' *'they, they, they speak …'*	2
Lexical register, for example, degree of formality as appropriate to the situation/context	3

1	2	3	4	5
Most informal		X		most formal

Feature	Number or level
Word stress correlates to intended meaning	4

1	2	3	4	5
No correlation			X	high correlation

Feature	Number or level
Grammar usage: accurate/inaccurate? use of *like* to signal the paraphrase	Accurate
Specific pronunciation features for example, speed, linking, pausing, pitch, intonation (using spectrograms created with Praat software to count number of student deviations from model)	

Table 11.4.1: Assessing reformulation

A major take-away from this session was increased awareness that ELF may be a temporary label serving as a place holder while we develop methods and materials for training teachers and instructing students. The session concluded with our assertion that we need Seidlhofer's EFL corpus work (see The Vienna–Oxford International Corpus of English (VOICE) at http://www.univie.ac.at/voice) and our agreement with linguists such as Maley, and Rajagopalan, who point out firstly that the pedagogical future of teaching NNS should be curricula and objectives driven by the learners' needs, and secondly that our common pedagogic goal is to help our students acquire forms and features of English that enable communication between them right now.

Email: mgparker@duke.edu <br> prousimb@umich.edu

References

Levis, J. 2006. *Guidelines for Promoting Intelligibility.* jlevis.public.iastate.edu/intelligibility.ppt

Maley, A. 2008. 'Review of A. Kirkpatrick. *World Englishes: Implications for International Communication and English Language Teaching* and R. Rudby and M. Saraceni (eds.). *English in the World: Global Rules, Global Roles'. ELT Journal* 62/2: 205–9.

Rajagopalan, K. 2008. 'Review of *English as a Lingua Franca: Attitudes and Identity.* J. Jenkins'. *ELT Journal* 62/2: 209–11.

11.5 Evaluating oral performance in teaching

Jody Skinner *Universität Koblenz, Germany*

Evaluating oral performance can be challenging, especially if language, presentation skills and content all count. I've devised an evaluation sheet that helps teachers provide feedback by using clearly defined criteria.

Reasons for detailed evaluations

For many years I'd simply presented my evaluations of student-taught lessons in key words and very general categories, hurriedly scribbled on a sheet of paper. Student feedback was limited to this handwritten sheet and to a brief discussion after the lesson. My tried-and-true method Learning through Teaching (Lernen durch Lehren, or LdL) with teams made up of three to five student-teachers in university seminars of circa 30 students encouraged student participation even without the carrot of receiving a grade at the end of the course—most courses weren't graded in pre-Bologna Germany. But the new modularised degrees necessitate far more formal grades, and so I began experimenting with a new detailed course grading system. Over a period of three years I tinkered with the system and used helpful student feedback. My goal was to come up with a way of combining all aspects of student-teaching performance in the classroom into one grade: oral language skills, didactic and presentation techniques, and content—with the proper emphasis on content since the seminars I teach in Anglo-American Studies are CLIL courses.

Evaluation procedure

My procedure for using evaluation sheets (see Figure 11.5.1) for oral assessment puts me in the back corner of the room, as far out of sight of all students and of the student-teachers at the front as possible, while still giving me a good view of what's going on. I keyboard in my comments during the student-taught lessons; the layout of the evaluation sheet makes it easy for me to do this quickly. I meet with the group immediately afterwards to discuss how the lesson went. During this private meeting in one part of the room with the student-teachers, the other students note what they've learned during the lesson for use in the detailed reviews they will write later about the lesson they've just experienced. I make my finalised evaluation sheet accessible to the student-teachers along with a collated anonymous version of the reviews of their fellow students. Thus all student-teachers have a written evaluation from me and from

EVALUATION SHEET TEMPLATE

Names of students for team teaching: Topic of student-taught lessons (date)

teamwork Honors, Pass, Fail homework Honors, Pass, Fail	media / props blackboard, OHP, video, audio, posters, PowerPoint, computer, internet, flip chart, maps, timeline, live sources, flags, food, …	teaching techniques lecturing, teacher talk with questions, guided group work, guided pair work, learning stations, guided discussions, role play, …	student participation passive listeners, note taking, answered questions, asked questions, reading aloud, group work, pair work, learning stations, active discussion, role play, individual / group presentations, reading comprehension, …
	highlights content	highlights didactics	
	problems content	problems didactics	

lexis / grammar / pronunciation [ŋ θ ð ʒ dʒ ʃ ʧ æ ə ʌ ɔ ʊ] / spelling examples

student names, evaluations	pronunciation + emunciation/fluency + lexis/accuracy = language				audience awareness + media use + interaction/eloquence = presentation				audience relevance + critical choice + personal touch = content *G// */3			
general comments // intonation + v/w & voicing + th/ths + vowels + linking =	pronun- ciation	emunciation / fluency	lexis / accuracy	grade	awareness	media use	interaction / eloquence	grade	Art relevance	audience	personal touch	grade
	√—	√—	√—	HPF	√—	√—	√—	HPF	√—	√—	√—	HPF
	√—	√—	√—	HPF	√—	√—	√—	HPF	√—	√—	√—	HPF
	√—	√—	√—	HPF	√—	√—	√—	HPF	√—	√—	√—	HPF
	√—	√—	√—	HPF	√—	√—	√—	HPF	√—	√—	√—	HPF
	√—	√—	√—	HPF	√—	√—	√—	HPF	√—	√—	√—	HPF

+ = excellent, √ = acceptable, — = problems, blank = no evidence; wf = weighted multiplication factor; H (honors) = 2 points, P (pass) = 1 point, F (poor or fail) = 0 points

+ = excellent, √ = acceptable, — = problems, blank = no evidence; wf = weighted multiplication factor; H (honors) = 4 points, P+ (strong pass) = 3 points, P (pass) = 2 points, P– (weak pass) = 1 point, F (poor or fail) = 0 points

Please let me know if you think I missed some important positive aspects of your lesson in this evaluation!

Figure 11.5.1: Evaluation sheet template
(See http://userpages.uni-koblenz.de/~jody/cv/harrogate.pdf for more details.)

their fellow students of their language and didactic skills as well as of the content of their lesson.

Evaluation sheets

While the evaluation sheet I've devised might look dauntingly complicated at first glance, the many boxes and categories allow me to keyboard my responses in quickly. I use two grading scales depending on the type of assignment. The symbols + (excellent), √ (good), and – or blank (poor, failure) are used to indicate achievement in the various aspects, which add up to grades of Honors, Pass, and Fail in the various criteria. Content is given a weighted factor to indicate importance. The students gain grades for language, presentation skills and content, and earn points towards a complete course grade.

My real reason for using such evaluation sheets ...

While on the surface I'm providing detailed feedback on concrete aspects involved in grading oral presentations, my real reason for the evaluation sheets is subversive: provoking students into thinking about the purpose of grading in general and about my system in particular. Some students don't know how exactly to challenge general grades or are too much in awe of teacher authority to do so. My very detailed analysis gives them the chance to see my individual assessment of all aspects more easily. By providing the entire group of team teachers with the evaluation of each individual student, I also encourage students to compare my assessments and test *my* fairness. Thus my grading should encourage them to think more critically. While I use modern technology for my evaluation sheet, my true purpose is based on ideals much older. The philosopher Kant famously defined enlightenment more than 200 years ago as our way out of self-induced immaturity not produced by a lack of understanding, but by a fear of thinking for ourselves. Kant's (1799/2010) command was 'Sapere aude: Dare to know!' My evaluation sheet encourages students to: 'Dare to question your teacher!' And daring to question the teacher can be enlightening—for both students and teachers.

Email: jody@uni-koblenz.de

Reference

Kant, I. 2010 (originally published 1799). *An Answer to the Question: What Is Enlightenment?* London: Penguin Books.

11.6 Insights from a collaborative error-correction policy

Zoë Graham *A Plus English Ltd* and **Tim Graham** *Sheffield Hallam University, Sheffield, UK*

This paper explores key aspects of a commonly agreed-upon error correction policy, implemented in a UK-based private language school some three years ago. As the policy has matured and established itself, we felt the time was right to reflect on the ideas and reactions of both teachers and learners involved.

The policy arose from a British Council inspection reporting unsystematic error correction by the school's teachers. Flowing from this, the school instituted some in-house workshops focusing on error correction. An agreed-upon and commonly practised error-correction policy was drawn up by the teachers. The policy was originally implemented in December 2006 and regularly reviewed. The most recent modification came in January 2010: the addition of a common written error code complementing the existing spoken English code.

In brief, the spoken errors policy comprised 'before the lesson' decisions as to what would be corrected; overt correction during what might be termed the secure practice/study phase; and a short reflection after free practice/activation based on any errors noted. The target language itself was the major recipient of remodelling, or recasting of spoken output, with a clear view to targeting anything compromising communication or task completion. At the latest review in February 2010 we gathered 34 questionnaires from learners responding to this policy, and seven from teachers.

Learner responses

In response to questions about how frequently teachers corrected mistakes, 23 learners responded with 'enough'; six thought 'too much' and five 'insufficient'; this was a similar result to previous findings. With regard to awareness of correction taking place the vast majority signalled positively (31) with only three unsure. A final question showed a difference between responses in 2006 and then those in 2010. When asked to respond to the statement 'The teachers all correct my mistakes in the same way', student responses from 2006 showed that 67 per cent of students answered 'yes' while 33 per cent answered 'no'. However, in 2010, 41 per cent answered 'yes' and 59 per cent 'no'. There would now seem to be more diversification in error-response strategy.

Teacher responses

When asked about grounds for error correction, teachers gave a variety of responses: a slight preference for wrong word selection was followed, in order, by grammar, communicative breakdown and, jointly, pronunciation and register.

When invited to say whether they corrected errors systematically, teachers' responses were mixed; most were neutral with two agreeing, one disagreeing. There is a slight shift towards systematisation compared with earlier pre-policy findings, when most disagreed, but given the focus of the policy this outcome is mildly surprising.

In other areas we detected some clear and significant shifts in response between 2006 and 2010. When asked to comment on the sentence 'My approach to error correction is linked to a particular theory', teachers responded as shown in Table 11.6.1, indicating that theory is now playing a key role:

	2006	2010
Strongly disagree	20%	—
Disagree	20%	—
Neutral	40%	43%
Agree	20%	43%
Strongly agree	—	14%

Table 11.6.1: The extent to which teachers are influenced by theory in error correction

When presented with the statement 'I vary the techniques I use for error correction', teachers responded as shown in Table 11.6.2.

	2006	2010
Strongly disagree	20%	—
Disagree	20%	14%
Neutral	60%	43%
Agree	—	43%
Strongly agree	—	—

Table 11.6.2: The extent to which teachers vary their error-correction techniques

Again we see a significant move. We believe this category chimes with feedback from learners reported above. Teachers are being intentionally more varied in their approaches to error correction.

In terms of when teachers corrected errors in stages of the lesson, we are unsure of the significance of the shifts demonstrated here. There seems to be a tendency to frontload correction as compared with before (3.2 as against 1.8 in terms of frequency on a Likert scale of 5 for the introductory stage of the lesson). Similarly back-loading of correction increased (3.7 as against 2.6). This is an area worthy of further exploration.

Where popularity of technique was concerned, encouraging self correction came first, followed by recasts and then hot cards (colour-coded cards prompting learners to identify the category of their error).

Finally, we offer a reflection by a teacher involved in the project which we feel aptly summarises the dilemma and challenge for teachers in this area:

> It is necessary to be aware of and clarify students' expectations of error correction. The danger is that at one extreme you will demotivate unconfident students or you will not meet your students' expectations of being corrected.

In conclusion we suggest that for the teachers involved, the theoretical underpinning of error correction has increased and the variety of technique used has widened; however, further exploration of systematicity of correction is warranted.

Email: z.graham@aplusenglish.co.uk
t.graham@shu.ac.uk

11.7 Symposium on responding to writing

Convenor: Nagwa Kassabgy *The American University in Cairo, Egypt* with
Yasmine Salah El Din *The American University in Cairo, Egypt*
Veena Bhambhani *Mahavir Senior Model School, Delhi, India* and
Phyllis Wachob *The American University in Cairo, Egypt*

Although feedback has long been considered an essential part of the writing process, the research findings have not quite shown how teachers can make full use of its potential for writing development (Hyland and Hyland 2006). The speakers in this symposium reported on the findings of their action research in four different contexts, focusing on teacher and learner perceptions and preferences and on different feedback techniques in responding to writing.

Yasmine Salah El Din reported on a study which compared how native versus non-native speaking teachers respond to academic writing. Responding to students' written work is a tedious task for most teachers; it consumes the largest proportion of teachers' time, often without teachers knowing in any definitive way what effects their comments have in helping their students become better writers. That is why writing teachers often seek better ways to do their job more professionally. One effective way to achieve that goal is to find out how other teachers perform the task. Accordingly, comparing how native and non-native speaking teachers respond to students' writing could raise teachers' awareness of the commonly employed correction patterns each group use, with a view to improving inter-rater reliability and response strategies.

In this study, three EFL native and three non-native speaking teachers marked the same five essays written by students enrolled in a pre-freshman EAP programme. Based on a rubric, they read and graded the content, organisation and language use of each essay. Teachers made written comments as they saw necessary. Despite the similarities found between native and non-native speaking teachers in overall scores and the general use of a correction code, there were several differences in the types of errors each group focused on. While native speakers gave more attention to global errors, i.e. content and organisation, non-native speakers focused more on local errors, i.e. grammar and vocabulary. Results also indicated that the differences were more individual than based on L1 background. The researcher concluded that each group of teachers has points of strength that both teachers and students need to be aware of for more effective teaching to take place. More research needs to be conducted on different language backgrounds in order to reach more conclusive results.

Veena Bhambhani then reported on her action research study which investigated the gap in her perception as a teacher-researcher and her students' perception of what writing means, what the process of writing involves, and what review or revision of writing means. Belief in the process approach to writing made her give both written and oral feedback between drafts, and her feedback focused on meaning-making. On the other hand, her students, who considered writing a tool for transmitting or conveying knowledge, took up piecemeal revision necessitated by the teacher's comments. As a result, students continued to report difficulties in the areas for which no direct feedback was given. They continued to consider writing a problematic area in language learning, even though the teacher observed a definite and gradual improvement in coherence and clarity in the students' work. Even in the syntax, there was improvement in all cases, including in the work of the least skilled writers.

She then presented the implications of her study. Firstly, she contended that there is a need to fulfill students' affective needs and reduce their anxiety, to give them a sense of control over their learning, and to encourage them to become independent thinkers and writers. Secondly, she emphasised that students need to be made aware of specific difficulties they face in the writing process. This awareness empowers learners and helps them find better solutions to difficulties. Thirdly, making students aware of the recursive process of writing is essential. This awareness and experience of going through the recursive process creates the need to question or reflect on various ideas in the process of writing. Subsequently, it can enhance reflection and critical thinking. Following these implications, Veena suggested using tools, such as questionnaires, observations, journal writing, letters to the teacher, etc., that provide valuable data on students' perceived needs, and that can feed into a teacher's instructional strategies as well as make the students aware of their difficulties.

Nagwa Kassabgy's discussion focused on an action research study which compared the effectiveness of providing learner-preferred versus teacher-preferred corrective feedback (CF) on learner uptake and repair. Research has suggested that 'students be given a range of options by their teachers and that written CF be tailored to their preferences' (Ferris 2002: 37). Accordingly, this study investigated both the immediate and the delayed effect of providing learner-preferred CF versus teacher-preferred CF, focusing on one linguistic category, namely relative clauses, a structure which poses problems for native speakers of Arabic. Subjects were 32 EFL/EAP undergraduate students, 16 in the learner-preferred CF group (Group 1) and 16 in the teacher-preferred CF group (Group 2). Students were exposed to three different CF mechanisms: explicit direct; implicit indirect coded; and implicit indirect un-coded feedback; they were then asked to respond to a questionnaire that investigated the type they preferred. Both groups' use of relative clauses in Essay 1 was analysed and errors were categorised. Subsequently, Group 1 were provided with their stated preferred CF on Essays 2 and 3. Group 2 were provided with teacher-preferred CF, (implicit indirect coded and requiring greater cognitive effort). Subjects rewrote each essay based on the CF provided. Errors in Essay 4 were then analysed to determine the immediate effect, and errors in Essay 8 were analysed for the delayed effects.

Results showed significant gains in the acquisition of relative clauses for both groups, indicating that form-focused feedback does enhance acquisition. Moreover, although no significant difference was found between both groups on the immediate test, there was a significant effect on the delayed test. This suggested that although providing the learners with their preferred type of form-focused feedback seems 'challenging and cumbersome for teachers' (Ferris 2002: 37), it did have an effect on their acquisition of relative clauses.

Phyllis Wachob then reported on her study which investigated the writing feedback process using audio files instead of traditional written feedback, which helps in giving more extensive and affective feedback. The presentation described a research project with MA students who received audio (mp3) files from their instructor instead of written notes or comments on a soft copy. Previous research has shown that students in general respond very positively towards this type of feedback in both regular classrooms (Sipple 2007) and in distance learning venues (Ice *et al.* 2007). Data included: (a) student reactions to the new style of feedback; (b) comparison of number of words, positive comments, negative comments and neutral questions and/or invitations for rewrite in the written versus audio feedback; and (c) interviews with three students regarding their attitudes and how they 'read' the audio files.

Student reaction was positive and they overwhelmingly preferred the audio files. The most frequent comment was how personal the feedback was. The instructor used personal details to tailor the audio feedback and emphasis was more on positive than negative feedback than in written feedback. Also, instead of giving mostly positive or negative feedback, the researcher found that she frequently asked questions that gave cues to what the students could include in a second draft. The interviews revealed that the students who preferred audio feedback both listened and took notes on their own copies of the essay and used that to rewrite. The one student who preferred written feedback listened only and made no notes.

Implications for teachers are that they should try audio feedback as students seem to prefer it, that students may need training on how to 'read' and interpret audio files, and that teachers should ask students their preference and give them what they want as in Kassabgy's study. More research is needed on student preference, how students 'read' audio files, and how audio feedback helps students achieve. An obvious advantage of creating audio files is saving time as it is easier to make a short recording than to type or write on paper. This gives teachers more time to make more and better comments.

In conclusion, for feedback to be effective, L2 writers need to actively engage with it, and one way to enhance active engagement is to consider their preferences and perceptions. Our findings contribute to the research investigating how teachers can evaluate their practices in responding to writing and provide feedback that will feed forward.

Email: nagwa@aucegypt.edu
yasmine@aucegypt.edu
veena.bhambhani@gmail.com
pwachob@aucegypt.edu

References

Ferris, D. 2002. *Treatment of Error in Second Language Writing*. Ann Arbor: University of Michigan Press.

Hyland, K. and F. Hyland. 2006. 'Feedback on second language students' writing'. *Language Teaching* 39: 83–101.

Ice, P., R. Curtis, P. Phillips and J. Wells. 2007. 'Using asynchronous audio feedback to enhance teaching presence and students' sense of community'. *Journal of Asynchronous Learning Networks* 11/2: 2–25.

Sipple, S. 2007. 'Ideas in practice: developmental writers' attitudes toward audio and written feedback'. *Journal of Developmental Education* 30/3: 22–31.

11.8 Student-centred feedback

Jane Nolan and **Elizabeth Poynter** *Leeds Metropolitan University, Leeds, UK*

Giving feedback to students on their writing is a crucial role for (EAP) teachers seeking to support both the language development and the motivation of their students. However, our experience at Leeds Met is that students do not always take in or respond effectively to detailed teacher feedback. Indeed, research suggests that even rich, high-quality feedback may not be easily interpreted by students (Hyland and Hyland 2006). Feedback needs to be part of an ongoing dialogue between teachers and students, supporting students in taking responsibility for evaluating and improving their own performance (Nicol and Macfarlane-Dick 2006). This workshop built on a research project which had taken place over the previous two years to investigate the use of a range of feedback mechanisms in helping to actively engage students and support them in improving their writing. Two main feedback approaches were used. While written feedback was used to comment on students' weekly academic writing tasks, audio feedback was used for students' progress on extended research projects and more general academic skills.

Written feedback

Regular written feedback took two main forms. Firstly, errors were highlighted with a correction code on the students' scripts and sentences from these scripts containing typical errors were then made into a worksheet which students worked on in pairs in the following class. This was intended to help students process the input they received and notice discrepancies between their own work and the patterns they were aiming to achieve (Hyland and Hyland 2006). Each student also received comments on the accuracy, range, content and structure of his/her work with three specific suggestions for improvement. After four assignments, students performed an in-class analysis of their own strengths and weaknesses using a table provided by the tutor, and thereafter students were encouraged to determine their own three focus points for each assignment. It was hoped that this 'scaffolded' approach, which offered considerable support to students in identifying their strengths and weaknesses, would aid them in becoming more effective independent learners, and the results on this are encouraging so far. Samples of the worksheets and feedback sheets used were handed out at the workshop for the participants to discuss and offer 'feedback' on (see below).

Audio feedback

Audio feedback potentially helps to overcome some of the barriers students experience in understanding and taking action on feedback, as speech can be considered a richer and warmer medium than written language. Research on the 'affective' aspect of feedback shows that it can influence how positive or negative students feel; it can also influence student response (Hyland and Hyland 2006). Another advantage of audio for staff was the possibility of giving a substantial amount of feedback to a student in a shorter time than it might take to write it. The mp3 files could also be sent to the students either by email or uploaded through the VLE.

Feedback from students who received both formative and summative feedback in audio form was almost unanimously positive. All students found the mp3 files easy to access and use, and all listened to the files more than once, the majority making notes from the comments and claiming to use them to improve their drafts. It seems that for a number of students, audio feedback, which would generally be expressed in simpler language than written feedback, seems to better enable students to make sense of and interpret the feedback, and seems possibly also to motivate them to act on it. Other research (for example, Sipple 2007) has also highlighted how personal and affective factors are stronger in audio feedback, increasing students' perceptions of their motivation, self confidence and a more personal student–teacher relationship. For this reason the workshop gave participants the opportunity to plan, record and play back an audio file (while giving us feedback on the worksheets and feedback sheets used in our research), allowing them to get some idea of the process involved and how it might be incorporated into their own feedback processes.

Conclusion

Hopefully, the workshop will have stimulated participants to reflect on the feedback mechanisms they use and given them the confidence to try out new ones. Overall, a range of feedback mechanisms may be important to help all students to improve, but in particular, mechanisms that actively engage and motivate students may be most successful in supporting them in judging and improving their achievement in writing.

Email: j.nolan@leedsmet.ac.uk

e.poynter@leedsmet.ac.uk

References

Hyland, K. and F. Hyland. 2006. 'Feedback on second language students' writing'. *Language Teaching* 39: 83–101.

Nicol, D. and D. Macfarlane-Dick. 2006. 'Formative assessment and self-regulated learning: a model and seven principles of good feedback practice'. *Studies in Higher Education* 31/2: 199–218.

Sipple, S. 2007. 'Ideas in practice: developmental writers' attitudes toward audio and written Feedback'. *Journal of Developmental Education* 30/3: 22–31.

11.9 Anonymous peer review online: can it stimulate autonomous learning?

Tilly Harrison *University of Warwick, Coventry, UK*

The inspiration for my talk at IATEFL Harrogate 2010 came from seeing a presentation by Christian Schunn at the EATAW (European Association for Teaching Academic Writing) conference at Coventry University in July 2009. He showed the SWoRD (Scaffolded Writing and Reviewing in the Discipline) website for writing development. The free online system automatically redistributes students' uploaded drafts so that each student receives a small number to peer review; his/her own paper is also peer-reviewed. What I liked about this idea was that it is completely anonymous: students do not know who is reviewing their paper nor whose paper they are reviewing since all students take a pseudonym on registration.

The advantages of peer review

I immediately felt that this technique would work well with my Chinese undergraduate students at the University of Warwick. I had tried peer review of writing in groups, but they were reluctant to participate and preferred teacher feedback, even though they rarely acted on it. Nevertheless I had discovered that when asked to give written feedback on each other's oral presentations they often gave thoughtful, constructive comments and so were not averse to peer feedback *per se*. I guessed that the 'safety' of anonymity might overcome the problems of peer reviewing of writing. I also speculated that the stimulus of reading other students' work and having their own work critiqued might push them to seek to solve their language problems more actively, and thus become more autonomous. This was my ultimate goal—creating a 'hunger to improve' in relatively unmotivated students.

I could also see other advantages in the peer-review process. Not least of these would be the fact that it allowed larger classes to gain a lot more chances for feedback on their writing than I as the teacher could hope to give them. The act of reviewing itself would hopefully become a learning process. Best of all, it seems that multiple peer feedback is just as reliable, valid and helpful as teacher feedback (Cho *et al.* 2006). I did not plan to go so far as to use the peer-review marks as part of the official assessment, but the website is set up to allow that.

Measuring autonomy

Holec (1981) characterised autonomy as the ability to take charge of one's learning. In order to test my hypothesis about the project increasing this ability, I needed a way to measure it. Luckily I could use a tool developed by David Dixon at the University of Warwick as part of his PhD research: an Online Measure of Autonomous Language Learning or OMALL (Dixon 2009). This is an online questionnaire that is easy to administer. I asked the students to take it in November 2009 and March 2010 after the project ended. Interestingly the OMALL showed lower overall results in the second test. Since the OMALL is a self-report this possibly captures a loss of confidence rather than a lack of autonomy. A more explicit questionnaire showed that many students had indeed both benefited from the project and found a stimulus to language learning. Some student comments were:

- Yes, in the past, when I finished my writing, I would not check it but now I will check my writing after finish my writing.
- Yes. When I review others' essays, it is easy to find their grammar mistakes that I also make but without consciousness. I can improve my writing by reviewing others' essays and learning from other's mistakes.

The SWoRD website

In my talk I showed how the website works, and we looked at some of the results so far—see Figure 11.9.1.

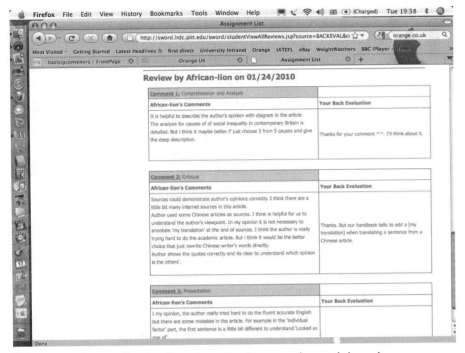

Figure 11.9.1: Example of a review given by one student and the reply comments

All the 32 students had uploaded their work and there had been a high level of peer-review comment. This decreased on the second draft but even on the third draft at least a third of the students were actively commenting and giving suggestions (with each draft they are randomly sent a different set of papers to review). The main complaint was that some students either did not review or did not take it seriously enough, even though all students had followed the website's review-writing training. Unfortunately anonymity allows lazy students to hide unless the teacher (who knows their identities) chases them up. However this is not an insurmountable problem and for the benefits gained I will certainly be using this site again.

Email: Tilly.Harrison@warwick.ac.uk

References

Cho, K., C. D. Schunn and R. Wilson. 2006. 'Validity and reliability of scaffolded peer assessment of writing from instructor and student perspectives'. *Journal of Educational Psychology*, 98/4: 891–901.

Dixon, D. 2009. *Language Learner Autonomy in Tertiary-Level Learners of English*. Draft of unpublished PhD thesis, University of Warwick.

Holec, H. 1981. *Autonomy and Foreign Language Learning*. Oxford: Pergamon.

12 Stories for all ages

12.1 Symposium on using narrative in ELT

Convenor: **Brian Tomlinson** *Leeds Metropolitan University, Leeds, UK* with
Hitomi Masuhara *Leeds Metropolitan University, Leeds, UK*
Jaya Mukundan *University Putra, Malaysia*
Ivor Timmis *Leeds Metropolitan University, Leeds, UK* and
Alan Maley *Leeds Metropolitan University, Leeds, UK*

Brian Tomlinson claimed we do almost everything through narrative except learn English from EFL coursebooks. He then demonstrated the value of narrative in providing rich and engaging exposure to the language, as well as opportunities for creative expression. Brian demonstrated the following uses of narrative:

Task-free activities

The teacher starts a lesson by telling a story. There are no questions or tasks, just exposure to language in use. At the end of the lesson learners can take a copy of the story for their folder. Sometimes they ask questions about it days later and they re-visit it and deepen their understanding.

Text-driven approach

The teacher uses an engaging narrative text to drive a lesson. She devises activities which do the following:

- activate the learners' minds in relation to the topic of the text,
- give the learners something to think about whilst experiencing the text,
- help the learners to develop and articulate their personal response to the text,
- encourage the learners to create a development from the text, and
- return the learners to the text to make discoveries to help them to improve their own text.

The creative use of English

Circle Story: The learners experience the beginning of a story. They then sit in a circle and continue the story one sentence at a time. One group retells their story and the teacher writes it on the board. The class suggest improvements and the teacher writes them on the board. The learners copy the story and complete it for homework.

Novel: The learners are told to visualise their area and an interesting person they know there. They are encouraged to see this person doing something interesting and to write this down as the beginning of their novel. Brian reported doing this with a low-level class in Vanuatu and after 30 lessons they had each written a 50–60-page novel. They asked each other and Brian for help, they gained self-esteem and they learned a lot of English too.

Hitomi Masuhara argued that all students have stories to tell if only they are encouraged to express themselves in various ways and are given the kinds of support they need at the times they need it. Hitomi firstly pointed out that L2 learners' difficulties derive from various gaps, including those between their mental maturity and language ability and also those between their aspiration and actual achievement. She then showed that the solutions offered by recent coursebooks seem to consist of linguistic simplification of unengaging texts and language practice, with very few free speaking or writing activities at all (Masuhara *et al.* 2008). She argued that the typical PPP approach (Present, Practice, Produce and be Punished for making errors) fails to address L2 learners' problems in self-expression.

Hitomi proposed an alternative approach, namely EEEE (i.e. Engage, Express, Enjoy and be Empowered). In EEEE approaches the learners are firstly given rich and varied exposure to language in use in an engaging manner. They are then enticed to express themselves so they can share and appreciate the fruits of their creativity for their enjoyment. She demonstrated some examples of creative writing (including Photo Haiku) that seem to help L2 learners reduce frustrations and start enjoying expressing themselves. She also explained how accuracy can be encouraged without spoiling the joy of self-expression through self- and peer-correction, through awareness activities and through learning from authentic texts. Hitomi discussed the principles behind her examples so that teachers and materials writers could apply them to the classroom or to materials development.

Jaya Mukundan said that two things are obvious when he visits classrooms for observations: lessons are usually teacher-centred, and the textbook is the most commonly used teaching material. Textbooks have never really helped with language learning, and their negative aspects (Mukundan 2009) seem to have influenced teachers more than the positive.

One reason why textbooks rarely help with learner language development is that learners rarely have to contribute to their own learning, which means they don't invest in their own learning. Jaya suggests that for learning to be successful, teachers need to show learners that materials that help them learn a language are often found within their own lives.

Jaya presented a small study (Mukundan 2009) that shows that free, non-textbook material like the use of learners' photographs can bring about a lot more discussion amongst learners than a textbook unit that features unreal, textbook families. Apart from photographs from home, he has also got learners to use technology like video camcorders to work on special group projects like Malaysian festivals (there is one almost every month!) and has got them to do final presentations in class (his students appreciated this more than reading the unit on Malaysian festivals, which featured only the most common ones celebrated by the main races). Jaya's learners created their own stories from their own materials when they invested in their own learning.

Ivor Timmis' take on narrative is that teachers' stories provide a very promising site for exploring aspects of spoken language with our learners. One of the challenges of developing materials for spoken language is that many typical features are found in the most mundane conversations. Ivor argued that using our own stories provides motivational value (Davies 2002) and also allows the teacher to explain cultural references in the story, which can sometimes be problematic in spoken-language material. A further benefit is that spoken-language features in teachers' language are less likely to be dismissed as slang or deviant forms.

Ivor recorded colleagues' anecdotes and showed that these are replete with features of potential use to learners, though ultimately it is learners and teachers who decide which features are of value to them. He also produced a provisional framework which can help teachers to analyse such material. In terms of methodology, he suggested that teachers can follow typical procedures for dealing with listening tasks, but they can add language-noticing tasks. The main principle of the tasks he proposed is that they focus learners on the difference between their expectations of spoken language and the reality of spoken language. An added benefit of these tasks is that they function both as intensive listening tasks and language awareness tasks. He argued that we should accept that learners will choose whether their priority lies with listening or language. In sum, when it comes to spoken language, frequent light showers are better than occasional heavy thunderstorms.

Finally, **Alan Maley**'s presentation suggested that classes not only be exposed to stories but that the class itself should be regarded as a texture of narratives. Further, classes with a richer narrative texture will be better learning communities.

After detailing the centrality of story to our lives and to our learning, and setting out the benefits to be had from a richly-storied approach, Alan went on to discuss what Wajnryb (2003) has termed a 'storied class'. He suggested that a storied class might be created in a number of ways:

- making story-telling a regular part of every lesson (this is echoed in Brian Tomlinson's proposal that every class be started with a story or poem, without commentary);
- encouraging the class to record its own unfolding story, through a class journal, website or blog—including the visual records, poems, songs, etc. arising from it;
- celebrating the class story (ethnic memory); this would involve the re-visiting of key incidents in the class story and encouraging learners to talk about the way their learning community is evolving;
- encouraging the exchange of stories from the world outside the class: from the press, TV, family, friends, self;
- encouraging the writing of stories (and 'publishing' them); the impact of creative writing on both students and teachers is only now beginning to be appreciated.

All these practical ways of implementing a 'storied' approach to learning are guaranteed to contribute to the formation of a 'learning community' committed to cooperative effort.

Email: brianjohntomlinson@gmail.com
hitomi.masuhara@gmail.com
jayakaranmukundan@yahoo.com
I.Timmis@leedsmet.ac.uk
yelamoo@yahoo.co.uk

References

Davies, A. 2002. 'Using teacher-generated biography as input material'. *ELT Journal* 56/4: 368–79.

Masuhara, H., M. Haan, Y. Yi, and B. Tomlinson. 2008. 'Adult EFL courses'. *ELT Journal* 62/3: 294–312.

Mukundan, J. (ed.). 2009. *Readings on ELT Materials III*. Petaling Jaya: Pearson-Longman.

Wajnryb, R. 2003. *Stories: Narrative Activities in the Language Classroom*. Cambridge: Cambridge University Press.

12.2 Symposium on meaning making through stories for young learners

Convenor: Rama Mathew *Delhi University, India* with
Caroline Linse *Queen's University, Belfast, UK*
Sandie Mourão *University of Aveiro, Portugal*
Teresa Fleta Guillén *Alcalá de Henares University, Madrid, Spain* and **M. Luisa García Bermejo** *Universidad Complutense, Madrid, Spain* and
Uma Raman *Freelance, Chennai, India*

Stories represent an imaginary world created by a variety of devices such as theme, characters, illustrations, vocabulary, humour, dialogue and the like, and help to promote not only language and literacy development, but also imagination and fantasy along with cognitive and aesthetic development (Wajnryb 2003). This symposium looked at ways of exploiting stories, both word-based and wordless ones, in the service of language teaching to young learners (YLs). Two of the five presentations demonstrated how teachers can, in fact, conceptualise and write stories and experiment with different methodologies that contribute to the development of YLs' multiple intelligences (MIs).

Caroline Linse's presentation on *wordless books* (picture books that contain illustrations but no printed words) explored ways of selecting and utilising this low-cost resource in the YL classroom. Wordless books often contain provocative storylines that appeal to children up to the age of 12 and can be very culturally relevant; they provide a rich context for learners who may be print-phobic or who have not had extensive book-based experiences. The teacher can easily tailor the language to meet varying proficiency levels, for example, by telling a very simple story for beginners or by providing a more complicated narrative accessible to more advanced learners. Learners who lack advanced English skills can often be challenged cognitively by the narratives found embedded in books without text. There are telescopic stories which require learners to try to decipher a location and what is taking place in the mystery locale.

Linse also elaborated on a variety of child-centred techniques that can be used with wordless books. Beginners can be prompted to *spy* or search for different items on the page. Learners at all stages of language proficiency can be led on a picture walk where they explore the pages of a book much as one would explore a neighbourhood. They can create story maps where they list the key elements of the story such as the setting, plot and characters. Finally, there are practical reasons for using wordless books in non-English speaking countries where it can be difficult and costly to access English language books.

Continuing with picture books, **Sandie Mourão**'s talk focused on the use of peri-textual features of the picture book. 'Peritext' is a term used to define the parts of a book which frame a text. Children's publishing brings illustrators, authors, editors and book designers together to exploit the peritext, bringing wholeness to picture books. Special attention is paid to the ways in which the front and back covers, endpapers, title pages, copyright and dedication pages all work together with text and accompanying illustrations to produce a unified end product, the picture book as object.

Following Lo (2008), Mourão demonstrated the broader 'ideological' view of literacy based on her own recent research: it was observed that children paid particular attention to the peritextual elements of picture books, especially when they were given the opportunity to use them to predict and confirm meaning. Through these features during shared reading sessions children used new and known language to discuss what they saw and their thoughts about it. On returning to these features once they had listened to the story, they made connections and discussed them. They talked about picture books using meta-language like cover, author, illustrator, publisher, logos and titles etc. and used the illustrations to develop a keener sense of what to look for and at, which contributed to their abilities in visual understanding and developed their visual literacy. There was no predetermined language-learning objective; instead, language and learning were shaped by social interaction, which enabled a co-constructed meaning through language given by the different communication modes, the word and the picture, within the picture book.

Teresa Fleta Guillén and **M. Luisa García Bermejo** reported on teaching techniques that promote language, content and literacy in English language. These techniques were tried out at school and at university with a twofold purpose: to stimulate the learners' imagination and creativity and to foster oral and written language in an enjoyable manner. While the learners (aged 6–8) from two different learning contexts were at their first stages of literacy, the student teachers from the School of Education experimented with the techniques in order to learn to put them into practice with their future pupils in the classroom.

The creative writing process consisted of several phases: visualisation, movement, drafting, story organizing, interaction, book making and storytelling. By being exposed to music (Brahms, Grieg or Vivaldi), or to music and art (Hovhaness and Munch), the learners developed visualisation abilities, created their own characters and invented stories. By moving freely to the music as they thought their character would move, the learners were able to express their emotions. Using graphic organisers helped them to make thinking visible, and participating in the process of making books and telling stories to an audience encouraged them to interact and to work collaboratively. Editing the story books and telling the created stories to an audience helped the learners to develop all four skills plus the cognitive skills, which are crucial because cognitive development and language development go hand in hand.

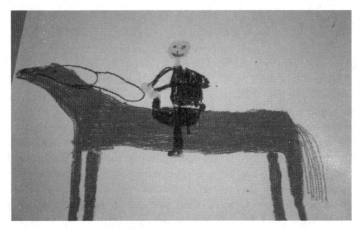

Figure 12.2.1: Combining art and storytelling in a YL classroom

The creation of stories was the departure point for the introduction of content learning through subject matters such as science, music, art, crafts and history. Learning through music, movement, art, story-making and story-telling involved learners holistically. They expressed their own messages in their stories and by doing so, the words, structures and content they use were easily retrieved from memory—see Figure 12.2.1 for an example. Offering students a variety of activities contributed to the development of their MIs and showed future teachers that we all have different intelligence profiles: not only do we learn differently, but we teach differently too.

Uma Raman's presentation focused on the creation of a set of English story books by teachers for use in government schools of Tamil Nadu, in southern India. The project, with support from Sarva Shiksha Abhiyan, the Government of India's flagship programme to universalise education, aimed to promote language learning through a new approach, namely, Activity-Based Learning (ABL) in primary schools. Since books in Tamil, their L1, proved very popular and useful, a similar project was undertaken for teaching English from Grade 1, for use by 300,000 students in some 37,000 government schools. Although teacher competency was a challenge, giving learners opportunities to read, hear and make meaning of language was an important strategy to promote language learning, and storybooks were considered an important resource. Further, since books available in the market are few and often not accessible to ESL learners culturally, linguistically or economically, it was decided to use the most easily available resource in the system, the teacher, to create the books in-house.

The books were conceptualised by English teachers in two writing workshops and illustrated by art teachers in three weeklong workshops. The set of about 75 English story books thus created and graded at four levels reflect, visually and thematically, concerns and contexts familiar to the learners. The editors facilitated the workshops, edited the stories, graded them for language level, provided a bilingual glossary and coordinated the production. The entire process was completed in about eight months. The books themselves range from normal alphabet books, wordbooks with illustrations, single line text on a page to 16-page storybooks with four or five lines of text on a page. The books are lively, brightly coloured and appealing. The initial response from teachers and learners has been positive and the project aims to collect systematic feedback for a more effective use of story books in the YL classroom.

Rama Mathew described an experiment conducted in a government school for about four months in which learners aged 9–11 were helped to develop the strategy of 'visualising' when a story was told/read aloud to them. Helping L2 learners to visualise, also known as 'mental/visual imaging', especially at early stages of L2 learning can enhance learners' reading comprehension and positive attitudes towards English, which can in turn improve their ability to visualise in their L2 (Tomlinson 1998).

As the teacher told/read the story, learners participated in it interactively by seeking clarifications, repeating after the teacher, allowing a more personal interpretation of stories which freed learners from the need for a complete and correct interpretation. There were instances of top-down strategies, bringing learners' world view knowledge outside the text to bear on their comprehension; not high-level inferencing but more global understanding of texts. The teacher used the L1 wherever necessary; similarly learners used the L1 very naturally to negotiate their learning. However, they progressively started using chunks/phrases in English, or imitated the teacher using English, and more importantly, they appeared to enjoy the activity. Explicit instructions for visualising, given at the beginning as well as during the story reading/rereading, helped learners to imagine the scene/incident they most wanted to draw on, as they made meaning of the story.

The drawings got more descriptive as the teaching continued; almost all of them showed a distinct improvement in terms of the coherence of the scene, relating specifically to particular dialogues in the story, imagination of extra detail or aspects that were implicit, facial expressions appropriate to the scene in question and captions

Figure 12.2.2: The use of visualisation during storytelling

that described the picture—see Figure 12.2.2 for an example. This way, the needs and interests of a heterogeneous group could also be addressed.

In sum, the symposium was a coherent story with a strong storyline: stories facilitate meaning-making and language-learning like magic.

Email: ramamathew@yahoo.co.in
C.Linse@qub.ac.uk
nettlehouse@mail.telepac.pt
tfleta@perlaunion.es
mlgarber@edu.ucm.es
ramanuma@gmail.com

References

Lo, M. M. 2008. 'Multilteracies in teaching young learners of English' in W. Arnold, K. Powell and H. Mol (eds.). *Literacy in the Language Classroom: The Role of the YL Professional in Developing Reading and Writing Skills in Young Learners.* Canterbury: IATEFL.

Tomlinson, B. 1998. 'Seeing what they mean: helping L2 readers to visualise' in B. Tomlinson (ed.). *Materials Development in Language Teaching.* Cambridge: Cambridge University Press.

Wajnryb, R. 2003. *Stories: Narrative Activities for the Language Classroom.* Cambridge: Cambridge University Press.

12.3 The use of picture books in a Norwegian L2 classroom

Hege Emma Rimmereide *Bergen University College, Norway*

This paper will describe a pilot study in a Norwegian classroom, in which authentic picture books rather than textbooks were used in the English lessons; I will reflect upon the impact on the learners' language. Our research questions were as follows:

- In what ways do young language learners read and understand picture books?
- What impact do pictures have on young learners' motivation, engagement and language learning?

The first question is related to the aesthetic approach as promoted by Bamford (2006), who found that good aesthetic education enhances the basic skills. The second research question is twofold and focuses both on motivation/engagement, where autonomy is a basis for motivation (Reeve 1992) and on language learning, taking into account such theories as Krashen's hypothesis of acquisition–learning (1985).

The study was carried out in one class of 21 pupils in Grade 6. The pupils had the choice of 60 books with pictures. The books presented authentic English, which is not found to the same extent in textbooks. The students were asked to read extensively during eight lessons, twice a week for four weeks; reading between lessons was optional. The pupils were asked to do the following:

- read as many books as possible, but a minimum of three books,
- write two texts; one before the reading project and one after the project,
- write a reading log for each book they read,
- write at least five expressions/words in context and indicate their meaning,
- answer a questionnaire,
- take part in an individual interview.

The reason for using picture books was to motivate and engage the pupils into reading. We experienced that having a selection of 60 titles to choose from provided the pupils with real alternatives, which promotes autonomy and thereby motivation (Reeve 1992). Thus, the pupils were able to decide for themselves which book to read according to their interests and their own levels of competence, which again promotes motivation and engagement. The pupils were very enthusiastic, and as one pupil stated in the interview, 'I really enjoyed the reading project because we didn't have to do so much work'. The pupils did not actually realise how much work they had put into it, as they had enjoyed the reading process. A number of pupils found that they were able to read longer texts than they had actually anticipated at first. The motivation and engagement in the pupils were clear; they read seven books on average.

Regardless of the input—in this case, reading—the output must be language production. One problem with the study is that although we considered the study a reading project, in order to determine the learning outcome, we asked the pupils to do a lot of writing. Thus, we learned that we need to find other measurements for reading. However, we were able to see progress in the pupils' writing through their increased use of adjectives and adverbials. In some instances we were able to trace adjectives from the texts they had read and saw how these were included in the texts they produced. Furthermore, we emphasised the importance of focusing on expressions rather than single words in order to enhance the pupils' understanding and knowledge of words in context; the pupils managed to find good Norwegian expressions, which is much harder than translating single words.

In the interesting and lively discussion after my presentation at the conference, it was pointed out—in hindsight, rather obvious and highly valuable—that we ought to go back and look at the material to see whether the pupils have actually been able to use the expressions they themselves had written down. Another point raised in our discussion referred to the actual material used in the classroom, as the quality and appropriateness of a picture book could vary. The questions raised by the audience reveal the necessity for further study of this material in the classroom and its potential as language learning material.

Email: her@hib.no

References

Bamford, A. 2006. *The Wow Factor*. Münster: Waxmann.

Krashen, S. 1985. *The Input Hypothesis: Issues and Implications*. London: Longman.

Reeve, J. 1992. *Understanding Motivation and Emotion*. Fort Worth: Harcourt Brace Jovanovich.

12.4 'I remember more when it's fun': teaching English through *Storyline*

Sharon Ahlquist *University College Kristianstad, Sweden*

The *Storyline* approach

The *Storyline* approach was developed in Scotland more than 40 years ago to facilitate cross-curricular teaching (Bell *et al.* 2007). It is based on a social-constructivist perspective which recognises the importance of learner interaction (Vygotsky 1978). In *Storyline* learners work in small groups to create a shared fictive world in the classroom, taking on and maintaining the role of a character throughout the story. Art, drama and movement are combined with language work. One of the benefits of the approach to second language education is that it provides a naturalistic context in the classroom where learners can use their language skills in a meaningful way.

The study

In 2009 I conducted a five-week study—*Storyline, The Street*—with a class of 32 Swedish 11–13 year olds, who had been learning English since the age of seven and who were used to working with a textbook. The mixed-method study was situated in a sociocultural theoretical framework, which recognises the influence of socio-affective factors on learning—see, for instance, Lantolf and Thorne 2006. In the story the learners were families who had just moved into a new street in the fictive English town of Danbury.

A *Storyline* develops through the use of so-called key questions, which are devised by the teacher on the basis of curriculum content to be covered—in this case, the national syllabus objectives for English in Year 5. By the end of this school year, learners are expected, for example, to be able to talk about themselves, write short descriptions, read short texts at an appropriate level, understand spoken information and know something about everyday life in an English-speaking country.

The first question, 'Who are you?' introduced the characters. The learners created their characters, introduced them to the rest of the class, wrote a short description of the family and their daily lives and drew a self-portrait. Whenever the class was working with the *Storyline*, each learner wore an item of clothing to represent his/her character. During the course of the *Storyline* the learners wrote an estate agent's advertisement for their house and drew a picture of it ('What is your home like?'); took part in a project to live in a more sustainable way (for example, by considering how they might reduce their impact on the environment); discovered that people had been illegally dumping rubbish on waste land at the end of their street; and dealt with an anti-social neighbour. These tasks involved writing a diary, petitioning the council about the dump, designing a park, and airing their grievances with the neighbour (teacher-in-role).

A key feature of a *Storyline* is the frieze, which both documents the developing story and anticipates future developments. At the outset only the street and plots of land were represented. As the families moved in, the plots were filled with the drawings and written descriptions of the houses as well as the portraits and descriptions of the characters. One plot of land remained unsold until the anti-social neighbours moved in.

The findings

The data consisted of learner questionnaires, interviews with teachers and learners, observation and video filming. Features that were highly rated by both boys and girls were *group work* and *art work*. For the girls *writing* and *using imagination* to create the characters was important, and *art work* was found to play an integral part in the character-creating process. For the boys, *variety* and *not using a textbook* were especially important. All the learners believed that they had improved in some way in English; for example, two thirds of both boys and girls believed that their spoken English had improved. They related this to the fact that *Storyline* work was *fun* (the word most commonly used in their responses) in that they did different things which were mostly interesting and enjoyable. The two class teachers observed a greater willingness to speak in the quieter learners and increases in lexical knowledge in all. In their opinion, the younger learners were pushed to perform by working with the older ones, benefitting from the latter group's greater linguistic resources. The older learners in turn were stretched by the subject content of sustainable development.

Email: sharon.ahlquist@hkr.se

References

Bell, S., S. Harkness and G. White (eds). 2007. *Storyline: Past, Present and Future*. Glasgow: University of Strathclyde Press.

Lantolf, J. P. and S. Thorne. 2006. *Sociocultural Theory and the Genesis of Second Language Development*. Oxford: Oxford University Press.

Vygotsky, L.S. 1978. *Mind in Society*. Cambridge, Mass.: Harvard University Press.

12.5 The role of young-adult literature in developing socio-cultural competency

Jennifer Schumm Fauster *University of Graz, Austria*

Introduction

The need for socio-cultural competence is growing every day. Through rapid developments in information and communication technology, globalisation of business and increasing travel opportunities, many people find themselves having more intercultural contact in both their private and professional lives. Interacting with people from different cultural backgrounds can be a very enriching experience, enabling us to expand our knowledge about specific cultures and in turn our intercultural understanding; however, it may also mean that people find their own cultural beliefs and values called into question. This can result in feelings of insecurity, where contact with foreign cultures is viewed as a threat instead of an intercultural opportunity. This presentation reported on an ongoing reading project carried out with tertiary-level EFL students in which young-adult literature (YAL) was used to enhance students' socio-cultural competence in order to help to prepare them for future intercultural encounters.

Using literature to enhance socio-cultural competence

Many convincing arguments have been given for using literature to enhance socio-cultural competence. Bredella (2000) suggests that when reading literary texts, readers are encouraged to imagine a world different from theirs and to see it through the eyes of 'the other'; thus we, as readers, 'become aware of the relativity of our attitudes, values and world views' (page 378). Delanoy (1993) compares reading literary texts to the experience we have when encountering different cultures. In both cases, we are required to come to terms with the unknown and try to make sense of it. Another reason for using literature is that it can be read on a more personal level. Readers are invited to reflect on various situations, issues, problems, etc. that occur in the given literary work and consider how they themselves would handle them, thus calling into question both their individual and cultural standpoints (Kramsch 1993, Bredella 2000). One final argument considers the different readings of literary texts people have. By reading a literary text and then discussing it collaboratively, readers often find themselves questioning their own cultural assumptions, which is a necessary skill in developing intercultural competence (Bredella 2000).

Criteria for choosing literature

Contemporary YAL was selected to provide students with a reading experience different from what they normally experience at university. Moreover, as most YAL is written in the first person, it was hoped students would gain more insight into the main character's world and thus better identify with it. Multicultural literature was chosen for the project because these texts portray encounters between different cultures which show points of commonality as well as conflict and thus can lead to deeper intercultural understanding.

Implementation of the reading project

The reading project was carried out in two parts. Firstly, students were required to read a multicultural short story. The three main objectives behind this reading task were as follows:

- to (re)acquaint tertiary-level students with YAL,
- to give them the opportunity to analyse a shorter literary text from a cultural standpoint before reading a young-adult novel,
- to sensitise students to the different communication styles and values addressed in the text.

In the second part of the project, students worked in small groups on a multicultural young-adult novel chosen from the reading list. The main objectives of this reading task were to carry out a collaborative reading and analysis from a socio-cultural standpoint and to present their findings in the form of a written review and oral presentations which highlighted the multicultural aspects in the novels. Students were also asked to write reflective papers on their YAL reading experience.

Findings

Based on an analysis of student reflective papers, five key findings emerged. Students reported that reading multicultural YAL did the following:

- expanded their cultural knowledge,
- promoted empathy for culturally related problems,
- helped them to relate to situations and thus better understand socio-cultural aspects due to the first-person perspective,
- challenged their cultural boundaries during the socio-cultural analysis of the literary texts, especially the novels, and
- provided a fresh, unique approach to addressing (inter)cultural issues.

Conclusion

Multicultural YAL has the potential to develop socio-cultural competence because students at the tertiary level can put themselves in the position of the teenage protagonists and thus empathise with the culture-specific situations/problems the teenage characters encounter. By being able to see things through the eyes of the first-person narrator, students gain a better understanding of the motivations behind the character's culturally-induced behavior. This understanding not only expands their (inter)cultural understanding but also promotes socio-cultural competency.

Email: jennifer.schumm@uni-graz.at

References

Bredella, L. 2000. 'Literary texts' in M. Byram (ed.). *Routledge Encyclopedia of Language Teaching and Learning*. London: Routledge.

Delanoy, W. 1993. 'Come to Mecca—assessing a literary text's potential for intercultural learning' in W. Delanoy, J. Köberl and H. Tschachler (eds.). *Experiencing a Foreign Culture*. Tübingen: Narr.

Kramsch, C. 1993. *Context and Culture in Language Teaching*. Oxford: Oxford University Press.

12.6 Shakespeare revisited or reinvented on an ESP syllabus

Stella Smyth *ELTU, University of Leicester, UK*

My workshop first clarified how I had used textual and film extracts from Shakespeare's *The Taming of the Shrew* (Miller 1980) with multicultural and multilingual overseas students taking a 20-credit undergraduate module at a British university. The module was entitled 'The study of English literacy and cultural issues through the media'. Its objectives were as follows:

- To extend students' awareness of the English language by exposing them to a variety of registers, literary and non-literary texts, academic texts and journalistic readings that corresponded to both *The Taming of the Shrew* and some topics in their main academic subjects: Law, Marketing and Media Studies.

- To analyse features of written genres, such as contracts, legal cases, excerpts from Shakespeare's *The Taming of the Shrew*, the lyrics, and screenplay extracts from both *Shrew* films.
- To examine 16th Century lexical items in Shakespeare's play to see how some words, for example, 'arms' and 'cobbler', develop different connotations over time and how knowledge of these earlier word meanings is essential to appreciating the verbal irony of Shakespeare's style.
- To encourage students to reflect on the link between language and gender and on why certain insults would generally be used to describe a female rather than a male and vice versa.
- To focus on contemporary linguistic trends, for example, the impact of political correctness on public documents, such as the *National Union of Journalist Guidelines*, or the way in which the BBC's *ShakespeaRe-Told* version of *The Shrew* (Richards 2005) revels in being so politically incorrect; the latter would suggest a deliberate attempt by screenplay writer, Sally Wainwright, to capture the anarchic spirit of the 1623 *Folio* play script.
- To assess the merits of reformulating Shakespeare's language and reducing his interwoven plots to a simplified storyline in Wainwright's screenplay.
- To compare attitudes to censorship and censorship laws in Shakespeare's time with ours.
- To analyse examples of intertexuality in popular magazines, tabloids and broadsheets, where Shakespearean quotations have been used for headings, or as allusions in journalistic articles. Students discussed the effects of reading the quotations literally and considered how meaning could become distorted; for example lines from Shakespeare's *Shrew* become very racist or sexist when removed from their original context and thus shredded of their irony.

Information about literacy practices in Elizabethan England and the role of the theatre was provided, so that students could consider the effects of modifying Elizabethan language and theatrical elements to comply with the conventions of director David Richards' (2005) romantic TV comedy. They could then see how the entertainment remit of the BBC is powered by the same kind of economic priorities that kept Shakespeare experimenting with language and genres, in the interest of satisfying public taste and staying ahead of the competition.

The overall selection of extracts, both on the original syllabus and in my workshop, constituted the comparative material for evaluating some of the screenplay writer's interpretations of critical issues in Shakespeare's drama, such as ownership of people and property, or marriage as an economic and political institution.

We considered how such a syllabus drew on *The Taming of the Shrew* as one of many resources on an English course, integrating legal, marketing and media content with the development of cultural knowledge and language awareness. Workshop participants matched some sample hands-on tasks to the above sample syllabus objectives, and then commented on how they could transpose activities such as 'the creative slander writing exercise' to their own classrooms.

The aim for both my original students and participants at the workshop was to engage with Shakespeare as iconic entertainment material that has also become the backbone of other contemporary cultural institutions, such as the BBC. We discussed what cultural changes in England drove the BBC to produce a very Renaissance film version of *The Taming of the Shrew* in 1980, in Shakespeare's language, only to reverse this decision in the 2005 BBC *ShakespeaRe-Told* version of *The Taming of the Shrew,* where almost all of Shakespeare's language is replaced by contemporary English.

We concluded by sharing how my approach to using Shakespeare as an ancillary film and textual resource is transferable to other ways of designing a syllabus, especially in the field of Literature, Media and Cultural Studies.

Email: sks6@leicester.ac.uk

References

Miller, J. (dir.). 1980. *The Taming of the Shrew.* BBC.

Richards, D. (dir.). 2005. *BBC ShakespeaRe-Told: The Taming of the Shrew.* (Film extracts available on YouTube.)

12.7 Transformation stories

Robert Hill *Black Cat Publishing, Rapallo, Italy*

Transformations pervade all kinds of narrative, from traditional children's stories to folk tales, from 'canonical' novels to TV talent shows and 'makeover' shows. Texts can be compared and similarities demonstrated through an intertextual approach: that is, looking for the relations of a text to other texts, of the same or different genre, both diachronically and synchronically. Although intertextuality is an academic term, it has real practical applications in the ESL class: in order for students to speak or write they have to have something to speak or write *about*, and comparing texts provides plenty of interesting material for practising all the skills.

Classic children's stories contain kinds of transformation also found in 'adult' literature. The ogre in *Puss in Boots* transforms himself into a lion and then a mouse—which means the cat can eat him! In current popular culture this is usually called 'shape-shifting' (although this term is first dated 1887 in Merriam-Webster's Dictionary) while for classical mythology the term is 'metamorphosis'—and Greek gods often changed themselves temporarily into animals or people. 'Shape-shifting' is common in science fiction films, the *Terminator* series providing just one example. In *The Gingerbread Man,* a freshly baked biscuit put on the table for tea jumps up and runs away; it is an example of transformation from inanimate to living. *Pinocchio* begins with this kind of spontaneous transformation, while stories that also involve a creator figure include the 'golem' from Jewish folklore and, I would suggest, *Frankenstein.*

The Ugly Duckling stages the change from unattractive to attractive which accompanies—hopefully!—growing up. This kind of transformation has given rise to the common phrase 'ugly duckling story', although nowadays such transformations are aided by fashion and make-up consultants or even surgeons in TV programmes that stage 'makeovers'. (Again, although the term seems modern, 'makeover' is dated 1927 in Merriam-Webster's Dictionary.) In *Cinderella* the fairy godmother's magic effects a 'makeover' for Cinderella, although this is only a preliminary transformation.

It is when the Prince falls in love with her that the poor-to-rich transformation—'rags to riches' is the common phrase in English—is guaranteed. The need for a *male* to transform the fortunes of a *female* doubtless reflects how society has been male-dominated—'Some day my prince will come', sings Snow White in the Disney film—and is clear in the 1990 film *Pretty Woman*. This film mixes the *Cinderella* transformation with the myth of the man who transforms a woman, as in the Greek myth of Pygmalion (a sculptor who fell in love with his own sculpture, which was then transformed into a real woman, Galatea), which inspired George Bernard Shaw's play *Pygmalion*, which inspired the Broadway musical *My Fair Lady*.

Transformation can also involve a change of personality or sentiment. Two 'canonical' novels, regularly voted as perennial favourites in readers' polls, are *Jane Eyre* by Charlotte Brontë and *Pride and Prejudice* by Jane Austen. Both centre on an aloof male apparently impervious to female interest being 'transformed' by the love of a woman. But even in *Jane Eyre* some physical transformation remains: Mr Rochester, blinded and disfigured in a fire, recovers some of his sight when Jane returns to him. Physical transformation may result from reciprocated love, as in *Beauty and the Beast*, but may *not* result from unreciprocated love, as in *The Phantom of the Opera*.

The Wife of Bath's Tale from Chaucer's 14th century *The Canterbury Tales* has elements found in other texts. The plot device of the 'rash promise' is found in the Bible (Herod, Salomé and the head of John the Baptist) and the Grimm Brothers' *The Frog Prince*, to name but two texts. And the 'loathly lady', beautiful by day but ugly by night—or some variation of this—is alive and well in the figure of Princess Fiona in *Shrek* (which is *such* an intertextual film!).

A recent phenomenon concluded the session, that of Susan Boyle on the TV show *Britain's Got Talent* on 11 April 2009 (and on YouTube, watched by millions). Why such success? Well, she was a 'loathly lady', transformed when she sang; an 'ugly duckling' in the light of her recent makeover; an example of 'rags to riches' transformation with her subsequent success; and an example of a society informed by male values—who says female singers should be 'glamorous'?

Email: robhill@tin.it

12.8 Plenary: What is a storyteller?

Jan Blake *The Akua Storytelling Project, London, UK*

I've been a storyteller for 23 years, touring, performing and hopefully inspiring others to get up and tell a tale or two themselves. Yet despite what might sound an obvious job description—storyteller—there's often confusion about what that actually means. When I tell people I'm a professional storyteller and that I perform stories for a living, I often hear, 'What does a storyteller do, then?' So let's explore the what, why, and how of storytelling and, in turn, use this to discover how stories and storytelling can enhance your own experience and enjoyment of performing in the classroom.

I was born in Manchester to Jamaican parents during the '60s and while I was growing up, my parents constantly talked about home, about Jamaica ... about how, in their opinion, second generation British–Jamaican children weren't quite as authentic as those children born in Jamaica. So, I grew up with a very strong sense that there was something missing within me: I hadn't been born in Jamaica; I didn't have the influences of Jamaica, my aunts, uncles, grandparents, and so on. My desire to connect with my parents, beyond them being my parents, and to bridge the gap between myself and Jamaica is one of the main driving forces behind me becoming a storyteller.

I'd always wanted to be a performer; I've always enjoyed getting up and showing off in front of people. However, when I started telling stories, my intentions changed. I was taking the first step towards bridging that gap between myself and my parents because I told exclusively in the vernacular, in Jamaican Patois, my first language, the language that my parents spoke at home and had also spoken growing up in Jamaica. I also chose to tell Ananse stories because these were the stories my parents would have heard as children, back in Jamaica. When I told these stories, I felt I was getting closer and closer to the thing that I felt was missing in me. So as a young, green storyteller, I told stories like this:

Synopsis of Story 1: *Ananse and Brer Patoo*

Call: 'Ananse!' Response: 'Story!'

Brer Ananse is seeking a wife and must go to Woman Town to find one. In order to impress the women there, he must sing a song to delight their hearts. To enhance his chances, he decides to ask the painfully shy Brer Patoo (owl), to join him, sure in the knowledge that by contrast, he, Ananse, will shine. When Ananse visits Brer Patoo he flatters him about his good looks and invites him along. Brer Patoo reminds Ananse that the women in Woman Town hate feathers and that, as an owl, he is covered in feathers.

Ananse reassures and encourages Brer Patoo, offering to lend him a hat, shirt, jacket, trousers, gloves and shoes to hide his feathers. Moved and impressed by Ananse's generosity, Patoo is persuaded to go. With his self-esteem greatly enhanced by his new attire, Brer Patoo is looking forward to meeting some women in Woman Town, but as he and Ananse approach their destination, Ananse breaks away from Brer Patoo, explaining that he can *'take it from here'* and begins to sing, lustily, a praise song in his own honour. The women of Woman Town emerge, surrounding Ananse and praising him highly for his song and good looks.

Poor Brer Patoo is ignored and feels dejected. He gives himself a good talking to, remarking that Ananse cannot be allowed to have the women *'all to 'imself'*. Plucking up the courage, he composes and sings a lively little number, which makes such an impact on the women, that they immediately abandon Ananse, declaring that they love Brer Patoo *'like cook food! We love yuh cyaan dun! We love yuh more dan him!'*

Brer Patoo has triumphed and is in his element; women surround him and he takes down their details, but Ananse is furious and demands that Brer Patoo return his clothes to him immediately. Brer Patoo is far too involved with the women to hear Ananse, who insists that Brer Patoo should *'gimmie back di close weh mi len yuh!'*

Finally, spiteful Ananse tears the clothes from Brer Patoo's body, revealing the *'naykid feddahs'*. Disgusted by what they see, the women of Woman Town make it clear to Brer Patoo that they don't intend to spend their lives cleaning up feathers and return to Woman Town, taking Ananse with them. Brer Patoo is so hurt and ashamed by the experience, that all he can say is *'Uhuh-Uhoo!'* which he's been saying ever since.

Ananse, language and colonialism

I believe stories have something to tell us; they have ancient wisdom in them, and I enjoyed telling Ananse stories in the vernacular. However, the response to the stories wasn't always a positive one, despite the fact that Ananse stories were part of the rich pantheon of trickster stories from around the world. I came to understand that this was because Jamaican Creole, the language I was using to tell them, had become an object of ridicule.

The colonialist relationship between Jamaica and the UK wasn't always a respectful one, and the complex nature of the Ananse stories became distorted by default. Because of this negative relationship, the value of the stories was being lost and, as they weren't able to do the job they were supposed to do, I found it increasingly difficult to tell these stories and to feel I was doing them justice. So I had to make a choice about whether to continue telling those stories and it is very rare these days for me to tell an Ananse story in the vernacular.

Awakening: Common Lore Storytellers and Musicians

In1986 I joined the storytelling group Common Lore Storytellers and Musicians, a group of people from all over the globe who get together every Sunday morning to tell each other stories and to teach each other games and songs from our own traditions. It was whilst I was with this group that I heard for the first time a story that had a huge teaching impact on me. It was a Ghanaian story, which I think some of you may have heard me tell before and which I'm going to tell again, if you'll forgive me. This story still resonates with me 24 years later, and it was hearing this story that made me recognise that story had a function beyond entertainment.

Synopsis of Story 2: *Tortoise and Hunter*

Call: 'Ho!' Response: 'Hey!'

Kwao, a young, ambitious hunter from the Ashanti region of Ghana is loved and respected by his community; every day, on his return from the hunt, the people sing his praises and the women ululate. However, Kwao is dissatisfied with his standing in the community and wants to be more than he is: he wants to be the chief hunter of the hunters' association, and the only way to receive the title is to bring an unknown species to the village and present it to his people.

Every day after bringing the meat to the village, Kwao returns to the forests, to his familiar hunting paths in search of the as-yet-undiscovered creature, every day going deeper and deeper into the forest. One day, Kwao is in the deepest part of the forest when he hears singing in the distance. He can't quite make out the words, but he knows that someone is singing. His curiosity aroused, Kwao goes even deeper still, using his machete to cut his way into the interior. The words of the song are:

A sem pon i po	*'Trouble doesn't go looking for Man*
O ni pa no pa semo	*Man goes looking for trouble'*
A sem pon i po	
O ni pa no pa semo	

Kwao isn't listening to the words; he is determined to know who could be singing in the heart of the forest.

Finally, he comes to a bush, parts its leaves and there finds a creature he's never seen before: a creature with its house on its back, a tortoise. Delighted, Kwao realises that this creature is exactly what he needs to become chief hunter of the hunters association and begs the tortoise to return home with him. The tortoise repeats the song again and again, but Kwao still does not hear the words and, losing all patience, scoops up the creature and takes it home. The tortoise continues to sing.

On his return Kwao immediately goes to see the chief and, speaking through his linguist, informs him of his wonderful, singing discovery. The chief is sceptical and, speaking through his linguist, assures Kwao that he realises his ambitions, but he also reminds him that to lie to the chief means death. Kwao insists that he wouldn't break such an important taboo and demands an opportunity to prove himself to the chief and his community. It is agreed that Kwao will present his creature the following afternoon, with a very strong admonition that if after three chances his creature does not sing, he will lose his head.

When Kwao returns to his home, the tortoise is still singing; it sings as Kwao makes preparation for the following day, singing throughout the day and though the night, but Kwao still hasn't heard the words:

A sem pon i po	*'Trouble doesn't go looking for Man*
O ni pa no pa semo	*Man goes looking for trouble'*
A sem pon i po	
O ni pa no pa semo	

The day finally arrives and Kwao makes ready to leave, but the tortoise has stopped singing. Unperturbed, Kwao gives the tortoise a good polish and makes his way to the village meeting place, where the whole community is gathered. They sing his praise song and the women ululate. Next, the chief arrives, accompanied by the sound of the royal drummers and flanked by his linguist and executioner. When the chief is seated, the signal is given for the creature to sing. *'My friend,'* says Kwao, *'the song you were singing when I found you in the forest, sing it for us now.'* The tortoise first smiles, then grins, but refuses to sing. With two of his chances gone, the linguist reminds Kwao that there is no turning back, his creature must sing or Kwao's head will roll. Kwao begs the tortoise on bended knee; this time the creature giggles but does not sing.

The shocked villagers watch as Kwao, protesting his innocence, is taken away to the place of execution; they stop their ears as they hear Kwao's life come to an abrupt end and are incredulous when the tortoise opens its mouth and sings:

A sem pon i po	*'Trouble doesn't go looking for Man*
O ni pa no pa semo	*Man goes looking for trouble'*
A sem pon i po	
O ni pa no pa semo	

The impact of stories

Stories like that never leave you; they kind of get under your skin because you can't believe what just happened, as you experienced for yourselves: 'It's really going to happen! It's *not* a funny story; well it *is* a funny story, but it's *not a funny story!* It's really going to happen!' So stories like that get under your skin, and once stories like that began to get under my skin, I began to leave behind the frivolity ... well that's how it felt; it felt frivolous to tell jokey Ananse stories. I felt I had to start telling stories with a bit more impact.

I don't judge the stories, the stories do their work; I'm a conduit, the stories tell themselves. Obviously, I choose stories that have great impact on me, stories that I love, stories that I've read that make me take a sharp intake of breath and that I simply *have* to tell. It's the impulse of a gossip; you hear a juicy bit of gossip and you just can't help saying, 'You're never going to guess what happened!!' That's the impulse behind my telling. There's just something in that story that begs to be told.

The storyteller: the silent character

People have said to me, 'When you tell your stories it seems as though we're really there. We can see every detail'. Did you have that experience when you heard me telling the story? Part of what that's about is that, as a storyteller, I have to ask myself, 'How do you know? How do *you* know?' If I'm not there, if I'm not walking alongside that hunter as he's making his way through the forest, how do I know? If I'm not sitting with that tortoise under that bush, how do I know? If I'm not with that linguist and that chief during their interaction, how do I know? How can I tell you what I don't know? So in a way, the storyteller is the silent character in the story, the character who's there watching everything, reacting and feeling compelled to tell someone; the silent character who hears everything, sees everything, tastes everything, touches everything, knows the inside thinking of everything. The storyteller zooms into everything, does a wide shot of everything, hears every whisper, every scream, every giggle, every teardrop; the storyteller has to be able to communicate all of those things. Not all of them are needed in every single story, all of the time, but the storyteller needs to have all those things in her toolkit, so that if anyone asks a question about any aspect of the story, she can answer. The stories are being told through me and I, therefore, have to know *everything* about the story.

Question from the audience

Do you have any stories from Asia?

Not specifically. I was going to tell you a story from the Middle East next; is that close enough for you? The reason I was going to tell you a story from the Middle East is because recently, I've been reading a lot of stories ... have you come across Idries Shah? Idries Shah put together a book called *World Tales*. He came to England in the '70s and is the reason why a storytelling revival really began in England. He created the College of Storytellers, a group of people who wanted to get together to tell stories and work on what it meant to be human. Idries Shah came to England and identified that because stories weren't being told on a regular basis and people weren't asking the questions of humanity through stories, there was something missing here. So the College of Storytellers began and alongside the College of Storytellers, the Company of Storytellers began; their focus was storytelling. At that point storytelling began to move in two different directions: storytelling as learning and teaching, and storytelling as performance. I now find myself straddling both positions, so this is a Sufi teaching story that I love so much and am going tell for you.

Synopsis of Story 3: *The Camel Driver*

Call: 'Let's be off!' Response: 'Pull away!'

A camel driver is taking his camels through a town. He passes an orchard, with trees heavy with peaches and covets the delicious fruit. At the same time, the orchard owner marvels at the beauty of the camels being driven by the stranger and covets the lead camel, which is particularly beautiful. At the same moment the lead camel stretches its neck and plucks some of the peaches from a branch which is overhanging the orchard wall. Incensed, the orchard owner throws a stone at the camel, killing it instantly. In retaliation the camel driver throws a stone at the orchard owner, killing him in return. He tries to flee the scene but is captured by the orchard owner's sons who take him to the judge, tell him their story and demand his death. The judge urges a more compassionate solution, a ransom for their father's life, but only death will satisfy them.

The judge passes sentence, at which point the murderer asks for three days' grace so he can return to his village and settle his affairs. He asks that someone take his place until his return. The local people, reluctant to offer themselves up, are incredulous when a grey-haired old man offers to swap places with the stranger. His neighbours try to persuade him otherwise, explaining that he will die in the stranger's place if he doesn't return. But the old man is undeterred and extends the hand of friendship to the camel driver, who, vowing to return in the allotted time, jumps on his camel and gallops off. The old man is led off to the dungeons and townspeople are convinced that his fate is sealed; they will never see the stranger again.

Three days later the town is gathered and the old man is kneeling before the executioner, who has his sword bared. The judge is expressing his regret that the old man should have to die for a stranger, when someone calls out, *'A rider is coming!'* In the distance they see someone riding furiously towards them; as he gets closer they realise that it's the stranger, who jumps down from his camel, thanks the old man, apologises for being late and prepares to take the elder's place. The judge, moved by the stranger's sincerity, asks him to explain where he had been. The stranger explains that a widow in his village had given him her jewels for safekeeping and, as only he knew of their location, for the sake of honour he couldn't die before restoring them to her. The judge then turns his attention to the old man, asking why he had been prepared to help the stranger. The old man explains that he had been brought up to believe that a man's honour and word were his bond, and therefore had no reason to doubt that the stranger would return.

The judge then explains that it took wisdom, mercy and compassion to be a true judge; the stranger had proven himself an honourable man, and therefore he would not die. He instructed the brothers, the sons of the orchard owner, to accept a ransom for their father's death and invited all four men to dine with him.

Conclusion

There are so many stories, more stories that I'd like to tell you, but I hope some of the important things that I've communicated to you are as follows. You have to tell the stories you love. Stories are for entertainment, but we have to be prepared to look at the lessons within them, not from a moralising point of view, but from the point of view that everybody takes a piece of the story with them; the piece of the story that you need is already lodged in your heart, you'll take that with you and it will work on you, slowly, slowly without you realising. There are some schools of thought that say you should sit with that shard of story and that you should discuss and unpack it and look at it, from a psychological point of view, as to why it's having that impact on you. I prefer to let the stories burn away slowly and gently.

The stories that you've heard today you may tell again and again, as I have. Each time you tell a story, it's like revisiting an old master, like going to a gallery and looking at a painting from a different perspective, seeing something that you never saw before, or revisiting that block of colour that makes your senses tingle. In so doing, that shard of story that is now lodged in your heart will make itself clearer and clearer to you, and I hope that it serves you some good.

I've got nothing more to add because we have five minutes left and I could talk forever, but there are five minutes left, and if anyone has a question, I'd be happy to (tell) answer it.

Question from the audience

Can you explain the significance of the call and response?

It's a contract. Well, for me it's a contract; that's what I understand its purpose to be. In the French Caribbean, the call goes like this;

Call:	*'Et Cric!'*
Response:	*'Et Crac!'*
Call:	*'Et Mistie Cric!'*
Response:	*'Et Mistie Crac!'*
Call:	*'Est-ce-que le court dors?'*
Response:	*'Non! Le court ne dors pas!'*

So you have to keep asking, 'Are you sleeping?' and you hear, 'No we're not sleeping, we want to hear the story'. Without the contract, why would I stand here telling you stories? It would be just about me; I can do that in front of a mirror at home. Thank you!

Email: akuajan@btinternet.com

Index of authors

Index of topics